The Walton Basin Project:

Excavation and Survey in a Prehistoric Landscape 1993–7

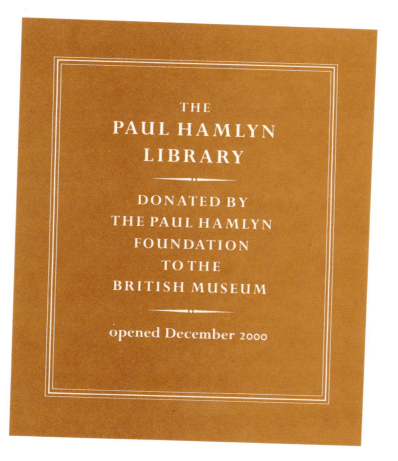

The Walton Basin Project:

Excavation and Survey in a Prehistoric Landscape 1993-7

Alex Gibson

With contributions by
Philippa Bradley, David Jenkins and John Williams,
Mark Walters, Randolph Donahue, Richard Evershed and
Stephanie Dudd, Julian Henderson, John Crowther,
Graham Morgan, Astrid Caseldine and Catherine Barrow,
Su Johnson

Project funded by
Cadw: Welsh Historic Monmuments, NERC, Cambrian Archaeological
Association, National Museums and Galleries of Wales

Project supported by
City Archaeology Service of Zwolle (Netherlands), University of
Staffordshire, University of Wales Cardiff, Trinity College Carmarthen,
British Museum, University College London

CBA Research Report 118
Council for British Archaeology
1999

Published 1999 by the Council for British Archaeology
Bowes Morrell House, 111 Walmgate, York YO1 9WA

British Library Cataloguing in Publication Data
A catalogue for this book is available from the British Library

ISSN 0141 7819

ISBN 1 872414 95 8

Typeset from authors' disks by Archetype IT Ltd, web site www.archetype-it.com

Printed by Pennine Printing Services Ltd

This book is published with the aid of a grant from
Cadw: Welsh Historic Monuments

Front cover: The Four Stones stone circle, Walton, from the south
Back cover: Structure 1 at Upper Ninepence. A partial reconstruction during the 1994 excavations

Contents

List of figures

List of tables

List of contributors

Alex Gibson
formerly:
Clwyd-Powys Archaeological Trust
7a Church Street
Welshpool
Powys
currently:
English Heritage
Central Archaeology Service
Fort Cumberland
Eastney
Portsmouth
Hampshire

Philippa Bradley
Oxford Archaeology Unit
Janus House
Osney Mead
Oxford
Oxfordshire

David Jenkins and John Williams
Dept of Agro-forestry
University of Wales, Bangor
Bangor
Gwynedd

R Donahue
Dept of Archaeological Science
The University of Bradford
Bradford
W Yorkshire

M Walters
Clwyd-Powys Archaeological Trust
7a Church Street
Welshpool
Powys

Richard Evershed and Stephanie Dudd
School of Chemistry
University of Bristol
Bristol

Julian Henderson
Dept of Archaeology
University of Nottingham
Nottingham

John Crowther
Dept of Geography
University of Wales, Lampeter
Lampeter
Ceredigion

Graham Morgan
School of Archaeology
The University of Leicester
Leicester

Astrid Caseldine and Kate Barrow
Dept of Archaeology
University of Wales, Lampeter
Lampeter
Ceredigion

Su Jonson
Dept of Archaeology
University of Wales, Lampeter
Lampeter
Ceredigion

Acknowledgements

This project has substantially gained from the help and wisdom of a large number of individuals. The specialists who have applied their expert knowledge to the benefit of the archaeology of the Walton Basin and whose names head their respective contributions are thanked for their enthusiasm and for keeping to an often tight timetable. The project was largely funded by Cadw: Welsh Historic Monuments with additional financial help from the National Museums and Galleries of Wales and the Cambrian Archaeological Association. Additional help 'in kind' was obtained from the University of Wales College Cardiff and Trinity College Carmarthen (student workforce), Department of Computing, University of Staffordshire (geophysical survey), Gemeente Zwolle, Netherlands (trainee supervisory staff), University College London (geophysical survey), British Museum (radiocarbon dates), University of Reading (loan of geophysical equipment) and Incom Training (fieldwalking help).

A number of individuals have been free with their time and advice and have generously supplied unpublished information: Dr Michael Meyer (Humboldt Universität, Berlin), Claude Burnez (Gensac-la Pallue), Derek Simpson, Jim Mallory and Barrie Hartwell (Queen's University Belfast), Helen Roche (University College Dublin), Conor Newman (University College Galway), Alisdair Whittle (University of Wales, Cardiff), Alistair Barclay (Oxford Archaeological Unit), Richard Bradley (University of Reading), Gordon Barclay (Historic Scotland), Graham Ritchie (RCAHMS), Aubrey Burl (Birmingham), Ros Cleal (Alexander Keiller Museum, Avebury), Chris Musson (RCAHMW), Chris Houlder (Aberystwyth), Frances Lynch (University of Wales, Bangor), Chris Wilson (Llandrindod Wells Museum), the late Peggy Guido (Devizes), David Wilson (CU-CAP, Cambridge), Robin Holgate (Luton Museum), Peter Topping (RCHME, Cambridge), Jan de Jong (formerly Monumentenzorg, Gemeente Zwolle), Humphrey Case (Warborough), Julie Gardiner (Wessex Archaeology), Stephen Aldhouse-Green (formerly National Museums and Galleries of Wales), Janet Ambers (British Museum), and Jonathan Cotton (Museum of London).

Chris Dunn (RCHME, Exeter) kindly allowed free access to his extensive collection of flints from Walton Basin and this collection, together with the artefacts from the present project, has been donated to the National Museums and Galleries of Wales. Rob Jones of Trehelig, Welshpool, was always ready to take to the air, often at minutes' notice, when weather and cropmarks demanded.

I owe a great debt to former colleagues at CPAT. The aerial photographic rectification, survey assistance and excavation supervision was by David Thomas. Additional survey was by Nigel Jones and Wendy Owen. Brian Hart, Gary Watson, Chris Lewis, Alice Meyer and Glyn Owen assisted during the survey and excavations. Marge Fenyok undertook fieldwalking. Caroline Earwood answered numerous SMR enquiries and Chris Martin and Bill Britnell offered valuable help and advice throughout the project.

A steering committee was established to guide the project through it's various phases and the members of that committee (Chris Musson, Jeff Davies, Sian Rees, Bill Britnell) are thanked for their enthusiasm and confidence.

The illustrations emanate from the skilled pen of Brian Williams with the exceptions of Figs 51–7 which were mostly by AMG with P33, P34, P35, and P68 being the work of Joanne Hutchinson. The Iron Age pot (Fig 59) was drawn by Alice Meyer.

The help and interest of the local individuals and landowners in the Walton Basin (or Radnor Valley) contributed significantly to the smooth running of the project. Roger Pye generously shared his extensive knowledge of the region. Excavation was kindly permitted by Mr and Mrs D Bufton (Lower Womaston), Mr E M Jones (Lower Harpton Farm), Mr J Hamer (Rough Close Farm) and Mr C R Evans (Knapp Farm). Especial thanks go to Colin and Anne Goodwin of Hindwell Farm for their unfailing help, interest and co-operation throughout the project; the unique and exceptional archaeology of the Walton Basin could not receive better stewardship.

Special thanks are extended to Ian Kinnes for his interest in the project, for approving radiocarbon samples, and for allowing me to benefit from his extensive knowledge of the British and French Neolithic. And finally to my long-suffering wife, Jane, who saw our house become variously an office, post-excavation unit, restaurant for hungry student archaeologists and hotel for British and European guests and for developing a tolerant sigh in response to the words 'sorry, love, I'm off to Walton'.

J Crowther would like to thank Ian Clewes for undertaking the laboratory analysis of the phosphate, loss on ignition and magnetic susceptibility samples, and Dr Richard Macphail for his assistance in the description and interpretation of the thin sections. S Dudd and R Evershed would like to thank NERC for funding and for mass spectrometry facilities, and Mr J Carter and Mr A Gledhill for technical assistance with GC-MS and GC-C-IRMS. Astrid Caseldine would like to thank both Kate Barrow and John James for helping with the fieldwork and also Kate for preparing the pollen samples.

Summary

The Walton Basin Project was intended to quantify and characterise the total archaeology of this rich and important area of the Welsh borderland. From this work, proposals would be made to Cadw: Welsh Historic Monuments, for the increased protection and better management of the archaeological resource. The initial desk-based study would be supported by survey, aerial survey, geophysical survey and trial excavation to build as complete a picture as possible of the basin's archaeological potential as well as the effects of the present agricultural regimes on the survival of the area's monuments. During the life of the project, the full potential of the basin's prehistoric archaeology was realised and this volume presents the results of work on the basin's prehistory. In particular the trial excavations of the Neolithic palisaded enclosure at Hindwell and the rescue excavation of a barrow and Neolithic settlement at Upper Ninepence are discussed. Scientific analysis of the finds and soils from these excavations also provide important information on the economy and environment of the area during the later Neolithic.

Crynodeb

Y bwriad gyda Phroject Basn Waltwn oedd mesur a disgrifio holl archeoleg yr ardal gyfoethog a phwysig hon ar y Gororau. Ar sail y gwaith hwn, byddai cynigion yn cael eu cyflwyno i Cadw: Henebion Cymru, ar gyfer cynyddu'r warchodaeth a gwella'r rheolaeth ar yr adnodd archeolegol. Gwaith a baratowyd wrth y ddesg fyddai'r astudiaeth gychwynnol gydag arolwg, arolwg o'r awyr, arolwg geoffisegol a chloddfa ragbrofol yn waith ategol, er mwyn creu darlun mor gyflawn â phosibl o botensial archeolegol y basn yn ogystal ag effeithiau'r arferion amaethyddol cyfoes ar oroesiad henebion yr ardal.

Yn ystod oes y project, sylweddolwyd y gwir botensial a oedd i archeoleg cynhanesyddol y basn ac mae'r gyfrol hon yn cyflwyno canlyniadau'r gwaith ar gynhanes y basn. Yn fwyaf arbennig, trafodir cloddfeydd rhagbrofol ar y lloc palis o Oes Newydd y Cerrig yn Hindwell, a'r gloddfa achub ar y garnedd ac ar yr aneddiad o Oes Newydd y Cerrig yn Upper Ninepence. Mae dadansoddi gwyddonol ar y darganfyddiadau a'r priddoedd a ddaeth o'r cloddfeydd hyn yn darparu gwybodaeth bwysig hefyd am economi ac amgylchedd yr ardal yn ystod cyfnod diweddar Oes Newydd y Cerrig.

Zusammenfassung

Das Walton Basin Project (Walton-Becken-Projekt) wurde ins Leben gerufen, um die gesamte Archäologie dieser reichen und wichtigen Gegend des walisischen Grenzlandgebietes zu quantifizieren und zu beschreiben. Die Folge der Resultate dieses Projekts wird sein, dass Vorschläge an das historische, walisische Denkmalamt (Welsh historic momuments) in Cadw gemacht werden, um verstärkten Schutz und bessere Verwaltung des archäologischen Quellenmaterials garantieren. Die zuerst an einen Schreibtisch gebundene Studie müßte durch Vermmmessungen aller Arten, wie Luftvermessungen und geophysikalische Vermessungen und Probeausgrabungen unterstützt werden, um sich dadurch ein möglichst vollkommenes Bild des archäologischen Potentials dieses Beckens machen zu können, sowie auch die

Überlebungschancen dieser Denkmäler aus dieser Gegend in der gegenwärtigen Lage zu überprüfen. Im Laufe dieses Projekts wurde man sich auch der vollständigen Möglichkeiten der vorgeschichtlichen Archäologie bewußt. Die Resultate dieser Arbeiten im Bereich der vorgeschichtlichen Archäologie werden in diesem Buch dargebracht. Dabei werden im besonderen die Probeausgrabungen der neolothis-chen eingepfählten Einfriedung bei Hindwell, die Rettungsausgrabung eines Hügelgrabes und einer neolithischen Ansiedlung bei Upper Ninepence besprochen. Eine wissenschaftliche Analyse der Funde und der bei dieser Ausgrabung gefundenen Erde vermitteln auch wichtige Informationen in bezug auf Wirtschaft und Umgebung in diesem Gebiet der späteren Neolothischen Periode.

Sommaire

Le projet du bassin de Walton était conçu pour quantifier et caractériser l'archéologie totale de cette riche et importante zone de la région frontalière du Pays de Galles. Sur la base de ce travail, des propositions seront soumises à Cadw: Monuments Historiques Gallois pour une sauvegarde accrue et une meilleure gestion des ressources archéologiques. La première étude sur papier sera soutenue par un levé, un levé aérien, un levé géophysique et des sondages afin de constituer une image aussi complète que possible du potentiel archéologique du bassin ainsi que des effets des régimes agricoles actuels sur la survie des monuments de la région. Au cours du projet, la totalité du potentiel de l'archéologie préhistorique du bassin avait été réalisé et ce volume présente les résultats du travail sur la préhistoire du bassin. En particulier, les sondages de l'enceinte néolithique avec palissade de Hindwell et les fouilles de sauvetage d'un tertre funéraire et d'un peuplement néolithique à Upper Ninepence sont examinés. L'analyse scientifique des découvertes et des sols provenant de ces fouilles fournissent également d'importantes informations sur l'économie et l'environnement de la région au néolithique supérieur.

1 Excavation and survey in the Walton (Radnor) Basin, Powys, Wales 1993–6

Introduction

The Walton (or Radnor) Basin has for many years been recognised as an area of great archaeological potential. Its well-drained and fertile soils, has made it an attractive area for settlement from the Mesolithic onwards but ironically it is these good soils and their potential for arable agriculture which today pose the main destructive threat to the archaeology of earthworks and cropmarks alike.

This study, largely funded by Cadw: Welsh Historic Monuments, was intended to quantify this threat to the total archaeology of the basin and make recommendations for the better management of the important sites in this rich and intensively farmed landscape. During the course of this project, two sites of national (even international) importance were discovered and excavated. The first of these is the Neolithic pit complex at Upper Ninepence where important data for our understanding of the interaction (or lack of it) between the users of Peterborough Ware and Grooved Ware was recovered using a variety of new methods of analyses. The second site is the palisaded enclosure at Hindwell II. Already published in interim form (Gibson 1996a; Gibson 1998a) this site is datable to the late Neolithic and covers some 34Ha. This site is the largest of its kind and date yet known in Western Europe and future work will be undertaken on trying to unravel its internal secrets.

This report deals exclusively with the prehistoric element of the project. The survey and trial excavations are dealt with first in chapter 1 followed by the results of the excavations at Hindwell II and Upper Ninepence. The finds section (chapter 2) considers the finds from fieldwalking and includes the well-documented Dunn collection of flints collected in the 1960s. The finds from the excavations are also discussed. A separate section (chapter 3) deals with the scientific analyses of the finds. It includes absorbed residue analysis of the Neolithic ceramics which has produced important results for our understanding of the economy in an area where faunal and non-carbonised floral remains are absent. This research is complemented by the microwear analysis of the flint assemblage. The palaeoenvironmental section (chapter 4) considers the data from the excavations. Finally the sites are placed in context in the discussion section which concludes the study.

The Roman and post-Roman archaeology, the archaeological survey plus elements of the geophysical survey have been published elsewhere (Gibson 1997), as have the land-use and agricultural threat assessments (Gibson 1998c). The preservation and management recommendations have been made in a CPAT in-house report (Gibson 1998b).

The survey area

The Walton Basin lies in the south-east part of Radnorshire, on the border with Herefordshire, just to the south-west of Presteigne and to the north-west of Kington (Fig 1). The survey area is a block of land roughly 10km by 10km covered by the map sheets SO25NW, SO25NE, SO26SW, SO26SE (Fig 2). The basin, situated in the centre of the block, is about 5km in diameter and is bounded on all sides by steeply rising uplands (Fig 3), including to the west the Radnor Forest and Glascwm Hill. The basin is thought to be the former bed of a post-glacial lake, now drained by the Summergil and Knobley Brooks. A relict shoreline of this lake, represented by a marked terrace, is particularly visible in the Hindwell area running from Hindwell pool to the Four Stones circle.

A low, broad ridge or spine runs roughly east–west along the axis of the basin rising to a maximum of c 25m above the surrounding countryside (Fig 2). From the crest of this ridge may be obtained good views of both the north and south halves of the valley and the well-drained soils afforded by this ridge have provided extensive evidence for prehistoric settlement in the form of flint scatters, round barrows, and occupation sites (see below).

The basin soils comprise well drained, fine loamy soils, some over stream terrace gravels but mostly over drift from Palaeozoic and Mesozoic sandstones and shales. Seasonal waterlogging is a property of some of these soils.

The rapid land-use survey

The rapid land-use survey of the Walton Basin was undertaken during August 1992 and was compiled from the observations made during a site visit to each field. The watershed was used to delimit the study area and encompassed the whole basin with upland areas defining the edges on all sides. The pass to the east and out of the basin between Burfa Bank (SO2861) and Herrock Hill (SO2759) is closed for the purposes of this present study by the English border.

The main land-uses in the basin are arable agricul-

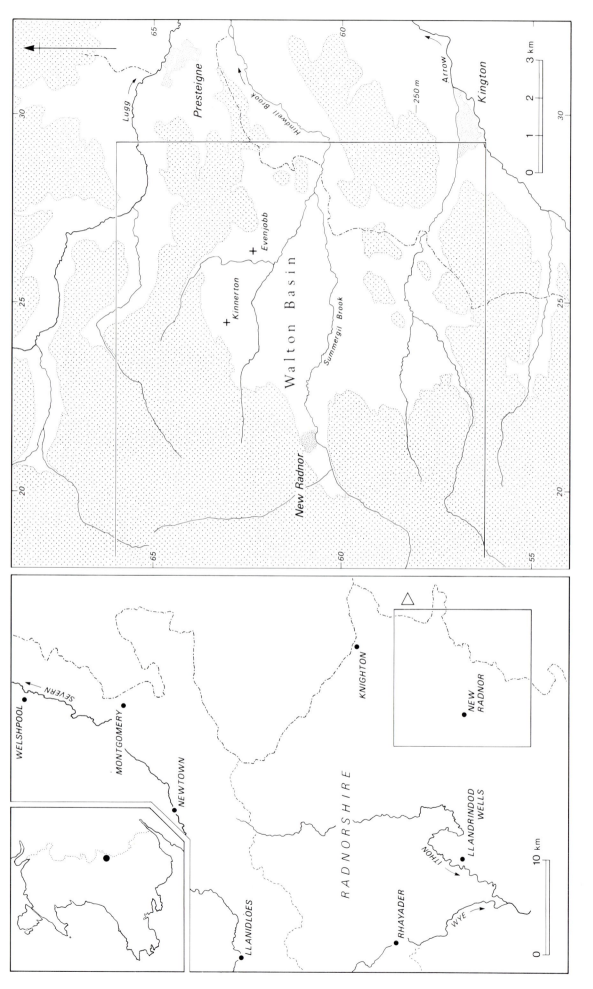

Figure 1 General location map of the Walton Basin

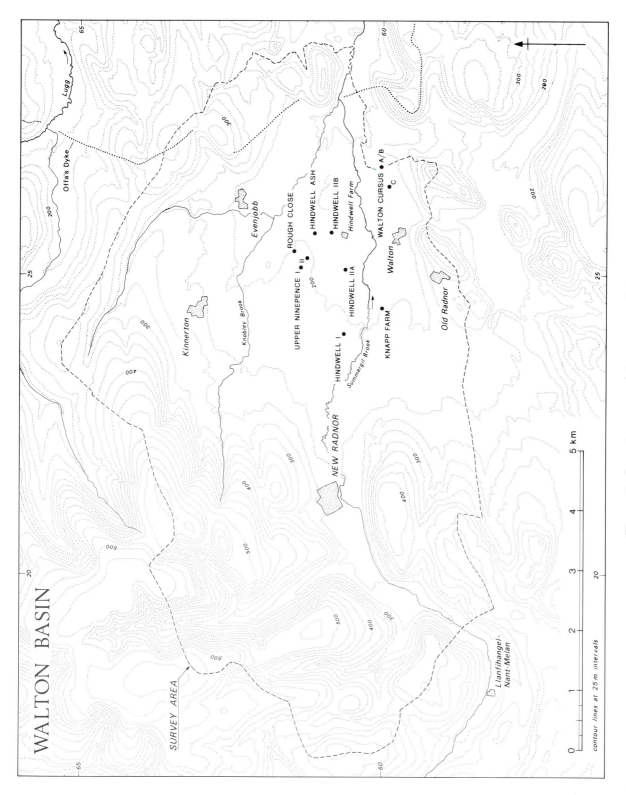

Figure 2 Location map of the excavated sites

Figure 3 Aerial photograph of the Walton Basin taken in 1968 looking north west. Hindwell Farm and pool are in the foreground. Photo No AWI–22, by permission of CUCAP, copyright reserved

ture (cereals and root crop), pasture, rough pasture/moorland, and woodland. The majority of the known earthwork, cropmark and artefactual archaeology is concentrated in the roughly rhomboid parcel of land limited by New Radnor in the west (SO2159), Beggar's Bush in the north (SO2664), Lower Harpton in the east (SO2760) and Walton in the south (SO2559). Furthermore, within this landparcel lies the greatest threat to the known archaeology through active arable agriculture.

The majority of pre-medieval archaeology is represented by cropmarks and artefact scatters themselves a result of a history of intensive arable agriculture and a testimony to the degradation of archaeological contexts. Prehistoric standing monuments are few, comprising a stone circle (Four Stones SO2460), standing stones (only three of which appear to be *in situ*) and round barrows. A further possible round barrow (PAR 3651) was discovered during the

survey. With few exceptions, ploughing continues over these mounds and around the stones irrespective of their scheduled/unscheduled status. All barrows are well-spread and low as a result of the erosive effect of the agricultural regime.

The Four Stones stone circle now stands on a slight knoll or spur as the surrounding land has been lowered by intensive ploughing. This might suggest that even cropmark sites, whose degradation might have been assumed to have stabilised, are in fact still deteriorating as a result of annual plough truncation. Furthermore, possible associated features outside this stone circle may now be difficult to recover.

Fieldwalking was undertaken on ploughed land over the valley floor and artefacts recovered at a number of points (see below). These can be added to the previously known flint scatters documented in the basin (Dunn 1964; 1965; 1966).

Methodology

The project was carried out as follows:

Stage 1 – preliminary assessment

The preliminary assessment comprised: 1 – aerial photograph consultation, 2 – cataloguing and mapping, 3 – library and SMR research, 4 – land-use survey and 5 – liaison with local landowners. Steps 1–3 were essentially desk-top exercises followed by field visits to complete steps 4 and 5 which ran concurrently. Further information on the archaeology of the region and the morphology of specific sites was obtained from steps 1 and 3 which were also the last tasks to be completed. This preliminary assessment allowed the characterisation of the basin's archaeology.

Stage 2 – survey

The survey comprised earthwork survey, geophysical survey, aerial photography and fieldwalking.

The main earthwork survey for the most part took place in November and December 1992 with a team of four people with the aim of assessing the agricultural effects on the archaeological monuments. The round barrows in the basin were judged to be most at risk from the present regime and therefore were selected as a group for survey. These results could be measured against the work of CJ Dunn (1974) which gave a point-in-time description of the condition and dimensions of the mounds. This comparison would enable a quantitative assessment to be made. Throughout the project other earthwork sites were surveyed where landowner permission allowed. The earthwork surveys have been discussed elsewhere (Gibson 1997; Gibson 1998b).

Geophysical survey took two main forms. Firstly it was undertaken over the areas of dense flint scatters in grid squares SO2461 and SO2561 to try and detect buried features from which the flints may have been derived. Secondly, specific sites were targeted either to provide extra information prior to excavation or to attempt to shed light on areas of poor cropmark cover. The geophysical survey has already been discussed (Gibson 1997). In general the results were good over known sites, where aerial photographic cover was informative, but was less successful at prospecting. Resistivity was more successful than magnetometry in these soils.

Aerial photography was undertaken principally in the dry summers of 1994–6 inclusive and was successful both in shedding new light on known monuments and in identifying previously unrecorded sites. The results of this element of the survey work have also been discussed elsewhere (Gibson 1997). Major discoveries made during flights over the valley included a triple-ditched enclosure at Hindwell, the palisaded enclosure at Hindwell, a possible second cursus near the Four Stones (though this may

also be part of a relict field system) and a possible Roman signal station at Harpton. More detailed information was also added to known sites.

Fieldwalking was undertaken during the winters and springs of 1993/4, 1994/5 and 1995/6. Some 'new' flint scatters were identified and post-medieval pottery was collected from several locations. The fieldwalking has been discussed in Gibson (1997) and the prehistoric finds are discussed below.

Stage 3 – excavation

The sites chosen for excavation were as follows:

PRN 307 Hindwell Ash barrow. The northern half of this barrow appeared to have been substantially destroyed and a trial excavation over the mound was designed to assess its condition.

PRN 305 Upper Ninepence barrow. This site comprised a low mound which had been substantially lowered since Dunn's survey. Furthermore Dunn had trial-trenched the site and found evidence for disturbed secondary burials. This degraded mound was completely excavated.

PRN 50187 Upper Ninepence enclosure. This enclosure was trial-trenched to obtain details of its morphology and date.

PRN 26548 Rough Close flint scatter. A small excavation was mounted to determine whether any features associated with the flint scatter had survived ploughing.

PRN 3664 Knapp Farm enclosure. The site was trial-trenched to determine its nature and date.

PRN 4222 Hindwell enclosure I. The site was trial-trenched to determine its nature and date.

PRN 5134 Walton Green cursus. The site was trial-trenched to confirm its identification and to obtain dating material.

PRN 19376 Hindwell enclosure II. The site was trial-trenched to determine its nature and date.

The results of these investigations are presented below.

Characterisation of the prehistoric archaeology of the Walton Basin

Introduction

The prehistoric archaeology of the Walton Basin is characterised and quantified in Table 1. In the majority of cases, the assignment of broad chronological periods to many of these untested and unexcavated sites has been largely intuitive and must be regarded as such.

The earliest signs of human activity are represented by a Palaeolithic artefact from the excavations in the medieval town of New Radnor (Jones, forthcoming). The flint is a shouldered point of Upper Palaeolithic date made of black translucent flint with a thick white patina and is dated to late-glacial

6

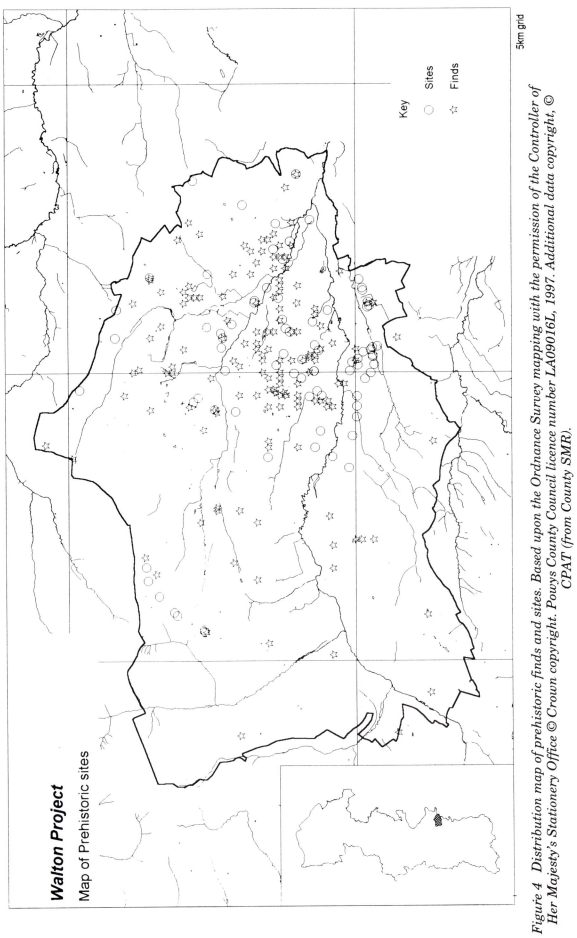

5km grid

Key

◯ Sites

☆ Finds

Walton Project

Map of Prehistoric sites

Figure 4   Distribution map of prehistoric finds and sites. Based upon the Ordnance Survey mapping with the permission of the Controller of Her Majesty's Stationery Office © Crown copyright. Powys County Council licence number LA09016L, 1997. Additional data copyright, © CPAT (from County SMR).

Table 1 Characterisation of the prehistoric archaeology of the Walton Basin

Period	Site type	Number	PRNs
Neolithic	Cursus	2	5134; 33109
	Enclosure	2	4255; 19376
	Mound?	1	359
	Pit alignment	1	5295
	Hengiform ?	1	375
Bronze Age	Enclosure	1	50187
	Ring-ditch	18	365; 373; 4223; 4224; 4254; 5650; 7022; 33100; 33111; 33112; 33113; 33118; 33128; 33129; 33148; 34059; 34400; 50188
	Round barrow	21	296; 300; 303; 305; 307; 309; 310; 314; 358; 369; 1078; 1081; 1991; 1992; 1994; 1995; 1996; 2184; 3651; 4464; 19242;
	Standing stone	6	299; 306; 1069; 1070; 1073; 4226
	Stone placename	4	2116; 2191; 2209; 2212
	Stone circle	1	1072
Iron Age	Ditch system	1	33122
	Enclosure	22	2207; 2274; 2275; 2276; 3664; 4222; 4225; 5133; 5137; 6121; 7025; 19358; 19374; 19427; 19428; 33101; 33117; 33120; 33127; 33131; 33134; 33135; 33155; 33156
	Hillfort	2	297; 312
	Pit alignment	1	50186
	Round house	1	33126
Undated	Bank	5	6831; 7899; 19010; 26297; 26298
	Ditch	2	33130; 33188
	Enclosure	3	6098; 6839; 33108
	Mound	1	6830
	Scoop	1	6837

interstadial and before the Younger Dryas stadial (13,000–11,800BP).

The majority of evidence for earlier prehistoric occupation, however, is to be seen in the lithic scatters which have been found after ploughing on stream terraces and low ridges – the ridge to the south of Rough Close Farm for instance has produced over 6000 flints (Fig 4). Mesolithic forms are well represented in these assemblages, although the majority show Neolithic and early Bronze Age affinities. It is likely that these scatters represent plough-truncated settlement sites though it is not known whether the settlement was permanent, temporary, continuous or intermittent. The flint scatters are dealt with separately below.

Other than the lithic scatters, no Mesolithic monuments have been identified and the earliest visible earthwork monuments date from the late Neolithic and early Bronze Age and include 21 round barrows

(see Table 1). A further eighteen ring-ditches, visible only as cropmarks, probably represent former barrows. The distribution of these sites falls into four main groups. The first is a linear group running along the horizon on the northern edge of the basin. The second, also linear, forms a chain from Kinnerton to Burfa and may represent a former route way. A similar distribution may be detected amongst the standing stones (see below). A third group runs approximately from Downton Farm (SO2360), east to Walton Green (SO2659) (corresponding to the present A44 to Walton) then continues east to the Walton cursus and the English border. The final group is more clustered and occupies the top and southern slopes of the central ridge of the basin between Hindwell and Rough Close farms, within and to the north of the Hindwell palisaded enclosure. This is an area of dense flint scatter attesting Neolithic and Bronze Age settlement and the south-

Figure 5 Aerial photograph of the Walton marching camps and the 'Meldon Bridge-type' enclosure looking north. Photo No BUG–41, by permission of CUCAP, copyright reserved

ern linear arrangement of standing stones also cuts through this barrow cluster.

Other cropmark sites may also be attributable to the Neolithic and Bronze Age, for instance a rather enigmatic large curvilinear enclosure defined by individual evenly-spaced pits (PRN 4255). This monument (Fig 5), with a possible pit-avenue to the south-west, resembles the later Neolithic enclosure at Meldon Bridge, Peeblesshire (Burgess 1976). The recently discovered palisaded enclosure at Hindwell (PRN 19376) also broadly dates to this period (see below) and two possible cursus monuments have been identified on Walton Farm (PRN 5134) and immediately south of the Four Stones (PRN 33109). A large ring-ditch west of Walton village (PRN 375) may

represent a hengiform monument though it appears on the SMR as a possible Roman *gyrus* or horse-training site. A multiple pit alignment at Upper Ninepence (PRN 4281) may also date to this period or may represent a later land boundary or even be the result of agricultural activity (inf Chris Musson).

There are six standing stones in the basin (see below, Table 1) as well as 'stone' placenames. Only three of the stones appear to be *in situ* (Fig 6), though the displaced stones need not have been moved far from their original positions. Like the barrows and ring-ditches, they form two linear arrangements. The first runs from the Four Stones stone circle towards Burfa Bank (PRN 1073, 306, 4226) and the second runs from Downton (Carreg placename PRN 2191) to Hindwell Ash and then to the same point (incorporating PRN 1069, 1070, 299). Both these routes are followed by present routes or tracks and may well represent ancient routes from the basin interior to the pass into the Midlands plain. The Four Stones stone circle (PRN 1072) is of four-poster type (Fig 7) and is one of only two in Wales, the other being at Cwm Saesan, six miles north of Rhayader (Burl 1988, 202–3).

The large mound at Knapp Farm (PRN 359) may possibly be a prehistoric monument rather than a motte which it is generally assumed to be. Firstly, there is no trace of a surrounding ditch or a bailey, nor are there the traces of the ridge and furrow cultivation which generally occurs in the vicinity of the mottes. Secondly the top of the mound is remarkably rounded rather than flat-topped like the other mottes in the basin (Fig 8). That this site should be seen alongside other large prehistoric mounds such as Silbury Hill, Marlborough, Hatfield Barrow or Duggleby Howe is a distinct possibility.

Two spectacular finds were made during ploughing in 1981 on Maesmelan Farm (PRN 5141; SO19455875). They comprise two gold Capel Isaf type hook-fastened bracelets of the middle to late Bronze Age (Green *et al* 1983). Now in the collections of the National Museum and Galleries of Wales, these bracelets had been deposited together, one inside the other, close to the surface and were declared Treasure Trove. Subsequent excavation at the site failed to provide a context for the finds.

Later prehistoric sites include the hillforts of Burfa Camp and Pen Offa (PRN 297, 312) and possibly

Figure 6 Kinnerton Court standing stone from the south east. One of the few in situ *standing stones in the basin*

Figure 7 Photograph of the Four Stones stone circle from the south

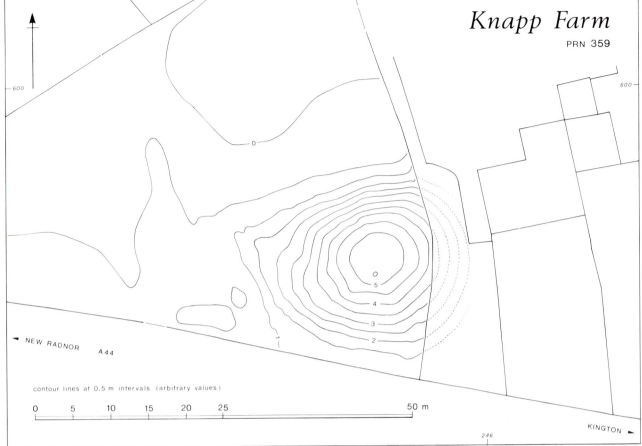

NEW RADNOR   A44

contour lines at 0.5 m intervals (arbitrary values)

0   5   10   15   20   25   50 m

246   KINGTON

Figure 8   Survey of the Knapp Farm mound. Generally considered a motte, the rounded top and lack of a bailey or remnant ridge and furrow in the immediate area suggests it is more possibly a monumental barrow

some of the 22 recorded cropmark enclosures in the basin (Fig 4). These include a rectilinear enclosure on Hindwell Farm (PRN 4222) another at Harpton (PRN 5225) and a larger enclosure below the present road at Knapp (PRN 3664). Other enclosures (PRN 5137, 5123, 6121) are visible amongst the cropmark complex at Walton Farm and a rectilinear enclosure north of Rough Close (PRN 19374) was located during project-based aerial photography in 1994.

Relict field ditches visible on aerial photographs may also belong to this later prehistoric phase. None of these cropmark ditches have been tested by excavation, but their disregard for the present field system suggests that they are earlier and they may well be associated with the later prehistoric enclosures.

Trial excavations

Trial excavation at Rough Close (PRN 26548: SO253617)

Introduction

The site at Rough Close was an area of flint scatter which forms a more generalised scatter along the northern edge of the central ridge of the basin within grid square SO2561. The site was initially investi-

gated as part of a general magnetic susceptibility survey of the subsoil and topsoil along this ridge (Gibson 1997), and was identified as an area with a strong positive response and therefore having a high potential for anthropogenic ground alteration. Consequently an area was investigated in more detail using magnetometer and resistivity surveys and when the results were again positive, a small trench was opened over an area of high response.

Excavation

An area measuring 15m by 5m (Fig 9) was excavated over an area of anomalies revealed by both the magnetometer and resistivity surveys. The stubble and topsoil was removed by machine and the surface subsequently cleaned and excavated by hand.

The subsoil was found to be very irregular in composition from gleyed stone-free patches to areas of dense shale in a yellow soil matrix. Towards the eastern end of the trench was a patch of smooth stone-free hillwash filling a natural gulley running approximately north–south in line with the natural slope. Within this hillwash was a small circular pit (F300) 0.44m in diameter and with a rounded bowl-shaped profile upto 0.2m deep. This pit was filled with a charcoal-rich dark brown soil but was

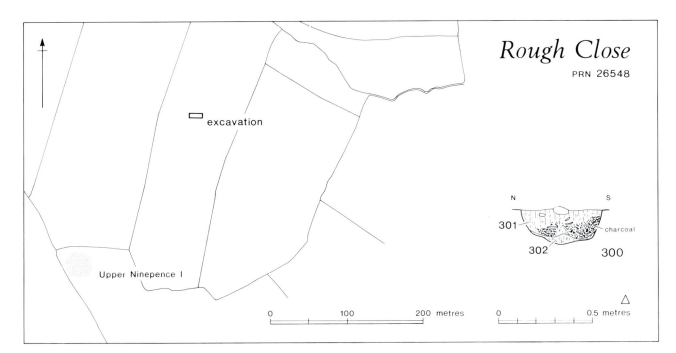

Figure 9 Excavations at Rough Close. Despite the density of flints from the area and the optimistic geophysical survey, only one late Mesolithic pit was recorded

Table 2 Radiocarbon date from Rough Close

Context	Lab No.	Date BP	Cal BC 68%	Cal BC 95%
Pit F300, basal fill	SWAN-114	5860 ± 70	4900–4880 or 4850–4670	4940–4540

devoid of artefacts. There were no traces of *in situ* burning on the sides or base of the pit and its function remains unresolved.

Charcoal from the fill of the pit has been identified as oak, hazel and gorse. A radiocarbon determination has been obtained from the hazel and gorse within the sample and is given in Table 2. This late Mesolithic date provides evidence for the early occupation of the area but this evidence is clearly insufficient to elucidate the nature of the settlement.

The identification of a Mesolithic presence at this site is particularly interesting since analysis of the flint scatter located in the Dunn collection (see below) has highlighted a largely Neolithic and Bronze Age affinity with the possibility of a single, lightly burnt, end scraper, possibly dating to the Mesolithic. Doubtless further Neolithic and Bronze Age features remain to be located at other points within the field.

The Mesolithic presence in the Walton Basin is a sparse one with only some nineteen findspots being located through the Dunn collection. Many of the microlithic finds may well result from accidental loss but nevertheless ten of these findspots occur in grid squares SO2461 and SO2561, in the vicinity of Rough Close and on the north facing slope of the central ridge. It must be here that future work on the Mesolithic occupation of the basin must be centred and the Rough Close pit must be regarded as a small but important physical representation of this period attesting the survival of Mesolithic features. The other nine findspots form no real clustering but are distributed evenly on a broad (1km wide) line from Evenjobb in the north to Walton.

Trial excavation at the Walton Green cursus (PRN 5134)

Introduction

The Walton Green cursus extends from the east of Walton Green Farm (NGR SO26195978) to the field immediately east of Watery Lane (NGR SO26826001). It comprises two parallel ditches running for a distance of 680m and 60m apart (Fig 10). At intervals the cursus is overlain by enclosures considered to be of Iron Age date (PRN 6121, 19427, 19428) while a round barrow (PRN 369) is situated to the west of the western terminal. The cursus is of Loveday's (1985) Bi type having well-spaced parallel ditches and square terminals.

The cursus has never shown up in its entirety as a cropmark but instead has been recognised from composite plots taken over a number of years (Musson 1994).

Excavation (Fig 11)

Three trenches were excavated through the ditches of the cursus monument, two (trenches A and B) at the east terminal (SO26826001) and the third

Figure 10 Aerial photograph of the western end of the Walton cursus with overlying later prehistoric enclosure. Photo by Chris Mussson, CPAT, copyright reserved

(trench C) across the north ditch (at SO 265599). These trenches were intended to obtain dating material from sealed contexts to confirm the identification of the monument as a cursus, and to enable it to be placed in its chronological context within the Walton complex. Accordingly, the topsoil and alluvium were removed by machine and the ditch contexts excavated by hand but no dating evidence was recovered.

Trench A

This excavation measured 3m × 5.5m and was located at what appeared to be the mid-point of the cursus terminal where it became indistinct in both the geophysical survey and on the aerial photographs. The trench was designed to test for a causeway at this point.

The cursus ditch was located in the hard natural riverine gravel below 1m of hard-packed grey alluvium. The ditch measured 2.8m across at the gravel surface in the north section and attained a depth of 0.3m below the gravel. It was shallow and rounded in profile and decreased in depth towards the south section where it faded out into a rounded terminal confirming both the cropmark and geophysical evidence.

The fill of the ditch comprised fine-fractioned leached silts with occasional small pebbles and with

no indication of silting patterns. The only finds comprised three flint flakes and a possible piercer (see below) from high in the ditch silts.

Trench B

This trench measured 7m × 2m and was located at the north-east corner of the monument (Fig 11) where the cursus ditch was located below 0.9m of alluvium. At the natural gravel surface, the ditch measured 2m across and 0.8m deep and was filled with fine-fractioned silt and gravel lenses (Fig 11). The tip lines indicated that the ditch had silted from the interior of the monument attesting the presence of internal banks.

Flint flakes were recovered from the upper silts of the ditch (see below).

Trench C

Trench C measured 2.5m × 8m and was located over the north ditch which at the time of excavation was showing as a well-defined cropmark. The turf and topsoil overlay the natural yellow-brown subsoil which was scarred with modern ploughmarks and at which point the cursus ditch could be recognised.

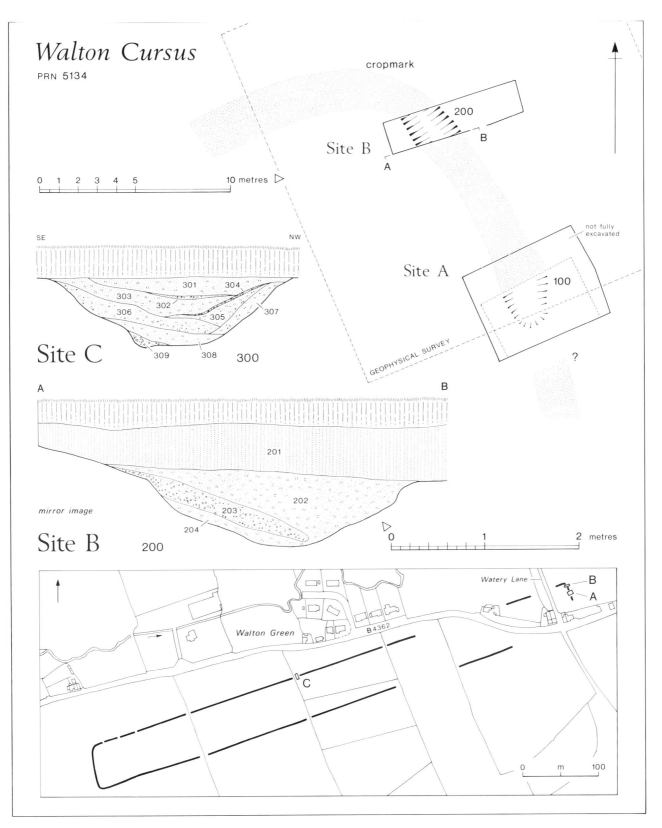

Figure 11 Walton cursus: excavation plans

The ditch was 3m wide and 0.7–0.8m deep below the natural subsoil. It was flat-bottomed and filled with silts indicating filling from the interior.

The only find from this trench was a large, possibly Neolithic flint end-and-side scraper from the upper silts towards the outer edge of the ditch.

Results

While the excavations succeeded in locating the ditches of the monument, the results of the excavations were poor in that no datable materials were found. Ditch morphology was recorded, however, and

Figure 12   Aerial photograph of the western end of Hindwell II. The first excavation was in the field corner towards the bottom of the photograph. Photo Alex Gibson, CPAT, copyright reserved

they proved to be shallow and narrow in keeping with other cursus monuments excavated in Wales (Gibson 1994; Houlder 1968). Some flint finds were recovered and while they are consistent in indicating a third or second millennium date (see finds below), their recovery from high in the silts implies that they cannot be regarded as reliable chronological indicators.

Trial excavations at Hindwell II palisaded enclosure (PRN 19376)

Introduction

A large arc of ditch (Fig 12) was discovered from the air during routine flying in 1994 (Gibson 1995c; 1998a). It lay on Hindwell Farm in the field known as 'Little Monster', the field in which the possible Four Stones cursus is expected to terminate, and it described an arc from a circle with an approximate diameter of 400m. Possible traces of an external bank showed on the aerial photograph and, when combined with perceived breaks in the ditch circumference, suggested the possibility of a Neolithic date for the monument. Accordingly geophysical survey and a small excavation were mounted to elucidate on the nature of the site and to try and recover dating material from secure contexts (site A). The geophysical survey (resistivity) located the ditch of the enclosure which was invisible on the

ground and also located the post-ramps though these were only recognised with hindsight after the excavation (Gibson 1997).

In 1995 further aerial photography produced evidence for a ditch of similar character in Berry Meadow field at SO257607. This ditch appeared to be coming out from beneath the modern minor road which described a peculiar curve at this point. It was a distinct probability that the track fossilised the line of the earthwork and that the Berry Meadow ditch was indeed part of the same site. If this was the case, then the ditch described an oval some 800m × 400m. Accordingly a second season of geophysical survey (with similar results, see Gibson 1997) and excavation (site B) was mounted to test the character of the new discovery. Subsequent air photography in 1996 located further arcs of ditch comprising the southern perimeter of the enclosure with the result that some 75% of the circumference can now be traced (Fig 13).

Site A (Little Monster)

An area measuring 20m × 20m was subject to geophysical survey by magnetometer, resistivity and ground probing radar (Gibson 1997). During the summer of 1995, a small trench measuring 5m × 15m was opened over the line of the ditch at SO25076065. The trench was placed at an oblique

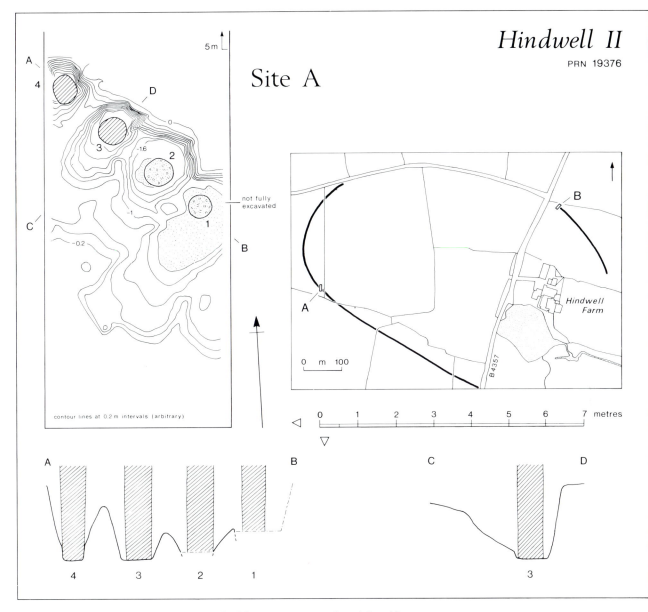

Figure 13   Plan of Hindwell II: Little Monster excavation (site A)

angle over the ditch to keep it close to the present hedge line and thus to minimise damage to the growing crop. The topsoil and ploughsoil were removed by machine and all cleaning and subsequent excavation was done by hand. The subsoil was generally an orange-yellow soil with a large (90%) ill-sorted stone content which made the recognition of features difficult.

A line of darker, relatively stone-free, soil was visible running at an angle across the centre of the trench on the estimated line of the enclosure ditch. This appeared to be much narrower than the wide ditch revealed in the geophysical survey. Further cleaning produced the traces of a post-pipe with carbonised outer rings still present in the western end of this trench. This darker soil proved to be the slow fill of the settling hollow in the backfill of the trench. The edges of the trench proved difficult to locate in the plough-disturbed stony subsoil until a depth of *c* 0.3m had been reached when natural

banding lines in the gravel could be noted. The ditch could then be widened out to a solid wall at the north (interior) but to a series of elongated post-ramps on the outer edge. These ramps were up to 4m long in the area excavated and provide the reason for the broad geophysical anomaly.

On excavation the trench proved to comprise a series of four intersecting postpits each with attendant post-ramp (Fig 14). It was not possible to completely excavate all the pits as a consequence of time and safety considerations. On average they measured 1.75m in diameter at the top and the two which were completely excavated, postholes 3 and 4 respectively proved to be 0.75 and 0.6m in diameter at the base and 2.10 and 1.80m deep. The filling of each posthole was a mixture of coarse mixed gravel. Each posthole contained a well-defined post-pipe which was filled with pinkish-brown sandy clay and was relatively stone-free. The carbonised outer rings of *in situ* posts were found at all levels in all four

Figure 14   The postpits at Hindwell II, site A, after excavation

postholes and indicated regularly-spaced oak posts *c* 0.7m in diameter and at intervals of between 0.7m and 0.9m edge to edge (Figs 12–14).

There were no finds of any date from stratified contexts within the area of excavation but sufficient charcoal was obtained from the outer rings of the oak posts for radiocarbon dating (see below).

Site B (Berry Meadow)

Site B was situated at SO257618 and measured 16m × 5m. It was laid out at right angles to the ditch as located both on the aerial photographs and by geophysical survey. The topsoil and turf was 0.3m thick and overlay up to 0.4m of fine-fractioned hillwash. Therefore the gravel surface was deeply covered, which may account for the ephemeral nature of the cropmark.

Traces of four large postholes were found excavated into the gravel surface (Fig 15). These were identical in nature to those located in site A. They intersected, measured 2m in diameter at the gravel surface, and each contained a post-pipe 0.9–1m in diameter. Once again the posts had been carbonised and charcoal from the outer rings was recovered *in situ*.

Strictures of time did not permit the complete excavation of any of the postholes but the attendant post-ramps were visible against the natural gravel surface and extended up to 3m from the post-pipe. Like the postholes, they were filled with loose jumbled gravel, difficult to distinguish from the natural. Charcoal from posts 2 and 3 was submitted for radiocarbon dating.

Also in site B were traces of six other pits describing an arc from a circle some 4m in diameter (Fig 15). These pits varied from 0.4–0.6m in diameter and from 0.12–0.4m deep, and were noted both in the natural gravel outside the enclosure and cutting through the filling of the post-ramps. The fill of these pits was remarkably similar to the fills of the post-pipes of the main enclosure and it may be that the pits themselves held posts which had rotted *in situ*. There were, however, neither packing stones nor indications within the fill of each pit to confirm the former presence of posts. These features clearly post-date the palisaded enclosure but no dating evidence or datable material was recovered from the fills and their nature and date remain elusive.

Radiocarbon determinations

Four radiocarbon determinations were obtained from the excavations on Hindwell II, two from trench A and two from trench B. The results of these determinations are given in Table 3.

All four determinations are remarkably similar and statistically indistinguishable, despite the large margins of error and the apparent lateness of Swan–116. They may be combined as in Table 3 to provide a date

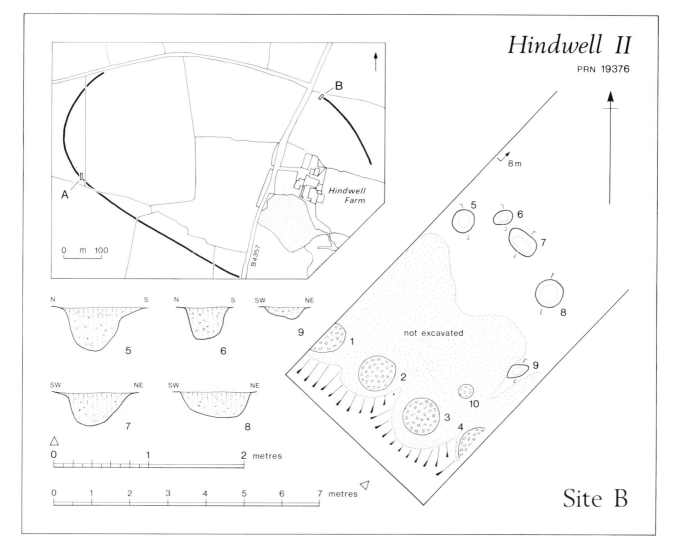

Figure 15 Plan of Hindwell II: Berry Meadow excavation (site B)

Table 3 Radiocarbon dates from Hindwell II

Context	Lab No	Date BP	Cal BC 68%	Cal BC 95%
Trench A: post 1	Swan-116	3960 ± 70	2590–2350	2900–2800 or 2700–2200
Trench A: post 4	Swan-117	4070 ± 70	2870–2810 or 2750–2720 or 2700–2560 or 2540–2500	2880–2800 or 2780–2460
Trench A combined date		4015 ± 49	2610–2470	2870–2810 or 2700–2450
Trench B: post 2	Swan-230	4040 ± 80	2860–2810 or 2700–2470	2900–2350
Trench B: post 3	Swan-231	4130 ± 80	2880–2800 or 2780–2600	2910–2500
Trench B combined date		4085 ± 56	2870–2810 or 2750–2720 or 2700–2570 or 2530–2510	2880–2800 or 2780–2490
Trenches A & B combined dates		4045 ± 37	2860–2830 or 2660–2640 or 2620–2560 or 2540–2500	2870–2810 or 2740–2720 or 2700–2470

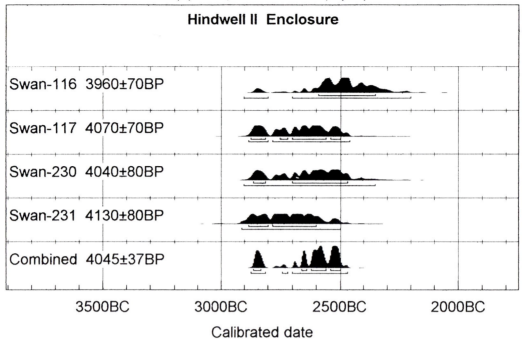

Figure 16   C14 dates from Hindwell II

Figure 17   Aerial photograph of the Upper Ninepence enclosure. Photo Alex Gibson, CPAT, copyright reserved

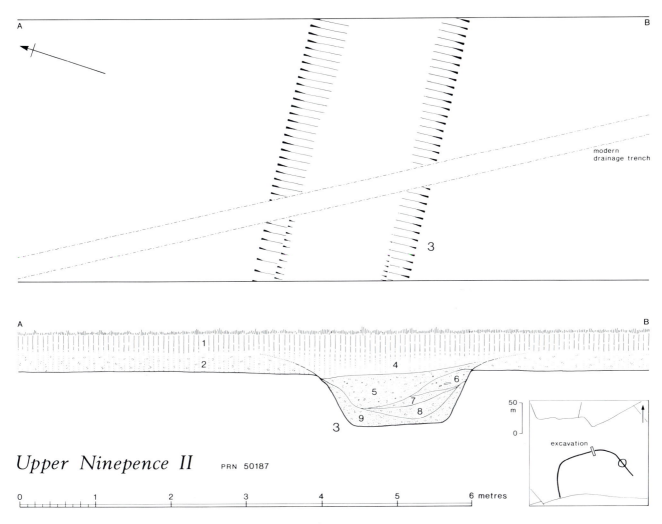

A   B

modern
drainage trench

3

A   B

1

2

4

6

5

7

8

9

3

50
m

0

excavation

Upper Ninepence II   PRN 50187

0   1   2   3   4   5   6 metres

Figure 18   Upper Ninepence enclosure: excavation plan

of 4045 ± 37 BP. They clearly place the construction of the palisade between *c* 2800–2500 Cal BC (Fig 16).

Results

Excavation at two widely separated points on the circumference of this monument has confirmed its unity in terms of date and building construction. The site can now be identified as a large enclosure covering some 34Ha and with a circumference of over 2km. No finds were recovered from the site and its cultural affinities cannot be established with certainty, though its contemporaneity with the Grooved Ware phase at Upper Ninepence (see below) is noteworthy. The site is discussed in greater detail below.

Trial excavation at the Upper Ninepence enclosure, Hindwell (PRN 50187; SO253613)

Introduction

The Upper Ninepence enclosure was discovered from the air in 1969 by Professor St Joseph (CUCAP AP No AYB34). It showed as a continuous irregular

curve emanating from and returning to the southern hedgeline of the field (Fig 17). It intersects a ring-ditch at the north-eastern arc and a cropmark resembling a multiple pit alignment runs south-south-west–north-north-east through the centre of the enclosure. Ground observation in 1995 and 1996 suggests that this cropmark may be of an agricultural, rather than archaeological, origin.

Though the southern circuit of the enclosure has not been identified, it is obvious that it lies on moderately sloping ground on the middle to lower slopes of the south side of the basin's central ridge and does not appear to encompass any level ground. It's date and function was therefore difficult to determine. Excavation was designed to obtain datable material from the ditch silts and to shed further light on the morphology of the monument.

Excavation (Fig 18)

A small trench measuring 15m × 4.5m was opened over the ditch. The modern turf and humus (context 1) and ploughsoil (context 2) were removed by machine and the remaining contexts were cleaned and excavated by hand. The ditch was located near the centre of the trench. It proved to be 2m across at the top where it showed in the natural subsoil, and 1.2m wide at the base. It was flat-bottomed and measured 0.7m deep. The fill was fairly homogenous, comprising fine-fractioned silts in which silting episodes could be detected. These silts suggest that the ditch had silted from the interior and that the site therefore had had an internal bank. Flint flakes (see below) were found in all levels of the ditch. They comprised five flint flakes, one retouched, and a core fragment.

Radiocarbon dating

Charcoal was recovered from the base of the ditch (context 9) and from the top of the uppermost silts (context 5). The upper sample has been identified as short-lived material comprising ash, rowan, poplar, hawthorn and gorse. The lower sample also comprised short-lived material including hazel, blackthorn and small diameter oak. The radiocarbon dates are given in Table 4.

The difference in date between these two determinations confirms the slow silting of the ditch, but interestingly illustrates that the enclosure is early Bronze Age in origin.

Results

The limited excavation has demonstrated a reasonably shallow flat-bottomed ditch with traces of silting from the interior. Diagnostic finds were once more absent but securely stratified charcoal deposits have allowed the enclosure to be dated. The site is discussed in more detail below.

Trial excavation at Hindwell Ash (PRN 307) (NGR 257611)

Introduction

The Hindwell Ash barrow straddled a field boundary and appeared to have been greatly destroyed by ploughing in its northern half, dropping from 1m in height to field level over a distance of only 7m (Fig 19). A trench 10m × 10m was opened over the central area of the visible mound during December and January 1992/3 with a workforce of four people. The work was hindered by wet weather followed by extreme frosts over the Christmas/New Year period making excavation impossible.

The purpose of the excavation was to test the actual (as opposed to estimated) plough-damage to the site and this barrow was chosen for two reasons. Firstly, the degree of damage to the northern half was considerable and it appeared that little stratigraphy remained. Secondly, flints had been recorded in the fields around this mound as well as from the barrow itself, and it was possible that pre-barrow features from which the flint was derived might still have been protected beneath the surviving stratigraphy.

The topsoil was removed using a JCB and the site otherwise excavated by hand. The archaeological features encountered are not fully understood but the sequence of events on the site as revealed by excavation is as follows.

Pre-barrow features

Postholes

Seven certain and eleven possible features were found excavated into the clay subsoil (Fig 20). The certain features comprised postholes 10 and 12–15, a shallow flat-bottomed gully (11), and a possible pit (21) which largely underlay the section and consequently was not investigated. The postholes ranged from 0.3–0.5m in diameter and from 0.15–0.3m deep. Each contained traces of a central post c 0.2m in diameter in the form of a softer, darker post-pipe in the generally yellow-grey clayey backfill. Fragments of oak charcoal (see below) were recovered from postholes 10 and 12. The postholes formed an irregular setting of unknown form and purpose. Taken with the features of uncertain origin, postholes 10 and 12–14 formed a rectangular setting 1.6m × 1.2m.

The following radiocarbon date was recovered from oak charcoal from one of the postholes (12). This calibrated date clearly places the postholes in the early Bronze Age and also acts as a *terminus post quem* for the barrow mound (Table 5).

Table 4   The radiocarbon dates from the Upper Ninepence enclosure

Context	Lab No	Date BP	Cal BC 68%	Cal BC 95%
U9D II. Basal ditch silts	SWAN-21	3390 ± 70	1870–1840 or 1780–1610	1880–1520
U9D II. Upper ditch silts	SWAN-22	2010 ± 70	110–AD60	200–AD130

Table 5   Radiocarbon date from posthole 12, Hindwell Ash

Context	Date BP	Lab No	Cal BC 68%	Cal BC 95%
Posthole 12	3730 ± 70	CAR-1480	2280–2230 or 2210–2030	2500–1900

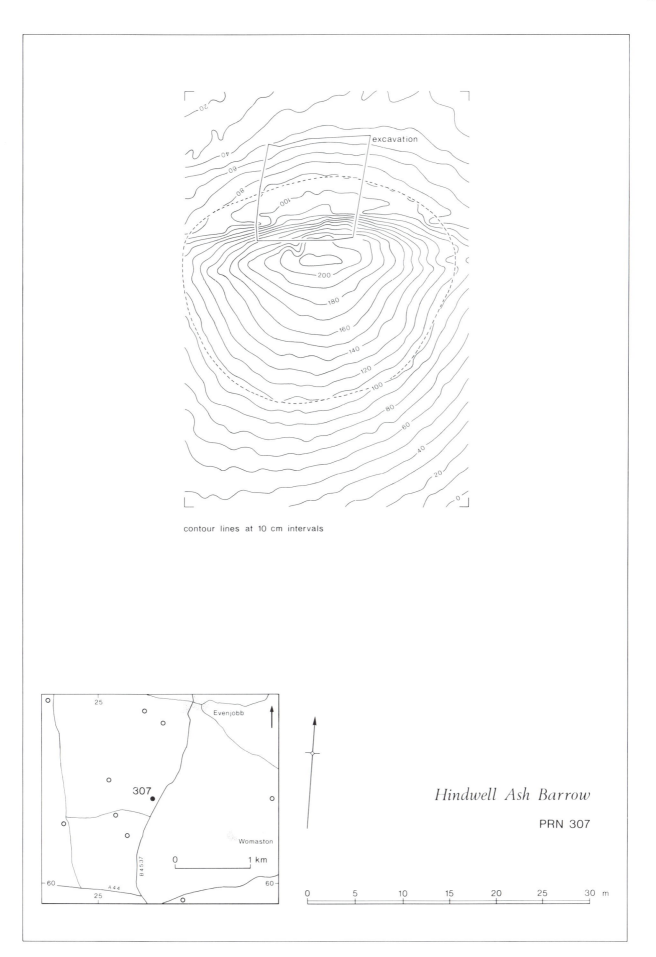

contour lines at 10 cm intervals

Hindwell Ash Barrow

PRN 307

Figure 19 Survey of the barrow at Hindwell Ash

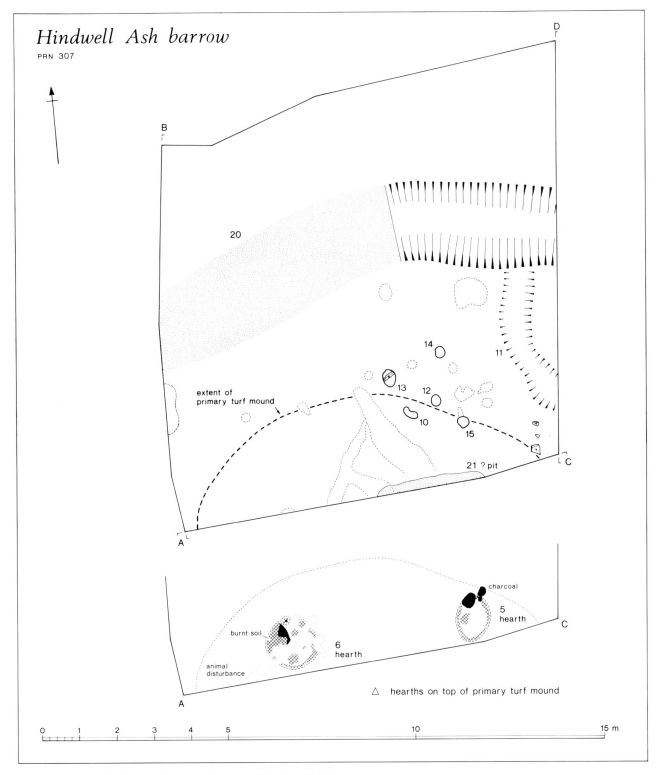

Figure 20 Plan of the trial excavations at Hindwell Ash

The gully

The flat-bottomed gully (11) measured 0.8m wide by 0.15m deep. It was filled with a uniform stiff, leached grey clay with occasional flecks of elm, poplar, hazel and hawthorn charcoal (see below). A small fragment of pottery with a smooth inner surface and containing abundant finely-crushed quartz and igneous inclusions was recovered from the lowest levels of the fill of this feature. The sherd weighs only 8g and the majority of the outer surface is missing. It is not possible to attribute a style or date to this pottery, but the angular crushed quartz inclusions recall the Neolithic sherds from Bromfield (Stanford 1982, 283–5), and the Peterborough Ware from Upper Ninepence (see below).

The buried soil

The features described above were only recognised in the natural yellow stony clay subsoil. This was overlain by an orange-brown stony soil with a smooth clayey texture (context 10), which achieved a maximum depth of 0.2m (Fig 21; sections A–C and C–D). A utilised flint blade fragment was recovered from this buried soil.

Pit 21

This pit cut through the buried soil (Fig 21; section A–C) and was filled with a grey sandy clay including manganese and iron oxide flecks (context 13). The pit measured 2.9m long where it entered the section and projected 0.3m into the excavated area. It was investigated to a depth of 0.16m, at which point excavation became both dangerous and futile, in view of the small area concerned. It is likely that this pit represents a central grave.

The barrow sequence

The turf mound

Overlying the buried soil and separated from it by a thin layer of iron pan, possibly representing a former turfline, were the remains of a turf mound (Fig 21; section A–C, context 12). This comprised soft sandy grey clay interspersed with intermittent lenses of iron pan. The mound had suffered considerable damage from burrowing animals. It projected 2.8m into the excavated area and was recorded as a chord of 9.3m with a height of 0.7m in the exposed section. Finds from this context comprised three flint flakes (two calcined) and a small blue glass bead (Fig 49 no 3). A high quality bifacially retouched oblique arrowhead (Fig 49 no 1) in a brown flint, and with an impact fracture at the tip, was recovered from the lowermost layers of the mound close to the section and c 0.3m north-west of and 0.2m above pit 21. Two fragments of pottery were found close together in the upper levels of the mound. One, weighing 6g is in an identical fabric to the sherd from gully 11. The second is in a much finer fabric, only 6mm thick with smooth surfaces, weighs only 1g and is probably Beaker. Both sherds are undecorated.

The turf mound appears to be a central or near-central core to the barrow and may well be associated with pit 21 which was cut through the underlying iron pan and was directly covered by the turf mound. Finds from this context may represent residual material already present in the turves at the time of the construction of the turf mound and thus may provide a *terminus post quem* for this phase of the barrow. However, the possibility that these finds, particularly the glass bead and the pottery, may have been introduced by the animal burrowing cannot be discounted.

The ditch

A large curving ditch (Fig 20 no 20) was located running through the centre of the trench. It measured c 2m wide by 0.6m deep below the natural subsoil. It had widely splayed straight sides and a rounded base, though the exact profile was difficult to determine with absolute confidence due to the ditch being waterlogged throughout the excavation. The ditch was filled with grey silty sand and contained fragments of hazel and blackthorn charcoal in its uppermost fill (see below). A utilised flint flake (Fig 49 no 2) was found in a similar context.

The ditch formed the irregular arc of a circle of c 30m in diameter and appeared to be slightly eccentric to the turf mound and the surviving earthwork barrow. The ditch was also unexpected not having been recorded previously by ground observation, survey or aerial photography, since it was apparently covered by the material of the plough-spread barrow. No material which could be certainly identified as being derived from the ditch was found within either the turf mound or earlier contexts; therefore the ditch seems to represent a later (though perhaps only slightly later) eccentric enlargement of the original mound.

The secondary mound

Material from the ditch described above appears to have been deposited as a capping over the turf mound (Fig 21, context 3). This is clearly secondary in sequence, though it may not have a chronological significance. There were no finds from this layer. As mentioned above, the mound enlargement seems to have been slightly eccentric to the turf mound – if indeed it is correct to see this phase of activity as being associated with the ditch. Nor was this ditch concentric with the surviving earthwork. It therefore remains a possibility that a third phase, perhaps represented by the orange-brown context 2 (Fig 21), further seals the surviving contexts and that this material may well be derived from a second, outer ditch beyond the limits of the excavation. There were no finds from this context.

The hearths

Two hearths (Fig 20, 5–6) were located within layer 3 and over the surviving turf mound (12). They were recognised by the fire-reddened soil around them and their abundant charcoal. Both hearths were disturbed by animal burrows. Hearth 5 was oval, measuring 1.2m × 1m, and occupied a dished hollow 0.1m deep. Hazel, ash and oak charcoal (see below) was recovered from the hearth as well as a calcined flint flake. Hearth 6 was more circular, being 1.4m in diameter, and occupied a similar dished hollow. It was associated with hazel, elm and oak charcoal, a calcined flint flake and spall.

24

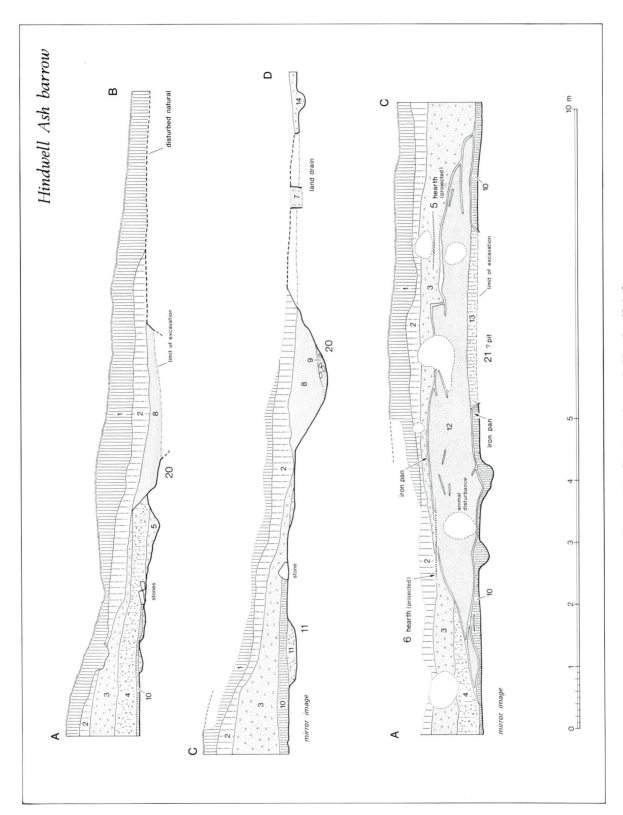

Figure 21 Sections through Hindwell Ash

Table 6 Radiocarbon date from hearth 5, Hindwell Ash

Context	Date BP	Lab No	Cal BC 68%	Cal BC 95%
Hearth context 5	1970 ± 60	CAR-1481	60BC–AD80	160–140 or 120BC–AD190

These hearths pose stratigraphic problems. A radiocarbon date (Table 6) was recovered from one of them (hearth 5). The calibrated date places the hearths in the late Iron Age or early Roman period, yet hearth 6 was situated on top of the turf mound and cut into it slightly, and hearth 5 was located in the grey-brown leached sandy clay (context 3) which overlay the turf mound (Fig 21).

Both features were either within or sealed by layer 3, which is interpreted as being the up-cast from the ditch representing a phase of barrow embellishment. The position of these hearths appears to suggest that this took place in the Roman period or later, thus the following may be suggested to explain the apparent discrepancy:

1 The radiocarbon date obtained is incorrect, perhaps from the incorporation in the sample of later material introduced by the animal activity noted above.
2 The date is acceptable and the hearths were inserted into the enlarged mound. If this is the case, no trace of this insertion was noted during the excavation, perhaps as a result of a combination of poor light, animal disturbance, and weather conditions.
3 The ditch and layer 3 are, in fact, unconnected. If this is the case then the whereabouts of the up-cast from the ditch has yet to be identified.
4 The irregularity of the turf mound at this point may suggest that the secondary mound had been damaged in this area, presumably in antiquity.

There are no supporting finds for this late date, although a glass bead (Fig 49 no 3) may possibly date to this phase, but nevertheless the use of the mound during this period is not incomprehensible. The mound offers a high vantage point over the surrounding fields from which an Iron Age pastoralist might keep watch over flocks and herds. Equally the Roman camps at Walton and Crossways Lane, and the fort at Hindwell Farm, are all visible from the Hindwell Ash barrow from which views to the northern half of the basin may be obtained. It would have provided an excellent vantage point for a Roman look-out. The lateness of the hearth also draws parallels with that discovered in the Upper Ninepence mound discussed below. The prominence of the mound is further attested by the presence of the Ordnance Survey triangulation pillar.

A domestic interpretation for the hearths seems likely. Amongst the charcoal from hearth 5 was 'a sample of vesicular charred material with traces of cereal grains and other vegetable matter. Assuming that bread would not have contained unground grains, this material could have been burnt "porridge" or burnt coprolite. There was a semicircular section about 20mm in diameter to part of it suggesting the latter' (note supplied by Dr G Morgan).

Results

Conclusions drawn from such a small-scale excavation of such damaged features must necessarily be tentative. Nevertheless some observations may be safely made. Firstly, the barrow appears to have had a complex history. Enigmatic pre-barrow features dated to *c* 2200–1985 BC (see above), with evidence for some structural activity and loosely associated with late Neolithic pottery, were covered by a turf barrow. This may have taken place after a considerable period of time, long enough for the buried soil (context 10) to develop. Alternatively, the features may have been cut through context 10 only becoming archaeologically visible in the light coloured subsoil. A *terminus post quem* for this turf mound may be provided by the oblique arrowhead and possible Beaker sherd from the mound material, and by the radiocarbon date obtained for the pre-barrow features. The site is discussed in more detail below.

Trial excavation at the Knapp Farm enclosure (PRN 3664; SO244600)

Introduction

The rectilinear enclosure at Knapp Farm (PRN3664) was discovered on aerial photographs in 1989 (Fig 22). The enclosure was bisected by the present road and the ditch, visible in grass, described an area 75m by 60m. A break in the cropmark in the south-east corner, may well represent an entrance causeway.

The excavations were concentrated on the ditch and were designed to shed light on the original form of the enclosure perimeter and to provide dating evidence for the site.

Excavation

A trench measuring 11m × 3m was excavated across the line of the ditch (Fig 22). The turf and ploughsoil were removed by machine and the surface cleaned by hand. The ditch was entirely hand-excavated.

The top of the ditch was visible as a less stony band crossing the trench. Its uppermost fill of sparse stones within grey clayey matrix stood out against

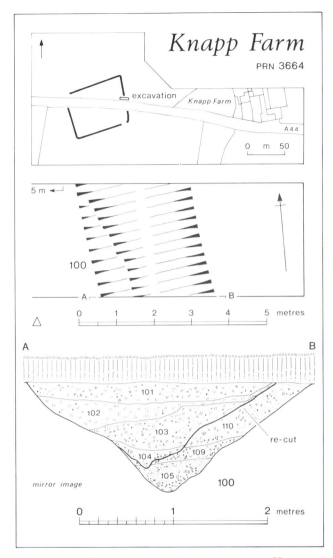

Figure 22 Plan of the trial excavations at Knapp Farm enclosure

the yellow ill-sorted gravel subsoil. It measured 3.5m wide.

The ditch was completely filled with varying lenses of gravel in a soil matrix. The dryness of the 1995 summer made the ditch difficult to excavate and the fills were difficult to identify: they were generally differentiated by their degree of stoniness. Nevertheless, the wetting of the section elucidated the fills, and indicated that the ditch had originally been V-sectioned and 1.15m deep below the gravel surface (Fig 22). This had been recut, apparently when the ditch had been more or less fully silted. The silting patterns appeared to be quite flat though there was a slight indication that the silting was from the inside suggesting an internal bank.

There were no finds from the ditch. Some sparse charcoal flecks and small fragments of calcined bone were recovered from context 102, a smooth grey silt representing the slow final silting of the second recut, but the charcoal was insufficient and too dispersed for reliable radiocarbon dating.

Interpretation

The dating of this enclosure remains unresolved but it appears to have been occupied over a considerable period of time though not necessarily continuously. The silting patterns within the ditch and the lack of features within the excavated part of the interior may be used to infer the presence of an internal bank. The ditch had been recut from a high level to a similar design. The V-section resembles the ditch at Hindwell I which had a similarly stony fill and which had also silted from the interior. The site may be assumed to be of later prehistoric date, but only by analogy with other sites (eg Hindwell I).

Trial excavation at Hindwell enclosure I (PRN 4222: NGR SO239606)

Introduction

Hindwell I is a trapezoidal enclosure situated in low-lying pasture at the western end of Hindwell Farm. It has appeared frequently as a cropmark in grass, particularly resulting from clover re-growth after hay or silage cropping (Fig 23). The cropmark reveals a single-ditched enclosure, orientated roughly east–west, with an entrance causeway near the north-east corner. The eastern, broader end is markedly bowed towards the exterior and the narrow western end is also bowed, though less dramatically, this time towards the interior. The north ditch frequently shows as a tramline cropmark (ie darker lines defining the edge of the ditch) which classically attests the truncation of the ditch silts. A large depression in the interior of the site is probably the result of gravel quarrying, and palaeochannels also show as cropmarks to the north of the site. Some aerial photographs reveal traces of a ring-ditch (PRN 33126) near the centre of the monument, to the east of the gravel quarry. This feature was also noted on analysis of the geophysical survey data (Gibson 1997), and may be a round house or may equally be a result of the gravel quarrying.

Hindwell I was selected for excavation to assess the plough damage to the site as a whole and to retrieve dating evidence for this strangely-shaped enclosure.

Excavation

Trench A (Fig 24)

Trench A measured 7.75m × 9m and was situated over the entrance causeway in order to locate and excavate the eastern ditch terminal and to unearth any features on the entrance causeway.

A length of ditch terminal 3.5m long was completely excavated. It is interesting that it did not exactly coincide with the cropmark but was as much

Figure 23 Aerial photograph of the excavations and cropmark at Hindwell I. Photo Chris Musson by permission of RCAHMW, Crown copyright reserved

as 1m north of where it was expected. The cropmark was also much broader than the ditch proved to be. The ditch was 2.15m wide at the gravel surface where it entered the section, was 1m deep, and was V-sectioned. It had been quickly filled with a few layers noted within the predominantly gravel fills. There is evidence in the form of context 504, a thick layer of yellow-brown loamy sand and gravel, to suggest that the ditch was filled from the interior and that there was, therefore, an internal bank.

The ditch was substantially recut as may be seen in the section (Fig 24). This recut feature was slightly narrower and shallower than the original and it is from layers in this recut that the finds are derived.

Occasional small flecks of comminuted charcoal were encountered from the upper levels of the ditch, and fragments of four vessels, in the Saucepan Pot tradition (see below) of the 4th and 2nd centuries BC (Fig 32), came from the upper silts in context 502.

The gravel subsoil was extremely dry and ill-sorted and, despite watering, locating the features was difficult. Nevertheless, six small pits were certainly identified and five of these were aligned on the centre of the causeway. The two largest of these features, pits 100 and 600, were oval and measured 0.9m × 1.3m × 0.3m deep and 1.75m × 1m × 0.4m deep

respectively. Their fills comprised dark loamy soil with gravel, and while no post-pipes were visible in the dry fills, there was the suggestion of a void in pit 600. Pit 700, also on the centre line of the causeway, measured 1.25m × 1m × 0.4m deep. The fill was as for the previously described features and once more there was the hint of a void in the centre of the feature which may suggest the former presence of a post. It is likely that these features were severely truncated, as the tramline ditch cropmark in this area shows, and that they represent postholes associated with some gate mechanism for the enclosure. However, it must be acknowledged that no datable material was recovered from any of the features and consequently their association with the enclosure can only be assumed.

Pit 900 also lay on the centre line of the causeway though some 3m outside the enclosure. It measured 0.6m across where it entered the section and was 0.35m deep. Feature 1200 also entered the north section and was either a ditch terminal or an oval pit. It was 0.95m wide where it entered the section and projected 1.5m from it. It was 0.5m deep and contained a sandy-clay and gravel fill. Once more no distinction in fill was noted, though there was suggestion of a void in the distribution of stone near the centre of the pit, perhaps indicating that this too was originally a posthole.

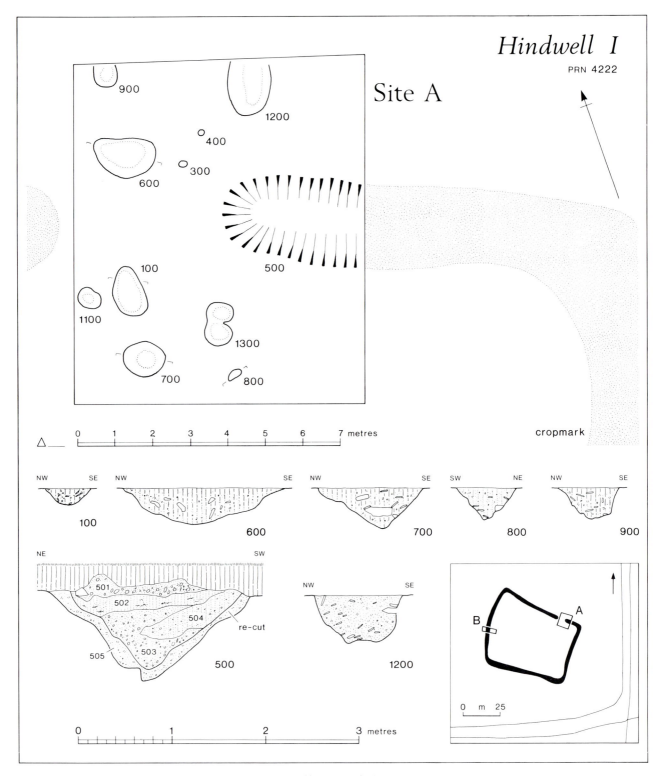

Figure 24 Plan of the trial excavations at Hindwell I, trench A

Trench B (Fig 25)

Measuring 10m × 3m, this trench was located over the west curving ditch. The cropmark did not show as a tramline here and it was therefore assumed that the preservation was better than it was on the north side. In this case, the cropmark and the archaeology coincided exactly. The ditch was 2.9m wide at the gravel surface and measured 1.1m deep in the north section and 1.2m deep in the south. Once again the

ditch was V-sectioned and had been backfilled rapidly with both loose gravel and gravel in a sandy matrix. There was the hint of silting from the interior in the north section but the south section was less convincing. The only finds recovered from the ditch in this trench comprised a single sherd of Iron Age pottery from the uppermost silts (context 101). Two possible postholes were located in the far eastern end of the trench. These were noted as two distinctly circular depressions filled with dark loamy

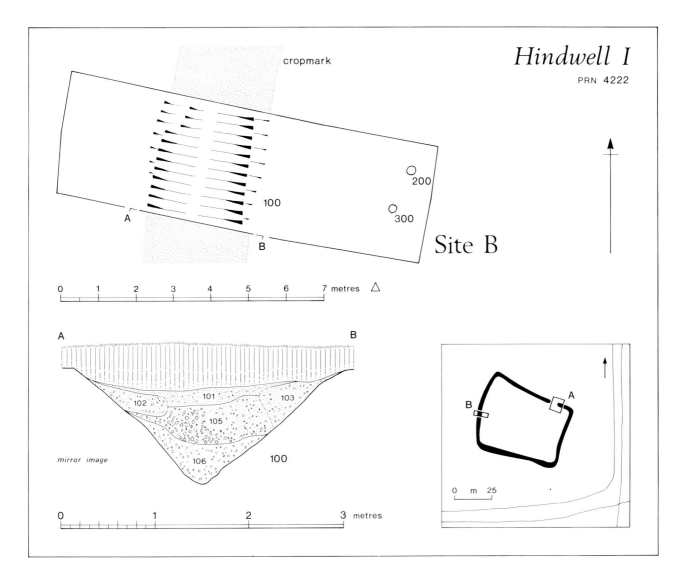

Figure 25   Plan of the trial excavations at Hindwell I, trench B

Discussion

The excavations at Hindwell I were limited in scale and scope on a site that had suffered considerably from agricultural processes. The features in trench A were all severely truncated and their interpretation remains tentative. Ceramic evidence does, however, confirm the middle Iron Age date of the enclosure. Admittedly these finds were from the upper silts and should provide a *terminus ante quem*, however, the ditch seems to have rapidly filled, perhaps suggesting that the internal bank had been deliberately slighted or that it was originally unstable. Therefore, these sherds can realistically be assumed to date the final phase of the occupation of the site. A line of possible postholes in trench A suggests the presence of a gate structure.

soil. They measured 0.2m in diameter but were only in the region of 0.1m deep. These too were devoid of finds.

Excavations at Upper Ninepence: a Neolithic settlement and possible Bronze Age barrow (PRN 305: NGR SO25126136)

Introduction

The barrow at Upper Ninepence, Hindwell, lies on the top of the ridge between the Knobley and Summergil brooks in a discreet corner of the field (Fig 26). It survived as a low spread mound some 20m in diameter and 0.3m high (Fig 27). Finds of around 700 flints had been recovered from the surface of this barrow (Dunn 1966), as well as fragments of pottery identified by Dunn as 'cinerary urn'. This ceramic find, coupled with the fragments of calcined bone and of an adult occipital bone found in the ploughsoil over the barrow, led Dunn to conclude that secondary burials had been ploughed. The flint artefacts generally comprised small flakes or knapping waste, though some artefactual material was also recognised, namely, a *petit tranchet* derivative arrowhead,

Figure 26   Photograph of the Upper Ninepence barrow before excavation

polished axe fragments, various points and scrapers. Analysis of this material has identified a mainly Neolithic assemblage but also with a Mesolithic and Bronze Age presence (see below).

Limited excavation in the mound confirmed that the barrow contained lithic material indicative of a nearby settlement and that ploughing was indeed having a detrimental effect on the mound (Dunn 1966, 14). A hearth was located in the top of the surviving barrow.

The barrow was surveyed by Dunn in 1973 (Dunn 1974) and was recorded as being 1m high and 30m in diameter (see Gibson 1997 for barrow dimensions). The site was re-surveyed in 1992 and was found to be only 0.35m high and 20m in diameter. Therefore, the barrow had lost 0.65m in height in the last 20 years and this despite only limited ploughing restricted to once or twice every ten years (inf Mr C Goodwin of Hindwell Farm).

Excavation

The mound and old ground surface

The archaeological potential of this site was clear from Dunn's fieldwalking and limited excavation. The site also had been shown to be at risk from the agricultural regime and as a result was chosen for rescue excavation. This took place over fourteen weeks during the summer of 1994. The barrow was excavated in quadrants (Fig 28) with the turf and topsoil (context 1) being removed by machine. The barrow mound (context 2) and old ground surface (OGS) (context 72) were also machined off in thin layers and, under close archaeological supervision, in the south-west and north-east quadrants. In these quadrants, the contexts were removed by hand. The OGS was sampled for palaeoenvironmental material, and phosphate analysis and soil micromorphology samples were taken at the mound/OGS interface, at the OGS/natural interface, and within the area of structure 1 (see below).

During the mechanical stripping of the south-west quadrant, the hearth described by Dunn (1966) was relocated immediately below the topsoil and was sampled (Fig 29). It measured 0.8m across and comprised a fire-reddened depression similar in size and appearance to the hearths located at Hindwell Ash (see above). There was no evidence to suggest that the hearth had been excavated into the mound. It was found to contain abundant charcoal (Pomoideae, oak, blackthorn, gorse and hazel) and charred grain (bread wheat and barley – see below). This was radiocarbon dated and the results are presented in Table 7.

This date, clearly in the Romano-British period, acts as a *terminus ante quem* for the construction of the mound, but raises questions on the observations made above regarding the survival of the barrow.

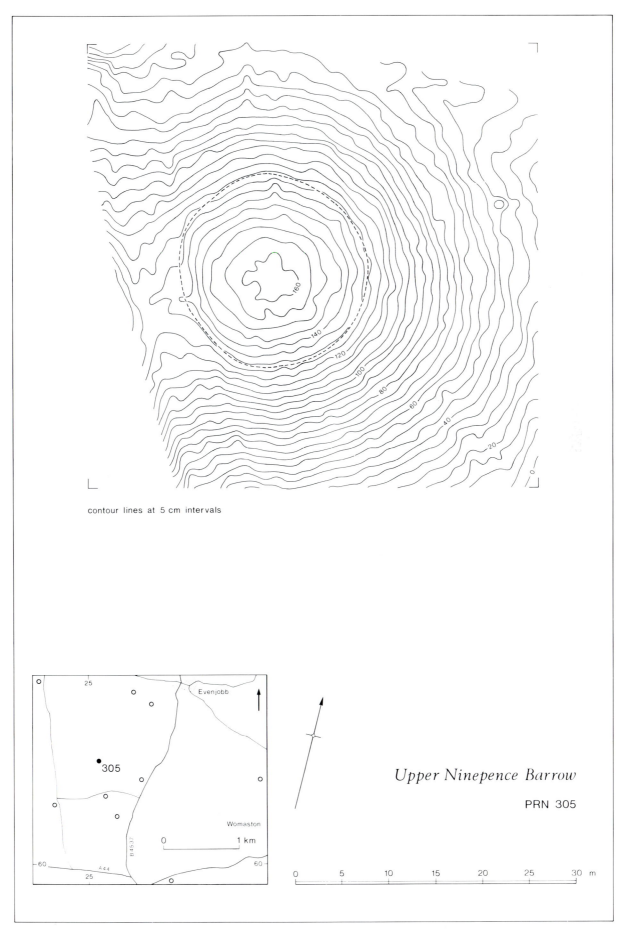

contour lines at 5 cm intervals

Upper Ninepence Barrow

PRN 305

Figure 27   Survey of the Upper Ninepence barrow before excavation

Figure 28   Aerial photograph of the excavations at Upper Ninepence. Photo Alex Gibson, CPAT, copyright reserved

Figure 29   Hearth (partially excavated) located in the top of the mound at the Upper Ninepence barrow

Table 7 Radiocarbon date from Upper Ninepence (hearth over mound)

Context	Lab No	Date BP	Cal AD 68%	Cal AD 95%
Hearth – 195	SWAN-115	1640 ± 70	260–290 or 330–460 or 480–530	230–590

The mound had been shown to have lost 0.65m in height since 1973. Yet this Romano-British feature, which could only have been constructed on the top of the mound, survived more or less intact. This leaves us with two options.

Firstly, that the survey data are incorrect. This is a possibility since the mound sits on top of a rounded ridge into the slopes of which it merges. The discrepancy therefore may be one of definition. Secondly, that the mound had been augmented in the post-Roman period, and it is this later augmentation which was being plough-truncated. This augmentation may well have occurred in the 19th century when the site was used as a rabbit warren (see below). However, neither explanation is entirely satisfactory. For example, Dunn's measurements for the well-preserved and unploughed barrows on the uplands around the basin closely agree with those from the present survey (Gibson 1997), suggesting that the same criteria were being measured and confirming the accuracy of both surveys. Regarding mound-augmentation, there was no archaeologically recognisable evidence for this, although ploughing may well have destroyed it totally. A similar discussion applies to the broadly contemporary hearths located in the top of Hindwell Ash (see above).

The mound material, which comprised grey clayey soil with occasional flecks of iron panning, contained flint flakes and potsherds (see below). In the southern half of the barrow, particularly around its perimeter, there was severe rabbit damage which had also affected the OGS and underlying natural. The present landowner has given information from the farm accounts showing that in the mid 19th century, the farmer was buying rabbits from the local warrens at New Radnor and Presteigne. By the late 1870s, however, he was selling rabbits on a fairly large scale. It seems that in Upper Ninepence we have inadvertently discovered the farm's rabbit production centre!

The OGS was up to 0.1m thick and comprised a similar soil to that of the barrow mound, but was separated from that context by a well-defined layer of iron pan often up to 25mm thick (Fig 30). Rabbit disturbance could clearly be seen in this material in both the south-east and the north-west quadrants. Once more, small potsherds and flint flakes were recovered from throughout this layer.

There was no trace of any burials in or below the mound though sherds of two early Bronze Age vessels, possibly a Collared Urn and a Food Vessel Urn (see below Fig 57, P89 and P90) from the mound material and OGS respectively, may hint that the mound had had a sepulchral role at least during part of its history.

Features below the mound

A total of 41 pits were discovered in the buried natural subsoil (Fig 31). In addition, there were five hearths and 227 stakeholes (Fig 32). All of these features were only noticeable at subsoil level. The majority of them, particularly the stakeholes, are undated, but Peterborough and Grooved Ware pottery and associated flint assemblages were recovered from some of the pits. The artefacts and radiocarbon dates suggest that there were two main phases of activity at the site, the first, associated with Peterborough Ware and dating to c 3000 Cal BC and the second, associated with Grooved Ware and centring on c 2700 Cal BC (Fig 33).

The Peterborough phase

Peterborough Ware ceramics were located in fourteen contexts (Table 8).

In only one instance, pit 154, was it associated with Grooved Ware and in this case the collar from a Fengate style vessel was clearly residual. Analysis of the flint artefacts confirms the ceramic identifications but does little to extend the distribution of features belonging to this phase.

The distribution of the features containing Peterborough Ware was restricted to the east and north-east parts of the site (Fig 33). The exception to this rule was pit 500 which contained exclusively Fengate sherds. This pit was located on the west side of the excavated area and the reason for its isolation is uncertain. The pit contained only Fengate style Peterborough Ware yet its radiocarbon date is indistinguishable from the other dates obtained from this phase (Table 9).

The dates obtained from small diameter charcoals for pits containing Peterborough Ware are listed in Table 9. The dates are remarkably uniform and confirm the middle Neolithic dates for Peterborough Ware (Gibson and Kinnes 1997).

Other than the generally restricted distribution of the pits, there was little patterning in their distribution. The pits were generally circular to oval, single filled, and relatively shallow (Fig 34). The flint assemblage suggests a domestic origin, though clearly the deposition of the waste and artefacts in pits need not be solely a domestic act.

The environmental data are presented below, but

34

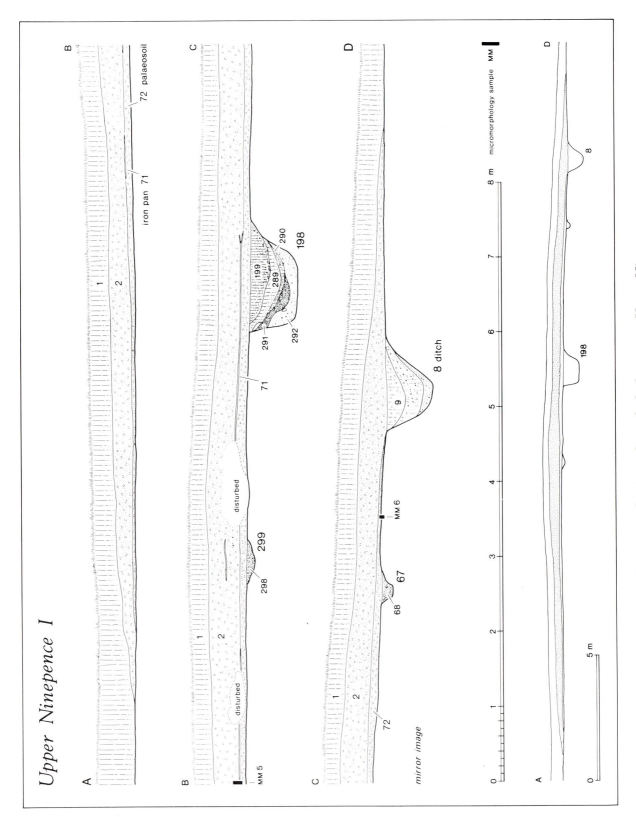

Figure 30 Sections through the barrow at Upper Ninepence

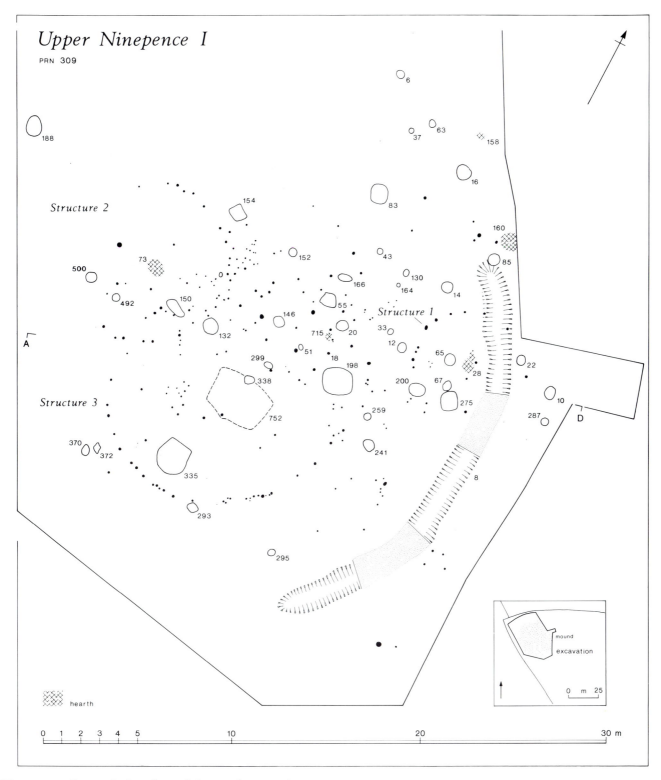

Figure 31   General site plan of the pre-barrow features at Upper Ninepence

in summary, it is worth noting the presence of emmer wheat in contexts associated with this phase, and weed species which indicate a grassland environment with some hazel scrub and cultivation nearby.

The Grooved Ware phase

Grooved Ware was found in the contexts listed in Table 10. These features were distributed more widely over the site and appear to have formed the main period of pre-mound activity (Fig 33). Some 68 Grooved Ware vessels are represented plus occasional and unidentifiable sherds from other contexts. The associated flint assemblage confirms the ceramic identifications but does not augment the Grooved Ware distribution; no diagnostic flints were recovered from contexts without ceramic associations.

Figure 32   General view of the pre-barrow features at Upper Ninepence during excavation

The pits varied from oval to circular to subrectangular. The majority were shallow with single fills (Figs 34 and 35) though a notable exception was the large subrectangular and generally flat-bottomed pit 198 which was 0.65m deep and contained five different fills, all of which were carbon-rich (see Fig 30). Grooved Ware was found throughout the fills of this feature with the exception of context 292 which was found at the base of the pit and lining the eastern edge. This material comprised yellow-brown clayey soil and is interpreted as being weathered and/or redeposited natural. This may represent material recently excavated from the pit, being replaced as part of a rapid, anthropogenic filling process.

Grooved Ware was also recovered from six post- or stakeholes (35, 180, 297, 422, 478, 448). These fall within the general Grooved Ware distribution on site and in the main comprise eroded and residual sherds. Sherds from four vessels (P42–5) were found in stakehole 297 representing by far the largest stakehole assemblage. In addition, a radiocarbon date was obtained from charcoal from stakehole 18 (Table 11) which places this feature within the same phase of the site's history.

Structure 1 (Fig 36)
Structure 1 has already been published in interim form (Gibson 1996b). It lay within the concentration of pits containing Peterborough Ware, but radiocarbon chronology (Table 12), and the association of possible Grooved Ware fragments in the central hearth, indicate that it postdates the Peterborough phase (see below).

The structure comprised a broken circle of thirteen stakeholes describing an area 6m in diameter (Figs 36 and 37). The stakeholes were only detectable at subsoil level and thus were undoubtedly truncated. The very bases of two stakes (753 and 754) were also found in the sides of ditch 4 which had cut through the eastern and consequently more damaged part of the structure. The stakeholes averaged about 100mm in diameter and 100–200mm deep. They had pointed bases and were clearly formed by driven stakes. The majority (24, 26, 47, 49, 57, 59, 279, 281) contained charcoal flecks suggesting that the posts may have been charred prior to their use, but there is no evidence for burning *in situ* and none contained sufficient charcoal for conventional radiocarbon dating. Four stakeholes outside the structure on the south-west arc (271, 273, 281, 283) formed what appears to have been a trapezoidal arrangement, perhaps representing some formalised porch or entrance feature, though the association of these stakeholes with the structure may only be surmised. Similarly, the association with the structure of the internal stakeholes is also uncertain, given the proliferation of these features over the site as a whole.

The central hearth (28) was probably originally

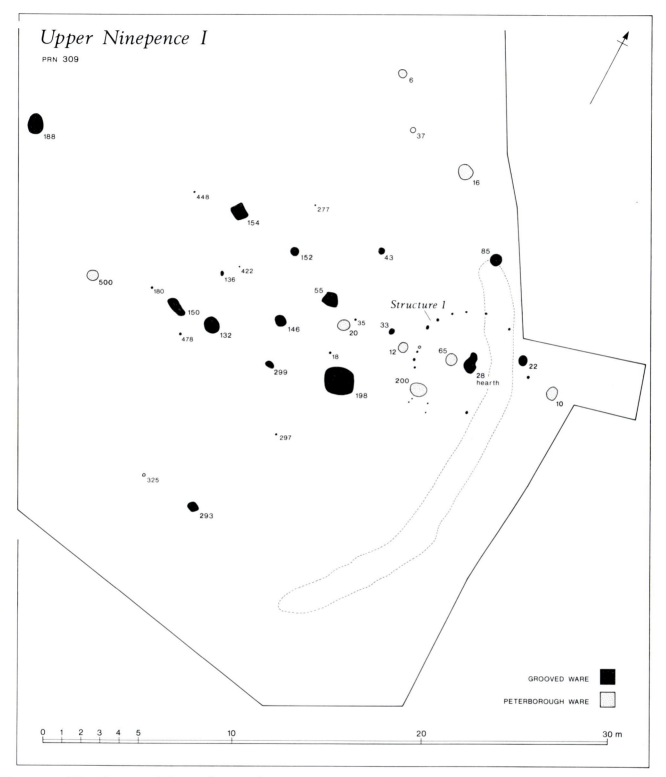

Figure 33 The phasing of the pre-barrow features at Upper Ninepence

oval measuring 1.25m × 0.6m but has been damaged on the north side by animal burrowing. It was set in a small scoop, 0.12m deep and the pink, burnt subsoil attested prolonged use. There was no trace of an associated floor level with this structure although soil micromorphology did suggest the trampling of the old ground surface in this area.

Ditch (context 8)

The penannular ditch (context 8) must also belong to the Grooved Ware phase. It cut structure 1 (dated to 4240 ± 70 BP) but was in turn cut by pit 85 which contained Grooved Ware and is dated to 4060 ± 40 BP (see Table 12). The ditch averaged 1.2m deep by 1.4m across and had sloping sides and a rounded

Table 8 Features associated with Peterborough Ware (Upper Ninepence)

Feature	Dimensions (m)				Description	Finds	Date BP
(context)	Diam	Length	Width	Depth			
Mound (2)						P3–4	
Pit 6 (7)	0.40			0.09	Roughly circular pit filled with dark sandy soil & stone	P10	
Pit 10 (11)	0.6			0.33	Oval pit filled with charcoal-rich loam	P8	
Pit 12 (13)	0.55			0.27	Large round-based pit filled with clayey loam & charcoal flecks	P1	
Pit 16 (17)	0.79			0.20	Round-based pit filled with clayey loam & charcoal flecks	P5–7	4400 ± 50 BM-2967
Pit 20 (21)	0.52			0.20	Round-based pit filled with clayey loam & charcoal flecks	P11	4410 ± 35 BM-2966
Pit 37 (38)	0.24			0.11	Round-based pit filled with clayey loam & charcoal flecks	P9	
Stakehole 47 (48)	0.12			0.22	Circular stakehole filled with clayey loam	P13	
Pit 65 (66)	0.60			0.15	Round-based pit filled with clayey loam & charcoal flecks	P2	4470 ± 80 SWAN-23
Pit 154 (155)		0.80	0.70	0.20	Rectangular pit filled with dark charcoal-rich soil and abundant pottery	P16	
Pit 200		0.92	0.72	0.25	Oval pit filled with dark carbonaceous soil	P15 P19	4590 ± 60 BM-3071
Stakehole 325 (326)	0.15			0.19	Stakehole filled with dark clayey loam	P14	
Pit 500 (502)	0.55			0.37	Round pit filled with grey clayey loam and charcoal flecks	P18 P20	4490 ± 60 BM-3070

Table 9 Radiocarbon dates from Peterborough Ware associated contexts (Upper Ninepence)

Context	Date BP	Lab No	Cal BC 68%	Cal BC 95%
Pit 16	4400 ± 50	BM-2967	3100–2920	3310–3230 or 3180–3160 or 3140–2910
Pit 20	4410 ± 35	BM-2966	3100–3020 or 3000–2920	3300–3240 or 3110–2920
Pit 65	4470 ± 80	SWAN-23	3340–3220 or 3190–3030	3360–2920
Pit 200	4590 ± 60	BM-3071	3500–3420 or 3380–3310 or 3240–3180 or 3160–3130	3520–3090
Pit 500	4490 ± 60	BM-3070	3340–3220 or 3190–3090 or 3060–3040	3360–3030 or 2980–2930

base. The fill of the ditch was almost totally mixed by burrowing animals, but where a silting pattern could be detected, the silts appeared to derive from redeposited subsoil piled on the inner (western) edge of the ditch (see below). The function of this ditch remains unresolved. It appears to have had the excavated material piled on the inside but the mound as excavated was composed entirely of turf and topsoil. The ditch was also full by the time that pit 85 was excavated and therefore seems to have

Table 10 Grooved Ware contexts from Upper Ninepence

Feature (Context)	Dimensions (m)				Description	Finds	Date BP
	Diam	Length	Width	Depth			
Mound (2)						P58, P83–5	
Palaeosol (72)						P51, P79–81	
Ditch 8 (9)			1.20	0.55	Curved ditch	P50, P54, P61	
Pit 22 (23)	0.40			0.25	Roughly circular round-based pit filled with dark charcoal-rich soil and burnt stones	P70	
Hearth 28 (29)		1.25	0.60	0.12	Hearth central to structure 1	frags	4240 ± 70 SWAN-24
Pit 33 (34)	0.35			0.08	Small circular shallow pit filled with dark charcoal-rich soil	frag	
Pit 35 (36)	0.10			0.07	Small circular round-bottomed pit filled with dark clayey loam	P56	
Pit 43 (44)	0.35			0.07	Small circular pit filled with clayey loam and charcoal flecks	P60	
Pit 55 (56)		0.90	0.70	0.27	Pit cut by animal disturbance filled with grey charcoal-rich soil	P32, P71–6	
Pit 85 (86)	0.65			0.26	Circular round-bottomed pit with brown charcoal-rich soil	P62–3, P78	4060 ± 40 BM-3069
Pit 132 (133)	0.83			0.23	Large roughly circular pit filled with dark soil, charcoal and stones	P66–9	4160 ± 35 BM-2968
Pit 136 (137)	0.35			0.07	Shallow circular pit filled with charcoal-rich soil	P49, P58–9	
Pit 146 (147)	0.48			0.22	Circular pit filled with charcoal-rich soil	P57	
Pit 152 (153)	0.53			0.10	Shallow circular pit filled with dark clayey loam	frag	
Pit 154 (155)		0.84	0.70	0.20	Large rectangular pit filled with charcoal-rich soil and abundant pottery	P33–6, P38–41	4050 ± 35 BM-2969
Stakehole 180 (181)	0.12			0.08	Stakehole filled with dark clay with charcoal flecks	P55	
Pit 188 (191)		1.10	0.84	0.21	Small oval pit filled with dark charcoal-rich soil	frag	
Pit 198 (289)	1.60			0.65	Large sub-rectangular pit. 289 comprises dark compressed charcoal-rich soil	P21–2, P25, P37, P77	
Pit 198 (291)					291 = compressed charcoal	P88	
Pit 198 (199)					199 = dark carbonaceous soil	P23–4, P26–31, P37, P48	
Stakehole 277 (278)	0.08			0.12	Stakehole filled with dark charcoal-rich soil	P87	
Pit 293 (294)		0.55	0.50	0.07	Pit filled with dark charcoal-rich soil	P64–5, frags	
Stakehole 297 (298)	0.10			0.17	Stakehole filled with dark charcoal-rich soil	P42–5	
Pit 299 (300)		0.48	0.34	0.11	Pit filled with dark charcoal-rich soil	P52, P86	
Stakehole 422 (423)	0.08			0.15	Stakehole filled with clayey loam and occasional charcoal	P46	
Stakehole 448 (449)	0.11			0.17	Stakehole with grey-brown clayey fill and charcoal flecks	frags	
Posthole 478 (479)	0.16			0.26	Posthole with grey-brown clayey fill and charcoal flecks	P82	

Table 11 Radiocarbon date from stakehole 18

Context	Date BP	Lab No	Cal BC 68%	Cal BC 95%
Stakehole 18	4170 ± 80	SWAN-25	2890–2850 or 2820–2660 or 2640–2620	2920–2570 or 2540–2500

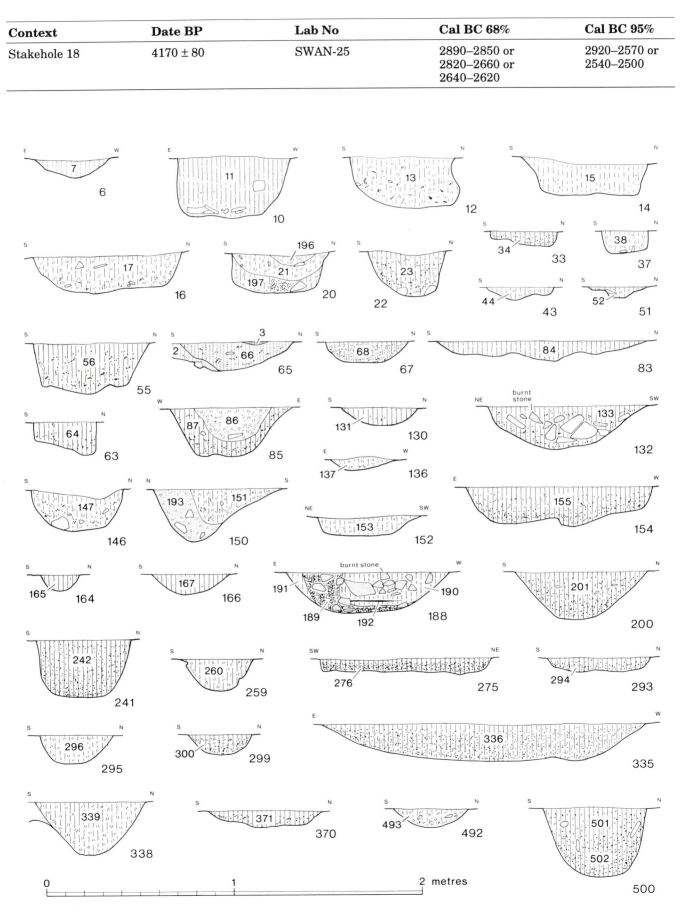

Figure 34 Upper Ninepence feature sections

Figure 35 Upper Ninepence: Grooved Ware pit 154 during excavation. Much of the pottery has been removed prior to the taking of this photograph

predated the mound by a considerable period. It remains the most puzzling feature of the pre-barrow complex.

Dating
Four radiocarbon dates have been obtained from contexts securely associated with Grooved Ware (Table 12). These dates cluster around 2700 Cal BC and represent a distinctly later period of activity than that associated with the Peterborough Ware (Fig 38).

In the interim statement on structure 1 (Gibson 1996b), a Peterborough association was postulated. Peterborough Ware, however, comes only from a circular pit (65) within the structure and from a stakehole (47) in the perimeter. The sherds from the latter context (P13) are small and abraded and are almost certainly residual. The sherd from context 65 (P2) is better stratified but there are no direct stratigraphical relationships between the pit and the structure. The radiocarbon date from this pit (SWAN–23) confirms its association with the Peterborough phase (Table 9; Fig 38)

The central position of the hearth suggests that it is more reliably associated with the structure despite the lack of unequivocal stratigraphy. The radiocarbon date from this feature (SWAN–24) is statistically later than that from pit 65 and is a more reliable

indicator, placing the structure within the Grooved Ware phase of the site, albeit early in that phase (Fig 38). There is, however, a large margin of error on this date which is especially significant at the 2σ calibrated date range (Table 12).

If the attribution of this structure to the Grooved Ware phase is correct, then the structure must belong to the earlier or middle part of this phase. This is supported not only by the radiocarbon date, but also by the stratigraphy, since the structure was cut by the curving ditch (8) which itself was cut by a Grooved Ware pit (85). It is interesting that this pit contained vessels very different from the rest of the assemblage (P62–3) in their pitted fabrics and Clacton style decoration. These vessels must be late in the pre-mound sequence, yet the radiocarbon dates show that they are broadly contemporary with, for example, the Durrington Walls style vessels from pit 154.

The radiocarbon dates from pit 85 and hearth 28 act as chronological brackets for the ditch. It would appear to have been constructed sometime during the two radiocarbon centuries which separate these dates, and this would agree with the site stratigraphy of house – ditch – pit. It can be demonstrated that structure 1 represents the earliest Grooved Ware activity on site, with the pit digging activity taking place after the structure has gone out of use.

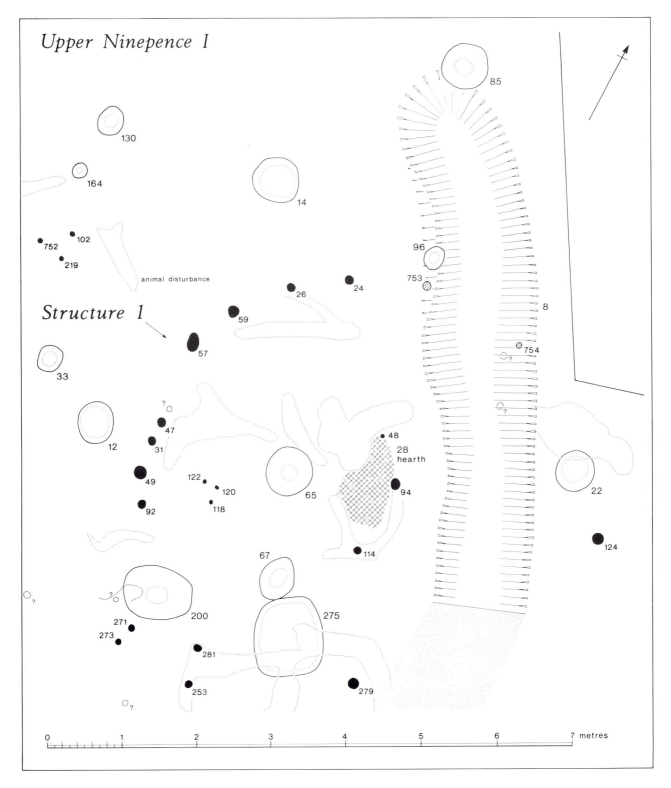

Figure 36 Upper Ninepence: detail of structure 1

While these dates position the ditch in the site's history, unfortunately they do not elucidate the ditch's function. It may, partly, define the area of pit-digging, but pit 22, also associated with Grooved Ware, lies outside this area and, as pit 85 demonstrates, the ditch was already substantially filled prior to *c* 4000 BP.

Undated Features (Fig 31)

The majority of the pre-barrow features remain undated. They consist in the main of small hearths, postholes and stakeholes which were generally dispersed, apparently randomly, throughout the excavated area. Within this general distribution there are

Figure 37   Upper Ninepence: structure 1 during excavation

three recognisable patterns identified as structures 2 and 3 (see Fig 40). These feature groups are discussed below.

Hearths
Of the apparently randomly distributed features, three are hearths (158, 160 and 715) or at least patches of fire-reddened subsoil. All were only recognised at the subsoil level and none penetrated the subsoil more than 50mm. Charcoal from these three features was sparse, comprising small flecks embedded within the burnt subsoil, and none contained the comparatively large quantities of charcoal noted in the upper layers of hearth 28 within structure 1. This may suggest that either the hearths were short-lived or, that they were originally open and that the dry ash and charcoal had blown away. Whatever the true explanation may be, they were, compared with hearth 28, fairly ephemeral features and none seem to be associated with any meaningful posthole or stakehole arrangements.

Stakeholes
A total of 227 stakeholes were recognised during the excavation in addition to a large number of possible stakeholes (see Fig 31). These were distributed over the whole of the excavated area, particularly where they had been protected by the barrow mound: few were discovered beyond the confines of the surviving barrow (Fig 39). The stakeholes were fairly uniform at around 100mm diameter, they were invariably pointed towards the base, and they were generally 100–200mm deep.

Within the stakehole spread, three groupings could be distinguished and are designated here as structures 1–3. Only structure 1, consisting of 16 stakeholes, could be dated and has been discussed above. Structures 2 and 3 are undated and are discussed below.

Pits
Fifteen pits remain undated and were generally devoid of datable material. They were spread over the whole excavated area and formed no recognisable pattern of distribution. Their dimensions are listed in Table 13. Pit 335 is remarkable by virtue of its large size and peculiar heel-shaped plan. This pit was devoid of finds and its purpose remains unresolved.

Table 12   Radiocarbon dates from Grooved Ware contexts (Upper Ninepence)

Feature (context)	Pot nos	C14 Date BP	Lab No	Cal BC (68%)	Cal BC (95%)
Hearth 28 (29)	crumbs	4240 ± 70	SWAN-24	2930–2860 or 2820–2660	3040–2850 or 2830–2610
Pit 132 (133)	P66–9	4160 ± 35	BM-2968	2880–2860 or 2820–2800 or 2780–2660 or 2640–2620	2890–2850 or 2830–2610
Pit 154 (155)	P33–6, 38–41	4050 ± 35	BM-2969	2860–2820 or 2660–2640 or 2540–2500	2870–2810 or 2740–2720 or 2700–2490
Pit 85 (86)	P62–3	4060 ± 40	BM-3069	2860–2820 or 2660–2640 or 2620–2570 or 2540–2500	2870–2810 or 2780–2720 or 2700–2490

44

M. Stuiver and R.S. Kra eds. 1986 Radiocarbon 28(2B): 805-1030; OxCal v2.17 cub r:4 sd:12 prob{chron}

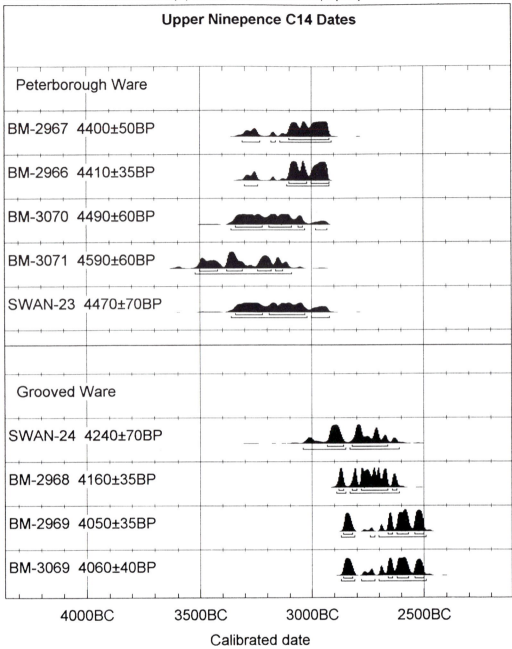

Figure 38 *Upper Ninepence radiocarbon dates*

Structure 2

The stakehole group tentatively identified as structure 2 is represented by a roughly circular arrangement of stakeholes in the western part of the site (Figs 31 and 40), defining an area some 8m in diameter, and with hearth 73 slightly south of centre. The perimeter of this structure would overlap with the projected perimeter of structure 3 in the area around pits 150 and 132, but there is no evidence defining the stratigraphic relationship between these two stakehole arrangements. None of the stakeholes, nor indeed hearth 73, provided sufficient charcoal for a conventional radiocarbon date.

The stakeholes averaged *c* 100mm in diameter and were generally 100–200mm deep. They had pointed profiles indicative of driven stakes. The spacing of these stakeholes in the better defined northern arc was in the region of 0.3m. No trace of a western arc was located and on the south and east, the structure appeared to merge with the large number of random stakeholes encountered near the middle of the site. An arc of stakeholes running from south-west of pit 492 round to pit 132 and incorporating stakehole 478 may be sufficiently regular to represent the southern arc of the arrangement (Fig 40).

The structure, if such it is, bears a strong resemblance in size, construction, and the presence of an internal hearth, to structure 1 and it may well be

Figure 39 Upper Ninepence: structure 2 during excavation. The positions of the stakeholes are marked by the sample bags

broadly contemporary. Indeed, Grooved Ware sherds were recovered from stakeholes 136, 448 and 478 which all lay on the proposed perimeter of the structure. It must be stressed, however, that the Grooved Ware sherds from these contexts cannot be regarded as anything but residual.

It is also interesting to point out the presence of pit 500 in close proximity to structure 2. Structure 1, while dated to the Grooved Ware phase, was nevertheless situated in an area of former Peterborough Ware activity. Structure 2 was therefore similarly placed, in this case adjacent to pit 500, which contained pottery in the Fengate style and was the only pit containing non-residual Peterborough Ware in this area of the site.

Structure 3
This comprised a circular arrangement of fairly uniform stakeholes in the southern half of the site (Figs 31 and 40) describing approximately 60% of a circle with a diameter of 12m. Near the centre of this assumed circle was context 752, a broadly rectangular patch of discoloured subsoil measuring 3.25m × 2.5m and orientated east–west.

The stakehole arc could be traced south from the west side of pit 150 round to pit 293 in the extreme south of the excavated area, then north and east to the southern edge of pit 198. The northern 40%

could not be identified with certainty, though it is possible that some of the larger stakeholes in this area (eg nos 18 and 41) belonged to this arrangement.

The stakeholes were close set and averaged 100mm in diameter and were generally 100–200mm deep. They had pointed bases indicative of driven stakes. The only finds came from stakehole 325 in the form of residual sherds of Peterborough Ware (P14).

Only stakehole 18 contained sufficient charcoal for a radiocarbon date. The date obtained is given in Table 13 above. It clearly places the feature within the Grooved Ware phase of the site but it cannot be demonstrated with certainty that stakehole 18 did in fact form part of the perimeter of structure 3.

Feature 752, apparently central to this stakehole arrangement, comprised a patch of discoloured subsoil. The area was investigated in the belief that this represented the upper fills of a primary grave pit. However, the feature appeared to have little depth (50mm max) and soon became indistinguishable from the surrounding natural. The high phosphate count from this feature, however (see below), is consistent with the depression having originally held an inhumation, presumably unaccompanied, which had entirely decayed. A sepul-

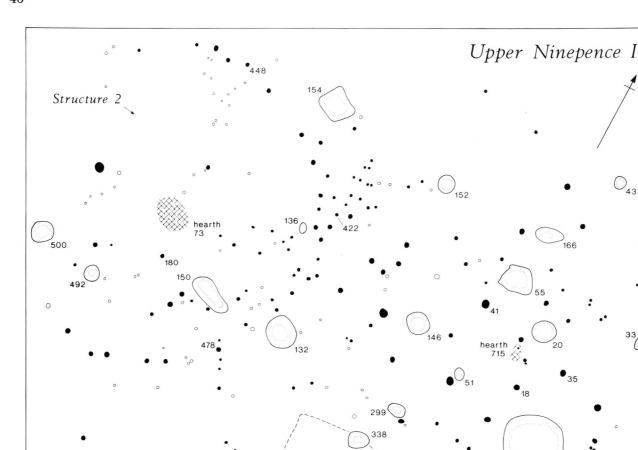

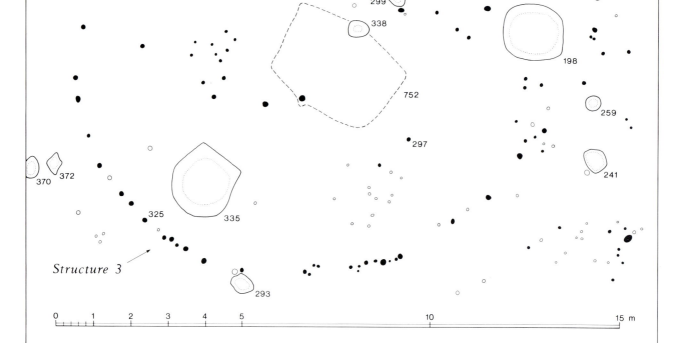

Figure 40   Upper Ninepence: detail of structures 2 and 3

chral role for this feature, therefore, remains a probability.

If the association of 752 with structure 3 is accepted, then these stakeholes may well be associated with the primary sepulchral phase of the barrow. Upper Ninepence would, then, have been a stake-circle barrow of a type common in Bronze Age Britain though admittedly the stake-circles below barrows are generally much more regular than this example.

Results

The excavation is discussed in detail below, but suffice it to say here that the exercise was successful in demonstrating the wealth of archaeological material that can survive below even severely degraded monuments. This serves to strengthen the argument for round barrows and related monuments being important not just for the data they contain but also, and perhaps arguably more

Table 13 Descriptions of undated pits

Pit (Fill)	Dimensions (m)				Description	Fill
	Diam	Length	Width	Depth		
14 (15)	0.67			0.16	Shallow flat-bottomed pit	Light brown soil with sparse stones
63 (64)	0.33			0.16	Small irregular pit	Dark brown loam with occasional charcoal
67 (68)		0.60	0.45	0.12	Oval flat-bottomed pit	Dark grey, charcoal-rich clayey soil
130 (131)	0.40			0.09	Small oval round-bottomed pit	Dark brown loam
150 (151)		1.25	0.54	0.28	Elongated oval pit	Dark brown clayey loam with charcoal flecks
164 (165)	0.20			0.08	Small circular pit	Dark brown loam
166 (167)		0.78	0.40	0.10	Oval pit	Dark brown loam
241 (242)		0.64	0.50	0.30	Oval pit	Dark brown loam
275 (276)		1.05	0.92	0.07	Large sub-rectangular pit	Dense charcoal-rich soil
287 (288)	0.20			0.10	Small circular pit	Grey clayey loam
295 (296)		0.44	0.40	0.16	Small oval pit	Brown clayey loam
299 (300)		0.48	0.34	0.11	Small oval pit	Dark grey charcoally clay loam
335 (336)		1.80	1.70	0.20	Large heel-shaped pit	Charcoal-rich soil
372 (373)		0.40	0.35	0.10	Small lozenge-shaped pit	Dark grey loamy clay with charcoal flecks
492 (493)	0.40			0.10	Small circular pit	Grey-brown clayey loam with charcoal flecks

importantly, for the earlier material they can preserve. Despite the recorded, demonstrable and quantifiable degradation of the mound, the survival of the Iron Age or Romano-British hearth poses a problem of interpretation unless the feature was originally dug into the mound to a considerable depth.

2 The finds

Lithics from the present survey

The number of flint and lithic artefacts recorded from the basin cannot be estimated. The Dunn collection alone numbers over 6000 flints and indeed, each farmer contacted during the present survey claimed to have found 'numerous' flints during the course of normal ploughing. The documented 'flint forays' of the Field Section of the Radnorshire Society (anon 1990, 6) have probably also produced numerous finds, most still in private possession and largely undocumented.

The previously recorded flint scatters are PAR 2150, 5239, 1074, 76, 3532, 2211, 2213, 305, and 307. The last two scatters numbered above are also barrow sites and represent flint from the mound material and surrounding area. Flint has also been recorded from the ploughed mounds of barrows 300, 303, 309, 310, 314, and 369.

In addition, during limited fieldwalking as part of the present survey, flint was recovered from the same field as the Four Stones stone circle (PAR 3652–3, 3658, 3661), from the field to the north (PAR 3656), and from the same field as barrows 309 and 314 (PAR 3657). Flint finds from the present survey are summarised in Table 14. A selection is presented in Fig 41.

These finds, combined with the recorded 6000 flints from PAR 76 and the 1000 from PAR 305 clearly demonstrate the wealth of the resource in this area but also demonstrate the destruction of archaeological contexts. While flints from mound material may have little contextual value other than providing a *terminus post quem* for the barrow and attesting the possible proximity of settlement, flints from other locations must clearly be derived from unknown but truncated contexts. The regularity with which flint finds occur in the basin demonstrates the rate at which these contexts are being destroyed.

Catalogue of illustrated pieces from the present survey (Fig 41)

1 SO254606, PRN3654. End scraper.
2 SO254606, PRN3654. Mesolithic blade.
3 SO254606, PRN3654. Mesolithic blade.
4 SO256623, PRN3655. Thumbnail scraper.
5 SO253608, PRN3657. Core from a polished flint axe in a milky grey flint.
6 SO253607, PRN 3660. Large retouched flake.
7 SO252609, PRN3659. Calcined retouched flake.
8 SO252609, PRN3659. Serrated flake with some cortex remaining.
9 SO252609, PRN3659. Awl with bifacial retouch and fine ripple-flaking on dorsal side.
10 SO253607, PRN 3660. Plano-convex knife fragment with some cortex remaining.

Table 14   Flint finds made and identified during the present survey

PRN	NGR	No of flints	Date
310	SO254606	3	
3652	SO244604	2	
3653	SO24506061	1	
3654	SO254606	8	
3655	SO258621	1	EBA
3656	SO244619	1	
3657	SO253608	1	N
3658	SO24506048	1	
3659	SO252609	3	BA
3660	SO253607	4	
3661	SO244605	6	
3662	SO262598	3	
3666	SO243624	1	
26300	SO24906150	39	N: BA
26301	SO24556100	5	
26302	SO22656240	5	
26303	SO22506046	4	
26304	SO24435990	2	
26305	SO22006040	7	
26307	SO28216120	2	
26308	SO25266080	1	
26309	SO23856546	2	
26310	SO24356360	9	BA
26311	SO26756027	8	
26312	SO24346155	2	
26313	SO20106045	14	M
26315	SO25056380	9	
26316	SO21976055	2	
26318	SO24006264	13	
26319	SO24676179	1	
26320	SO18755930	1	
26325	SO22966250	14	
26326	SO25056380	44	EBA
26327	SO24606405	8	
26328	SO23526493	1	

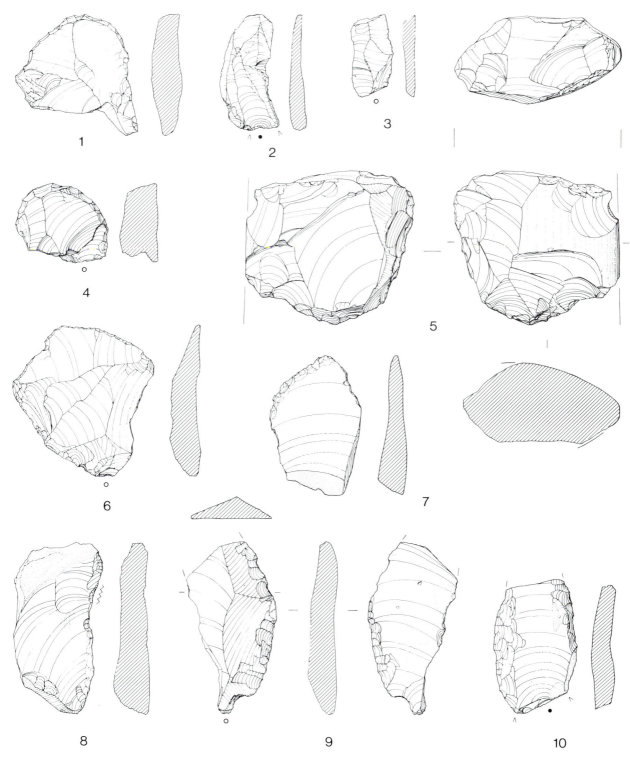

Figure 41   Flint finds recovered from fieldwalking

The worked flint from the Dunn Collection and the excavations
Philippa Bradley

Introduction

A total of 7901 pieces of worked flint were recovered from excavations and surface collections in the Walton Basin. This total includes a small quantity of burnt unworked flint and stone (42 pieces) and six pieces of worked stone. The largest group of material recovered forms the Dunn Collection from the National Museum of Wales, Cardiff, some of which has already been published (see for example Dunn 1965, 1966). The assemblages are summarised in Table 15 with selected pieces illustrated in Figures 42–46 and

Table 15 Flint assemblage composition

Site	Flake	Blade-like flake, blade	Chip	Irreg. waste	Core, core frag.	Retouched forms	Burnt unworked flint/stone	Total
Dunn Collection	4354	67	748	82	138	669	37	6095
Fieldwalk	159	5	6	3	13	53	2	241
76D	2	–	–	–	–	1	–	3
Walton Cursus	3	–	–	–	–	2	–	5
4222/I/501	2	–	–	–	–	–	–	2
Upper Ninepence	1122	27	271	8	16	93	3	1540
Upper Ninepence II	4	–	–	–	1	1	–	6
Hindwell Ash	5	–	1	–	1	2	–	9
TOTAL	5651	99	1026	93	169	821	42	7901

described in the catalogue. Further information about these assemblages may be found below. Selected groups of material were studied in greater detail and these are dealt with below by site.

Method

All of the material was examined but to different levels according to the context from which the assemblages came. The excavated assemblage from Upper Ninepence was therefore recorded in some detail, and was subjected to attribute analysis to facilitate the characterisation of the material. Metrical analysis was not undertaken, given the high proportion of burnt and broken pieces amongst the assemblage. The flint from the Dunn Collection was quantified and technological traits were recorded where relevant. The general appearance of the flint, including raw material and condition, was also noted. Diagnostic forms, particularly retouched pieces, are therefore the main dating tool for this collection. However, some use can be made of the more generalised attributes which were noted, but the unstratified nature of the collection must be remembered when drawing conclusions from the material.

Flint scatters – the Dunn Collection and other fieldwalked assemblages

The Dunn Collection comprises 6095 pieces of worked flint and stone. Another 241 pieces were collected from limited fieldwalking within the Walton Basin during 1992–4. The assemblages are summarised in Tables 15–18 and selected pieces are described in the catalogue and illustrated in Figures 42–46. A summary of each scatter is given below.

Raw materials and condition

The majority of the collection is composed of flint although quartzite, chert and various fine-grained rocks were used. A few pieces of probably unworked rock crystal were also recovered. Fourteen pieces of Bullhead flint (Shepherd 1972, 114) were found. This flint is particularly distinctive with a dark green to black cortex and a band of tan discolouration immediately underneath the cortex. Where discernable, the original colour of the flint is usually mid brown. The flint is good quality and seems to have been especially sought for its attractive appearance as well as for its flaking properties (Bradley in prep). Dark grey, light grey and a variety of orange and brown chert was also used. There appeared to be no period bias to the use of these other materials although they are perhaps more common amongst the Neolithic and Bronze Age flintwork. The flint was generally very good quality with excellent flaking properties. It varied in colour from dark grey/almost black to dark brown, light brown, buff, orange and grey. Cherty and crystalline inclusions were commonly noted but generally these did not affect the flaking properties of the raw materials. Cortex, where present, is either quite thick, buff, white and sometimes chalky, or brown, smooth and iron-stained. Cortication was recorded on much of the flintwork and was either light or medium; a few pieces were very heavily corticated. Plough damage to the edges of pieces was frequently recorded and many pieces were broken. Burning was recorded on approximately 32% of the assemblage, much of which was very heavy calcining.

Good quality flint does not occur in the locality and much of this material must have been imported; the nearest sources of high quality flint are the Berkshire Downs to the south and the Chiltern Hills to the south-east. Bullhead flint occurs in the southeast (Rayner 1981, 357) although it has been

Table 16   Surface collection: core typology

Single platform	Opposed platform flake/blade	Multi-platform	Keeled	Discoidal/ Levallois	Core on a flake	Other	Frags	Total
8	4	23	4	18	1	2	91	151

Table 17   Surface collection: retouched forms

1	2	3	4	5	6	7	8	9	10	11	12	13	14	15
204	29	144, 19	51	26	33	1, 7	1	5	1	179	3	7	12	722

1 = scrapers, 2 = knives, 3 = retouched and serrated flakes, 4 = arrowheads, 5 = polished flakes, 6 = piercers and awls, 7 = axes and axe frags, 8 = denticulates, 9 = fabricators, 10 = gunflint, 11 = miscellaneous retouch, 12 = notched, 13 = microliths, 14 = worked stone, 15 = total

Table 18   Upper Ninepence: flint from barrow surface

Flake	Blade-like flake, blade	Chip	Irregular waste	Core, core fragment	Retouched forms	Burnt unworked flint	Total
710	14	464	17	12	47	3	1267

recorded amongst flint from the Kennet Valley (Healy *et al* 1992, 48) and may occur more widely within gravel deposits. A small proportion of poorer quality iron-stained flint with a smooth, frequently worn cortex was also included in the collections. This material is derived flint and may have come from superficial deposits in the northern Cotswolds (Charlesworth 1957, 77; Tyler 1976, 4), or within gravel deposits around Cardiff and the Vale of Glamorgan (Dutton 1903, 111). Polished flint and stone axes were used as a source of raw material presumably once they had broken; reworked fragments and polished flakes are well represented amongst the collection (see Table 17). The flint used for axes includes a creamy white material which may originate around the Louth area of Lincolnshire (J Humble pers comm). A good quality grey flint was also used for axes.

The chert may derive from Carboniferous Limestones which occur in North Wales, for example in the Vale of Clwyd, although this raw material seems to have been used most extensively in the Mesolithic period. At Rhuddlan and Hendre, Clywd, for example, various coloured cherts including black, dark brown, grey and greyish-white were used (Berridge 1994, 95; Manley and Healey 1982, 21). Chert was also used in the Brenig Valley during the Mesolithic (Healey 1993, 187).

Technology and dating

Flint dating from the Mesolithic to the Bronze Age was included in the collection. However, the bulk of the material dates from the Neolithic and early Bronze Age. A small quantity of worked stone includes two spindlewhorls which are likely to be

Iron Age in date. The dating of surface collections is fraught with difficulties given the lack of stratigraphy, other associations, and the frequently large numbers of relatively undiagnostic pieces recovered. Dating has been based on certain diagnostic retouched forms such as arrowheads, some scraper types, and a variety of other well established forms which provide broad date ranges. Diagnostic pieces of debitage have also been used for dating purposes, although cores for example can only provide a general date range. Technological attributes may also be used to provide some indication of date (cf Holgate 1988; Brown 1991) which, together with the diagnostic forms, can be used to provide relatively firm dating.

Mesolithic flintwork is represented by seven microliths and a possible microburin; many of the numerous blades and blade-like flakes may also belong to this activity, although they may equally be of earlier Neolithic date. Two small opposed platform blade cores from grid reference SO254630 (bag 1675) and SO257615 (bag 1480) are also likely to be of Mesolithic date. A single large, quite crude fabricator from SO244615 (bag 1577; Fig 42 no 8) may also be of Mesolithic date. Although these artefacts occur in Bronze Age assemblages – this example can be paralleled at Oakhanger, Hampshire (Rankine and Rankine 1960, 250, fig 6, no 16) and Thatcham, Berkshire (Wymer 1962, 350, fig 12, nos 165–7) – Bronze Age examples tend to be smaller and less robustly worked. The microliths are simple, quite large obliquely blunted and edge blunted points. The simple microlith forms occur throughout the period (Pitts and Jacobi 1979, 169, fig 5) and are thus difficult to date precisely. However, their size, together with their relative simplicity in terms of retouching, would perhaps indicate an earlier Mesolithic date around 9800–8500 BP. Two probable microlith fragments were recovered from grid references SO246613 and SO270612 (bags 78 and 89). The latter are later Mesolithic in date and are forms which began to be made around 8500 BP. The possible microburin (bag 276, SO246612) attests microlith manufacture and the blade core indicates that knapping was occurring. Fabricators seem to have been multi-purpose tools, used for repeated rubbing and striking functions such as knapping, and in the production of fire. The sparse distribution of Mesolithic material, consisting mainly of microliths, indicates chance losses during hunting episodes. The fertile area of the Walton Basin would have provided good hunting opportunities and temporary camps would have been established.

Earlier Neolithic flintwork is chiefly indicated by the occurrence of leaf-shaped arrowheads. Sixteen leaf-shaped arrowheads and several other fragments were recovered. These ranged from finely retouched ones with little sign of use to cruder, perhaps purely utilitarian examples. A number of other retouched forms, including scrapers, piercers, serrated flakes, and simple flake knives, would also indicate Neolithic activity. Many of the blades and blade-like flakes may also be of earlier Neolithic date, although it is difficult to distinguish debitage, and these pieces may equally belong to the sparse Mesolithic activity identified. Earlier Neolithic core types tend to include the simpler examples such as single platform types. Platform preparation on some examples indicates the removal of overhangs and projections between knapping episodes. The removal of these projections strengthens the working platform edge and enables previous flake arises to be followed in subsequent flaking. The numerous polished implement fragments and flakes indicate Neolithic activity although the re-flaking of these objects may have occurred throughout the Neolithic and into the early Bronze Age.

Middle to later Neolithic flintwork is again mainly recognised by transverse arrowheads which were distributed quite widely. Both chisel and oblique arrowhead forms were recovered, although the former are more numerous. A single possible *petit tranchet* derivative arrowhead was recovered from grid reference SO252613 (bag 536), the scatter above the barrow at Upper Ninepence; another example was recovered from the subsequent excavation at the site (context 50). Diagnostic mid–later Neolithic debitage was also recovered, including Levallois and keeled cores (eg Figs 42 no 1; 45 no 39); other examples of these cores were recovered from the excavation at Upper Ninepence (eg Fig 47 no 10).

Beaker and Bronze Age activity is chiefly recognised by 'thumbnail' scrapers, barbed and tanged arrowheads, and a variety of flake knives. The arrowheads are quite varied in terms of quality of retouch. Some examples were clearly intended for use and some even have possible impact fractures indicating that they have been fired from a bow (eg bag numbers 320, 321 and 326, SO274627, SO274627 and SO250613). Other examples are in mint condition and may not have been intended for use. Approximately 40 'thumbnail' scrapers were recovered, these varied from very small extensively worked examples to larger, partly cortical ones (Figs 43 no 20, 44 no 30 and 45 no 48). Many fine scale-flaked knives including some plano-convex examples were recovered. Technically these are very accomplished pieces. Other retouched forms including small neatly retouched scrapers, piercers, and fabricators, may also be of Beaker and early Bronze Age date. Very little flintwork was demonstrably later Bronze Age. A single tanged arrowhead is likely to be of mid–later Bronze Age date. Debitage to accompany these diagnostic pieces is generally fairly uncharacteristic, although many of the small, hard-hammer struck flakes would appear to be contemporary.

A small quantity of post Bronze Age material includes two stone spindlewhorls which are likely to be of Iron Age date and a single post-medieval gunflint was recovered from SO254615 (bag 1512).

The flint scatters from the Walton Basin
P Bradley

Summary of flint scatters

The flint from each grid reference has been summarised below. Numbers in brackets refer to individual bag numbers. Illustrated material is referred to by catalogue number. Abbreviations: CRF – core rejuvenation flake.

Unprovenanced material

In all, 197 pieces of worked flint and a single piece of burnt unworked flint have no provenance. This material is summarised below and discussed in very general terms only, given the problems with its location.

Flake	142
Utilised flake	1
Blade-like flake	3
Bladelet	1
Blade	1
Chip	9
Irregular waste	4
Polished flake	2
Core	2
Core fragment	4
Axe fragment	1
Arrowhead	1
Scraper	3
Retouched flake	11
Knife	2
Miscellaneous retouch	10
Burnt unworked	1
Total	198

Burning was recorded on 45 flakes, 5 chips, 1 piece of irregular waste, 2 core fragments and 3 pieces of irregular waste.

Mesolithic material includes a possible obliquely blunted point (1588) and another microlith fragment which cannot be assigned to type (1984). Occasional blade-like flakes, blade, bladelet and soft-hammer struck flakes are probably Mesolithic also although they may equally be of earlier Neolithic date. Blade scars were also noted on the dorsal faces of some flakes and blades (for example, 45, 1676). A flake from an opposed platform blade core (1985) and an keeled core with blade scars support the Mesolithic date for some of this material.

Diagnostic retouched pieces include an oblique arrowhead (1986) and bifacially worked piece (1987) which is probably a fragmentary transverse arrowhead. A possible chisel arrowhead was also recovered (57). These arrowheads are of mid–late Neolithic date. A Levallois core on a polished implement fragment (30, Fig 42 no 1) is likely to be of mid–late Neolithic date. Less diagnostic artefacts include flakes from polished implements (31, 55) which are of Neolithic date. Beaker activity is indicated by the recovery of a 'thumbnail' scraper (1589) and a fragmentary barbed and tanged arrowhead (1590). An invasively retouched knife (1912) may be of early Bronze Age date.

Provenanced material

SO18755930 (PRN 26320) A single piece of miscellaneous retouch, possibly a scraper fragment was recovered from this grid reference.

SO20106045 (PRN26313) Fourteen pieces of worked flint were recovered from this grid reference. The material consists of ten flakes, four of which are burnt, a blade, a core fragment, a possible microlith fragment and a possible end-and-side scraper.

SO206629 (PRN unassigned) A single flake was recovered.

SO214617 (PRN 5239) A total of 101 pieces of worked flint and a single piece of burnt unworked flint were recovered. The material can be summarised as follows:

Flake	83
Chip	5
CRF	1
Polished flake	1
Core	1
Axe fragment	1
Arrowhead	1
Scraper	2
Scraper/piercer	1
Retouched flake	4
Miscellaneous retouch	1
Burnt unworked flint	1
Total	102

The leaf-shaped arrowhead, the axe fragment and the polished flake (283, 1594, 1812) indicate probable earlier Neolithic activity. Some of the other retouched forms would also be consistent with this date. An invasively retouched disc scraper (318, Fig 42 no 3) is likely to be early Bronze Age in date. The flakes include many hard-hammer struck examples and hinge fractures are common; this material would suggest a Neolithic to Bronze Age date.

SO2161 (PRN 23499) Eleven pieces of worked flint were recovered from this grid reference. The material consists of 3 flakes, a blade-like flake, 4 scrapers, a plano-convex knife, and 2 retouched flakes. Burning was recorded on 2 flakes. The diagnostic pieces recovered suggest an early Bronze Age date for this small scatter.

SO215635 (PRN 23326) A single, possibly reworked knife was recovered. The retouch cuts through the cortication indicating re-working. The blank is slightly blade-like with proximal and distal breaks. The left-hand side has been steeply retouched.

SO21976055 (PRN 26316) A single soft-hammer struck flake and a chip were recovered from this grid reference.

SO22006040 (PRN 26305) Seven pieces of worked flint were recovered from this grid reference. The material consists of two flakes, a polished flake, two pieces of irregular waste, a small opposed platform core and a scraper. The scraper and both of the flakes are burnt. The flakes are from a ?quartzite object.

SO224617 (PRN 19060) A single flake was recovered.

SO22506046 (PRN 26303) Four flakes, three of which are burnt, were recovered from this grid reference. One of the flakes is soft-hammer struck.

SO226620 (PRN19042) Two flakes, a polished flake, a discoidal core and a chip were recovered. The polished flake would indicate some Neolithic activity and the discoidal core points towards a later Neolithic date.

SO226624 (PRN 23329) A single flake was recovered.

SO22656240 (PRN 26302) Three flakes and a chip were recovered from this grid reference.

SO22966250 (PRN 26325) Fourteen pieces of worked flint were recovered from this grid reference. This material consists of eleven flakes, a notch on a core tablet and two scrapers. One of the flakes is burnt. One of the scrapers was on the end of a blade-like flake, the other was on an irregular flake.

SO23526493 (PRN 26328) A single flake was recovered.

SO237615 (PRN19041) Three flakes and a miscellaneous retouched piece were recovered. The miscellaneous retouched piece is a bifacially worked fragment, probably from an arrowhead, although not enough of the object survives to enable further identification.

SO23856546 (PRN 26309) Two flakes, one of which is burnt, were recovered from this grid reference.

SO238615 (PRN 23330) A finely retouched plano-convex knife (Fig 42 no 4) was found at this grid reference. An early Bronze Age date is indicated by this artefact type.

SO24006264 (PRN26318) A total of 13 pieces of worked flint were recovered. The material consists of 9 flakes, 1 core fragment, 1 end scraper and 2 pieces of miscellaneous retouch. Six of the flakes and 1 piece of miscellaneous retouch are burnt.

SO24346155 (PRN 26312) Two flakes, one soft-hammer struck, were recovered from this grid reference.

SO24356360 (PRN 26310) Eight pieces of worked flint, six flakes, a retouched flake and a barbed and tanged arrowhead, were recovered. Two of the flakes are burnt. The retouched flake has a worn area at its distal end and it may be an atypical fabricator. A late Neolithic to early Bronze Age date is indicated by the arrowhead. The possible fabricator may be Bronze Age in date.

SO243624 (PRN 3666) A multi-platform flake core (Fig 42 no 5) and two pieces of irregular waste were recovered from this grid reference. Subsequent field-walking at this location produced a possible knife fragment.

SO24435990 (PRN 26304) A flake and a core fragment were recovered from this grid reference.

SO244604 (PRN 3652) Two flakes were recovered from this grid reference.

SO244605 (PRN 3661) Six pieces of flint were recovered; four flakes, a serrated flake and a piece of miscellaneous retouch. The serrated flake is on Bullhead flint and is worn. It has been very finely serrated along its left side (approximately eight serrations per 10mm). One of the flakes has been soft-hammer struck.

SO244613 (PRN 23334) A total of 104 pieces of flint were recovered from this grid reference. The material is summarised below:

Flake	81
Chip	1
Irregular waste	1
Core	1
Scraper	11
Retouched flake	3
Piercer	1
Knife	3
Miscellaneous retouch	2
Total	104

Six flakes, the core, an end-and-side scraper and the chip are burnt. Diagnostic retouched forms recovered include five 'thumbnail' scrapers (1438, 1439, 1442, 1848, 1869) and an invasively retouched knife (1441). A later Neolithic to early Bronze Age date is provided by these artefacts. Many hinge fractures were recorded amongst the flakes and hard hammers seem to dominate. The single core (1936) recovered is a small multi-platform type which was rejected because it could not be reduced further due to the many hinge fractures covering its flaking faces.

An early Bronze Age date would be consistent with the debitage.

SO244615 (PRN 50222) Altogether, 299 pieces of worked flint were recovered from this grid reference. The material is summarised below:

Flake	233
Blade-like flake	1
Utilised flakes/blade	3
Chip	2
Irregular waste	7
Cores	3
Core fragment	2
Axe fragment	1
Arrowhead	3
Scraper	15
Retouched flake	11
Serrated flake	3
Knife	1
Fabricator	2
Miscellaneous retouch	12
Total	299

Burning was recorded on 70 flakes, a chip, a blade-like flake, a 'thumbnail' scraper, a retouched flake and six pieces of miscellaneous retouch. Diagnostic retouched forms can be dated to the mid Neolithic through to the early Bronze Age. Two chisel arrowheads and a broken transverse (probably another chisel arrowhead) are of mid to late Neolithic date (312, 313, 265). Five 'thumbnail' scrapers indicate Beaker activity (1546, 1552, 1565, 1578, 1579) and two other scrapers may also be of later Neolithic to early Bronze Age date (1558, 1575). A scale-flaked-knife is probably early Bronze Age in date (Fig 42 no 7; 1567). Less diagnostic artefacts include two fabricators of probable Bronze Age date (Fig 42 no 8, 1577, 1988). An axe fragment and serrated flakes indicate Neolithic activity (298, 1560, 1576, Fig 42 no 6; 1701). Two of the cores are discoidal (1257, 1697), a type which is more common in later Neolithic industries. The third core is a single platform type which cannot readily be dated. Many of the flakes were hard-hammer struck and hinge fractures were commonly noted. This material would be consistent with a later Neolithic to early Bronze Age date.

SO244619 (PRN 3656) A backed knife was recovered from this grid reference.

SO24506048 (PRN 3658) A retouched flake on an irregular flake was recovered from this grid reference.

SO24506061 (PRN 3653) A single flake was recovered.

SO24556100 (PRN 26301) Four flakes and a small discoidal core were recovered from this grid reference. The core might suggest a mid to later Neolithic date.

SO245607 (PRN 19026) Five flakes, a chip, a

'thumbnail' scraper and a retouched flake were recovered. The 'thumbnail' scraper, the chip and one flake are burnt. The 'thumbnail' scraper provides a later Neolithic to early Bronze Age date and the remaining material may also be of that date.

SO245610 (PRN 19059) A total of 39 pieces of flint were recovered from this grid reference. The material is summarised below:

Flake	27
Blade-like flake	2
Chip	1
Core fragment	2
Scraper	2
Retouched flake	1
Backed blade	1
Miscellaneous retouch	3
Total	39

One core fragment, the chip and ten flakes are burnt. The backed blade (1766) has been soft-hammer struck and may be of Mesolithic date. The distal break on this piece may be deliberate truncation. Two of the miscellaneous retouched pieces have bifacial retouch and both seem to belong to arrowheads, one possibly a leaf-shaped (286) and the other an oblique arrowhead (1906). The remaining miscellaneous piece may belong to a chisel arrowhead (1762). These pieces indicate earlier and mid–later Neolithic activity respectively. The scrapers are both end-and-side types, for example Fig 42 no 9, (304). One of these scrapers has shallow retouch and may have been broken during use (1928). This piece may be early Bronze Age in date. This small scatter has diagnostic retouched forms dating from the Mesolithic through to the later Neolithic, with the exception of the possible early Bronze Age scraper (1928).

SO246612 (PRN 50625) In all, 338 pieces of worked flint and two pieces of burnt unworked flint were recovered from this grid reference. The material is summarised below:

Flake	273
Blade-like flake	2
Chip	36
Irregular waste	2
CRF	1
Core	1
Core fragment	2
Micro-burin	1
Scraper	4
Retouched flake	7
Serrated flake	1
Notch	1
Miscellaneous retouch	7
Burnt unworked flint	2
Total	340

Altogether, 133 flakes, 4 chips, 1 scraper and a retouched flake are burnt. Mesolithic activity is indicated by the possible micro-burin, a notch and the blade-like flakes. Some soft-hammer struck flakes may also be Mesolithic in date. A small neatly retouched end-and-side scraper (1491) may be early Bronze Age in date. The majority of the debitage is, however, hard-hammer struck, with hinge fractures and other accidents of knapping being frequently recorded. The miscellaneous retouched pieces are mostly flakes with sporadic retouch although one possible scraper fragment was recovered (1490). The remaining retouched forms are not particularly diagnostic; these forms occur throughout Mesolithic, Neolithic and early Bronze Age flint assemblages. Edge gloss was recorded on the serrated flake. The core is a discoidal type which may suggest that some of the material is of later Neolithic date. The chips are mostly micro-flakes and burnt flake fragments.

SO246613 (PRN 23331) A microlith and a piece of miscellaneous retouch were recovered from this grid reference. The microlith is broken and may be part of a rod (Fig 42 no 10) which would indicate a later Mesolithic date. The miscellaneous retouched piece is a flake with steep retouch along its right-hand side and may be an unfinished microlith. Unfortunately the dating of these pieces cannot be refined as a result of their broken and unfinished state.

SO246617 (PRN 23333) A single flake was recovered.

SO246620 (PRN 50224) A total of 108 pieces of worked flint and two pieces of burnt unworked flint were recovered. The material is summarised below:

Flake	83
Blade-like flake	2
Chip	11
Irregular waste	1
Polished flake	1
Core fragment	1
Arrowhead	1
Scraper	5
Point	1
Miscellaneous retouch	2
Burnt unworked flint	2
Total	110

In all, 33 flakes, 9 chips, 1 'thumbnail' scraper and a piece of miscellaneous retouch are burnt. Earlier Neolithic activity is indicated by the leaf-shaped arrowhead (260) and possibly the polished flake (1463), although polished implements may have been reworked throughout the Neolithic and probably into the early Bronze Age. Beaker activity is indicated by the 'thumbnail' scraper (1460); a side scraper (1383) may be early Bronze Age in date. A bifacially worked point (281, Fig 42 no 11) may be a broken piercer, it has scale-flaking over much of both faces and is probably of early Bronze Age date. Fewer hinge fractures were recorded in this collection than in some of the other scatters and it is possible that more of this material is Neolithic in date. The remaining retouched forms would be consistent with a Neolithic date, although none is particularly diagnostic.

SO24606405 (PRN 26327) Eight pieces of worked flint were recovered. The material consists of four flakes, a serrated flake, a retouched flake on Bull-head flint, a piece of miscellaneous retouch, and a scraper. Three of the flakes are burnt. The serrated flake is worn, the right side has been serrated perhaps by use rather than formal retouch. The scraper may have been broken during use.

SO24676179 (PRN 26319) A retouched flake was recovered from this grid reference.

SO247614 (PRN 19037) A single possible end scraper on a core rejuvenation flake was recovered from this grid reference.

SO247615 (PRN 23335) A single retouched flake was recovered from this grid reference.

SO248610 (PRN 23336) Three flakes and a piece of irregular waste were recovered from this grid reference.

SO249613 (PRN23337) Four flakes, an arrowhead fragment (1968) and a piece of burnt unworked flint were recovered from this grid reference. The arrowhead fragment has been bifacially worked and may be part of either a leaf-shaped arrowhead or a barbed and tanged arrowhead.

SO249614 (PRN 13221) A flake from a polished implement was recovered.

SO249615 (PRN 50223) A total of 398 pieces of worked flint, a stone spindlewhorl and a piece of burnt stone were recovered from this grid reference. The material is summarised below:

Flake	292
Blade	2
Blade-like flake	2
Chips	17
Irregular waste	2
CRF	3
Polished flake	1
Core	4
Core fragment	12
Axe fragment	3
Arrowhead	1
Scraper	29
Retouched flake	13
Serrated flake	3
Piercer	1
Awl	1
Knife	2
Miscellaneous retouch	10
Spindlewhorl	1
Burnt stone	1
Total	400

Of these, 112 flakes, 2 core fragments, 5 chips, a core rejuvenation flake, a scraper and 2 pieces of miscellaneous retouch are burnt. Diagnostic retouched forms include a chisel arrowhead (mid–late Neolithic, 279, Fig 43 no 13) and 'thumbnail' scrapers (Beaker, 263, 1401, 1409, 1413, 1663, 1804, 1813, 1495). Less diagnostic forms include axe fragments (for example 1481) and a flake from a polished implement (69, Fig 42 no 12) which may suggest earlier Neolithic activity. Serrated flakes (for example 1386) occur in earlier and later assemblages The cores are keeled and discoidal forms; types which are more frequently found in later Neolithic assemblages. Amongst the miscellaneous retouched pieces there are two possible leaf-shaped arrowheads (34, 1658) and a single possible transverse arrowhead (299). Neatly retouched scrapers (for example 1380, 1431), knives (251, 1545) and an awl (522, Fig 43 no 14) may be of early Bronze Age date. The remaining retouched forms would belong equally well in a Neolithic or early Bronze Age context. The debitage is dominated by hard-hammer struck flakes, many of which end in hinge fractures. Such material would be consistent with a later Neolithic or Bronze Age date. The spindlewhorl (261) is probably Iron Age in date.

SO24906150 (PRN 26300) Altogether, 39 pieces of worked flint were recovered from this grid reference. The material is summarised below:

Flake	28
Blade	1
Core	2
Core fragment	1
Arrowhead	1
Scraper	3
Piercer	1
Knife	1
Miscellaneous retouch	1
Total	39

Three of the flakes and one of the scrapers are burnt. Diagnostic retouched forms include a later Neolithic/early Bronze Age chisel arrowhead, a possible Bronze Age piercer and an early Bronze Age knife. The cores are a discoidal and a multi-platform type, the former is probably of mid to late Neolithic date.

SO249625 (PRN 23338) A single piece of irregular waste was recovered.

SO250608 (PRN 23342) Two flakes, a fabricator and a serrated flake were recovered. The fabricator is a thick example (249) with a very worn distal end and is probably Mesolithic in date (Fig 43 no 15). The serrated flake (1323, Fig 43 no 16) may also be Mesolithic although these artefacts do occur in later assemblages.

SO250613 (PRN 3533) A total of 518 pieces of worked flint and a piece of worked stone were recovered from this grid reference. The material is summarised below:

Flake	407
Blade-like flake	1
Chip	31
Irregular waste	3
CRF	1
Polished flake	1
Core	1
Core fragment	10
Arrowhead	5
Scraper	21
Retouched flake	13
Serrated flake	4
Knife	2
Denticulate	1
Piercer	3
Miscellaneous retouch	14
Polished object	1
Total	519

Burning was recorded on 157 flakes, 16 chips, 3 pieces of irregular waste, 1 core fragment, a core, 5 scrapers, 2 retouched flakes and 5 pieces of miscellaneous retouch. This scatter contains diagnostic retouched forms of Neolithic and Bronze Age date. Less diagnostic pieces of probable Mesolithic date were also recorded, for example a scraper on a blade-like blank (111) and a retouched blade (109), both of which may be Mesolithic or earlier Neolithic in date. There are also occasional soft-hammer struck flakes and a flake from an opposed platform blade core (1769), which may be Mesolithic or earlier Neolithic in date.

The diagnostic forms include leaf-shaped arrowheads (for example, 315, 325, 527). Mid to later Neolithic activity is indicated by an oblique arrowhead (1352), and a piece of miscellaneous retouch (113) which may be a chisel arrowhead fragment. An invasively retouched knife fragment (110) may be later Neolithic or early Bronze Age in date. A Levallois core (1349) is also probably mid to later Neolithic in date.

Beaker activity is indicated by a barbed and tanged arrowhead (326) and 'thumbnail' scrapers, for example 314, 526, 1332, 1333 and 1334. Other artefacts which might be contemporary include a piercer (2) and a backed knife (75) with invasive retouch. Early Bronze Age flintwork comprises a variety of small, neatly retouched scrapers including 1331, 1336, 1337, 1341, 1343 and 1346 (Fig 43 no 19). A denticulate (77) may be mid to late Bronze Age although it is particularly neatly retouched to form four points. The polished object (90) is probably earlier as it has been re-worked as a core. It is a fine-grained rock with several areas of polishing and is probably a rubber or polisher.

Amongst the miscellaneous retouched pieces are three probable knife fragments, three scraper fragments and a piece which may be either a knife or scraper; the remainder are broken un-

identifiable pieces. The remaining retouched forms would be consistent with a Neolithic or Bronze Age date.

SO250614 (PRN 13222) A single burnt flake was recovered from this grid reference.

SO250616 (PRN 2200) In all, 306 pieces of worked flint were recovered from this grid reference. The material is summarised below:

Flake	224
Blade-like flake	2
Blade	2
Chip	35
Irregular waste	4
CRF	2
Core	3
Core fragment	4
Arrowhead	3
Scraper	4
Retouched flake	5
Microlith	2
Piercer	5
Knife	1
Miscellaneous retouch	9
Burnt unworked flint	1
Total	306

Burning was recorded on 78 flakes, 21 chips, 1 piece of irregular waste, a core fragment, a leaf-shaped arrowhead, and a scraper. Mesolithic, Neolithic and early Bronze Age activity is represented by a variety of diagnostic retouched forms. A small geometric microlith (519) is of later Mesolithic date. A sub-triangular blade fragment with steep retouch (521) may be of early Mesolithic date. A blade-like flake with truncations to its proximal and distal ends (844) and a flake with a proximal truncation (958) are also Mesolithic. A piercer on the end of a blade-like flake (991) may also be contemporary, as may the blade-like flakes and blades. Earlier Neolithic artefacts include a leaf-shaped arrowhead (4), and a chisel arrowhead (262) which is of mid to later Neolithic date. A keeled core (1026) and a discoidal core (1027) may also be mid to later Neolithic in date. Beaker activity is indicated by the barbed and tanged arrowhead (301). Two scrapers (770, 773) and a piercer (1) are probably early Bronze Age in date. A piercer with a worn and crushed point (1519) is probably of Bronze Age date.

SO250632 (PRN 19028) Two flakes and a retouched flake were recovered from this grid reference.

SO250633 (PRN 19027) Ten flakes, a piercer and an end-and-side scraper were recovered from this grid reference. One of the flakes is burnt.

SO2505638 (PRN 26315) A chip and a core fragment were recovered from this grid reference.

SO25056380 (PRN 26315) A total of 51 pieces of worked flint were recovered from this grid reference. The material is summarised below:

Flake	40
Chip	3
Core fragment	2
Scraper	2
Knife	1
Miscellaneous retouch	3
Total	51

Both of the core fragments, along with sixteen flakes, are burnt. The knife has been scale-flaked and is probably early Bronze Age in date. The scrapers are an end and an end and side.

SO250639 (PRN 19048) A single possible discoidal core fragment was recovered from this grid reference. The core is burnt.

SO25126136 (PRN 305) In all, 60 pieces of worked flint were recovered from this grid reference. The material is summarised below:

Flake	44
Chip	6
Irregular waste	5
Core fragment	1
Scraper	1
Piercer	1
Serrated flake	1
Miscellaneous retouch	1
Total	60

Twelve flakes, a chip, two pieces of irregular waste, and a piece of miscellaneous retouch are burnt. Two flakes are soft-hammer struck (675, 720) and a number of flakes have parallel blade scars on their dorsal faces. The core fragment (703) is from a blade core and one or two of the flakes are slightly blade-like (for example, 704, 705). The serrated flake (700) is on Bullhead flint and both edges have been finely serrated; macroscopic gloss was noted on both edges. This material may be Neolithic in date. A single 'thumbnail' scraper (672) indicates some Beaker activity. Many of the flakes end in hinge fractures and have been hard-hammer struck, and may be contemporary with the scraper. The miscellaneous retouched piece (683) may be an arrowhead but not enough of it survives for a full identification to be made.

SO251632 (PRN 19029) A single burnt core fragment was recovered.

SO252607 (PRN 19057) Sixteen pieces of worked flint were recovered from this grid reference (12 flakes, 1 blade, 2 core rejuvenation flakes and a piece of miscellaneous retouch). Three of the flakes and both of the core rejuvenation flakes are burnt.

SO252609 (PRN 3659) A tanged arrowhead was recovered from this grid reference, and it suggests an early Bronze Age date. Subsequent fieldwalking at this location produced a knife and two retouched flakes, one of which is burnt. The knife may be early Bronze Age in date.

SO25266080 (PRN 26308) A single flake was recovered from this grid reference.

SO252611 (PRN 19025) Sixteen pieces of worked flint were recovered from this grid reference (8 flakes, 3 blade-like flakes, 2 chips, a piece of irregular waste, a scraper and a piercer). Four of the flakes, a chip and the piercer are burnt.

SO252613 (PRN 19065) A total of 1264 pieces of worked flint and three pieces of burnt unworked flint were recovered from this grid reference, above the barrow in Upper Ninepence. Subsequent excavation produced an assemblage of 1540 pieces of worked flint and three pieces of burnt unworked flint. The excavated assemblage was mainly mid–late Neolithic in date but a small quantity of Mesolithic and early Bronze Age flintwork was also recovered. The surface collection is summarised below:

Flake	706
Blade-like flake	13
Blade	1
Chip	464
Irregular waste	17
Polished flake	5
Core	7
Core fragment	5
CRF	4
Arrowhead	3
Scraper	11
Retouched flake	3
Serrated flake	2
Microlith	1
Piercer	1
Awl	2
Knife	2
Miscellaneous retouch	17
Burnt unworked flint	3
Total	1267

Burning was recorded on 255 flakes, 242 chips, eleven pieces of irregular waste, a scraper and four pieces of miscellaneous retouch. Mesolithic activity is indicated by the recovery of an obliquely blunted point (1641), two truncated blade-like flakes (1595) and a blade and some blade-like flakes (for example, 1687, 1147, 1149, 634). Possible earlier Neolithic material includes flakes from polished implements (for example, 661, 1095, 1434). Mid to later Neolithic material includes a chisel arrowhead (290), a possible *petit tranchet* derivative (536) arrowhead and possible unfinished oblique arrowheads (1685, 1809). Beaker flintwork includes 'thumbnail' scrapers (for example, 264, 1902). A fine, bifacially worked piece (1685) may be a barbed and tanged or just possibly a leaf-shaped arrowhead. Early Bronze Age artefacts include a plano-convex knife (267), an end scraper (647), a backed knife (1081) and an awl (1142).

The debitage consists mainly of hard-hammer struck flakes, and hinge fractures were commonly recorded. This material is consistent with a mid to later Neolithic to early Bronze Age date. Occasional soft-hammer struck flakes and blade-like flakes (for example, 1112, 1147, 1176, 1595) are likely to be Mesolithic or earlier Neolithic in date and associated with the sporadic activity identified by diagnostic retouched forms. The cores recovered are either single platform or multi-platform types. One core fragment is a re-worked polished implement fragment (1059) with one flat facet remaining. A large number of chips were recovered from this scatter, many of which were burnt fragments, broken pieces from larger flakes, or microflakes. Very few diagnostic chip forms were recovered. This probably reflects the general low level of platform preparation which was recorded.

SO252616 (PRN 19055) Two flakes were recovered from this grid reference.

SO252621 (PRN 19036) A single flake was recovered from this grid reference.

SO253608 (PRN 3657) A core made on a fragment from a polished implement was recovered from this grid reference.

SO253613 (PRN 13223) Three pieces of miscellaneous retouch were recovered from this grid reference. Two of the pieces are flakes with sporadic retouch and the third piece is a burnt possible point. It may be a fabricator or rod but the piece is quite small.

SO253616 (PRN 6346) Altogether, 281 pieces of worked flint were recovered from this grid reference. The material is summarised below:

Flake	241
Chip	16
CRF	1
Polished flake	1
Core fragment	5
Arrowhead	1
Axe	1
Scraper	8
Retouched flake	4
Miscellaneous retouch	3
Total	281

Of these, 48 flakes, 13 chips, 3 core fragments, a polished flake, 3 scrapers and 2 pieces of miscellaneous retouch are burnt. Earlier Neolithic activity is indicated by the leaf-shaped arrowhead (287) and the complete polished stone axe (1596). The stone axe is a small flaked and lightly polished example, only the higher ridges and flake scars show any sign of polishing. The leaf-shaped arrowhead is a finely worked example. Amongst the debitage occasional soft-hammer struck flakes were recorded; this material would be consistent with a Neolithic date. A single burnt 'thumbnail' scraper (1623) indicates some Beaker activity. Many of the flakes are hard-hammer struck, and

hinge fractures and other accidents of debitage were also commonly recorded. An early Bronze Age date for this material is likely. A possible fabricator fragment (1633) may also be of early Bronze Age date. The scrapers are neatly retouched examples which may be Neolithic or Bronze Age, and a single, lightly burnt end scraper (1623) may be Mesolithic in date.

SO254600 (PRN 23344) Two flakes, one of which is burnt, and a core fragment were recovered from this grid reference. The core fragment has some platform edge abrasion and has a mixture of flake and bladelet scars.

SO254606 (PRN 3654) Three flakes and a blade were recovered from this grid reference. One of the flakes and the blade are soft-hammer struck. Subsequent fieldwalking at this location produced six flakes, two blade-like flakes, a core fragment, a core rejuvenation flake (face/edge) and an end-and-side scraper.

SO254615 (PRN 50174) A total of 106 pieces of worked flint and 4 pieces of burnt unworked flint were recovered from this grid reference. The material is summarised below:

Flake	76
Chip	5
Core	2
Core fragment	1
Polished flake	2
Arrowhead	1
Scraper	6
Retouched flake	3
Knife	2
Piercer	2
Miscellaneous retouch	5
Gunflint	1
Burnt unworked flint	4
Total	110

Of these, sixteen flakes, a scraper, a piece of miscellaneous retouch and a core fragment are burnt. Diagnostic retouched forms include a leaf-shaped arrowhead (291, earlier Neolithic), two 'thumbnail' scrapers (1513, 1736, Beaker) and a gunflint (1512, post-medieval). The leaf-shaped arrowhead is made on a flake from a polished implement. A miscellaneous retouched piece with fine bifacial retouch (1310) may be an oblique arrowhead Less diagnostic retouched forms include a possible Mesolithic piercer (5) which has been made on the distal end of a blade; its point is worn through use. The remaining retouched forms are probably Neolithic and early Bronze Age in date. A discoidal core (1517) may be of later Neolithic date. A miscellaneous retouched piece with inverse retouch may have been an arrowhead or a point.

SO254630 (PRN 23346) In all, 66 pieces of worked flint were recovered from this grid reference. The material is summarised below:

Flake	42
Blade-like flake	1
Chip	12
Irregular waste	2
Core	2
CRF	1
Arrowhead	1
Scraper	2
Retouched flake	2
Awl	1
Total	66

Burning was recorded on 17 flakes, 5 chips, 2 pieces of irregular waste and a scraper. An earlier Neolithic date for some of the material is indicated by a leaf-shaped arrowhead (1739); and a burnt end scraper (1604) on a thin blank may also be Neolithic in date. A single blade-like flake (1680) and a soft hammer-struck flake (1761) may also be contemporary. An opposed platform blade core (1675) may be Mesolithic in date. Later Neolithic material is represented by an awl with a long point (1739). Beaker activity is represented by a 'thumbnail' scraper (1679).

SO255617 (PRN50176) Altogether, 31 pieces of worked flint and a single piece of worked stone were recovered from this grid reference. The material is summarised below:

Flake	6
Blade	2
Blade-like flake	1
CRF	1
Arrowhead	4
Scraper	11
Retouched flake	2
Knife	1
Miscellaneous retouch	3
Polisher	1
Total	32

Burning was recorded on one flake, one piece of miscellaneous retouch, and a scraper. This multi-period scatter contained flint mainly of Neolithic and Bronze Age date. A small neatly retouched end scraper (1642) may be of Mesolithic date. Neolithic material is represented by a leaf-shaped arrowhead; the blades and blade-like flake may also be earlier Neolithic or possibly Mesolithic in date. A piece of miscellaneous retouch (294) may be either a leaf-shaped or barbed and tanged arrowhead, though unfortunately not enough of the object survives to enable identification. Mid to later Neolithic flintwork includes a chisel arrowhead (268) and a probable oblique arrowhead (295). Three 'thumbnail' scrapers (1667, 1669, 1670) and a barbed and tanged arrowhead (285) indicate Beaker activity. Early Bronze Age artefacts include an unfinished plano-convex knife (1821). A stone with a highly polished upper surface (1870) may be of earlier

prehistoric date and has certainly been used as a polisher or rubber.

SO255646 (PRN 19066) A total of 34 pieces of worked flint were recovered from this grid reference. The flint is summarised below:

Flake	21
Blade	1
Chip	5
Irregular waste	1
Core	1
Core fragment	2
Scraper	1
Retouched flake	1
Miscellaneous retouch	1
Total	34

Burning was recorded on seven flakes, five chips, two core fragments, a piece of irregular waste and a piece of miscellaneous retouch. No diagnostic retouched pieces were recovered, however, one steeply retouched scraper (1729) is probably of early Bronze Age date and the rest of the material may also be of this date.

SO257610 (PRN 50178) In all, 133 pieces of worked flint were recovered from this grid reference. The flint is summarised below:

Flake	105
Blade-like flake	1
Chip	2
Core	2
Core fragment	3
Irregular waste	3
CRF	1
Flake	2
Arrowhead	4
Scraper	4
Retouched flake	1
Miscellaneous retouch	4
Burnt unworked flint	1
Total	133

Burning was recorded on 40 flakes, a blade-like flake, a piece of irregular waste and a core. Earlier Neolithic material is represented by a leaf-shaped arrowhead (308) and flakes from polished implements (1305 – stone, 1306). The blade-like flake (1450) may also be Neolithic. Mid to later Neolithic flintwork includes two chisel arrowheads (300, 1313) and a probable oblique arrowhead (303). The scrapers are all neatly retouched and may be Neolithic or early Bronze Age in date. A possible fabricator fragment (1744) may be of early Bronze Age date. Many hinge fractures were recorded amongst the debitage and hard hammers dominate. Both of the cores are multi-platform types.

SO257614 (PRN 50177) Altogether, 519 pieces of worked flint were recovered from this grid reference. The flint is summarised below:

Flake	444
Blade-like flake	1
Chip	13
Irregular waste	5
CRF	1
Polished flake	2
Core	3
Core fragment	3
Arrowhead	3
Scraper	9
Retouched flake	13
Serrated flake	1
Awl	2
Miscellaneous retouch	19
Total	519

Burning was recorded on 131 flakes, five chips, seven miscellaneous retouched pieces and a scraper. Earlier Neolithic activity is indicated by two broken leaf-shaped arrowheads (250, 259), and also possibly early are two flakes from a polished implement (1722) and a serrated flake (1709). The blade-like flake may also be contemporary as may the occasional soft-hammer struck flakes that were recorded. Mid to later Neolithic activity is indicated by two chisel arrowheads (266, 1664). Another probable arrowhead fragment was also recovered (1661) although not enough of it survived to enable its type to be identified. Beaker activity is represented by a barbed and tanged arrowhead and two 'thumbnail' scrapers (252, 1714, 1720). Many of the other retouched forms such as the scrapers, retouched flakes, awls and miscellaneous pieces would be consistent with a Neolithic or Bronze Age date. Many of the miscellaneous pieces are broken scraper fragments. One scraper (1722) is made on a flake from a polished implement. Hard-hammer struck flakes dominate the debitage. Much of this would be consistent with a later Neolithic to early Bronze Age date. The cores include a Levallois type which would be consistent with a mid–late Neolithic date.

SO257615 (PRN 23345) Six pieces of worked flint were recovered from this grid reference. The material consists of three flakes, a core fragment, an opposed platform blade/bladelet core and a probable scraper fragment.

SO257617 (PRN 19054) A piece of burnt unworked flint was recovered from this grid reference.

SO257645 (PRN 23327) Three flakes, a leaf-shaped arrowhead and a possible leaf-shaped arrowhead fragment were recovered. An earlier Neolithic date is provided by the arrowheads.

SO258621 (PRN 3655) A single scraper, possibly of early Bronze Age date was recovered.

SO258634 (PRN 19063) Two flakes and a chip were recovered. One of the flakes is burnt.

SO258645 (PRN 19067) A total of 51 pieces of worked flint and a single piece of burnt unworked flint were recovered. The flint is summarised below:

Flake	36
Chip	7
Irregular waste	1
CRF	1
Core	1
Arrowhead	2
Retouched flake	3
Burnt unworked	1
Total	52

Fifteen flakes, five chips and a piece of irregular waste are burnt. Mid–late Neolithic activity is indicated by a chisel arrowhead (275). The core is a discoidal type which would be consistent with a mid–late Neolithic date. Beaker activity is indicated by the barbed and tanged arrowhead (273). Occasional soft-hammer struck flakes and retouched flakes (for example, 1207, 1221, 1232) may suggest earlier material, although this is a rather tentative suggestion.

SO259613 (PRN 50179) A total of 230 pieces of worked flint and twelve pieces of burnt unworked flint were recovered from this grid reference. The flint is summarised below.

Flake	165
Blade-like flake	5
Chip	8
Irregular waste	2
CRF	2
Polished flake	1
Core	8
Core fragment	6
Arrowhead	4
Scraper	8
Retouched flake	9
Awl	1
Piercer	1
Knife	1
Truncation	1
Miscellaneous retouch	7
Whetstone/hone	1
Burnt unworked flint	12
Total	242

Burning was recorded on 42 flakes and two cores. Diagnostic retouched forms dating from the mid to later Neolithic and the early Bronze Age were recovered. These artefacts are chiefly arrowheads, and mid–late Neolithic activity is indicated by the presence of chisel arrowheads (328, 1751, 1800). Less diagnostic but also probably contemporary are a number of other pieces including a keeled core (1740). Some of the scrapers (for example, 316, 1752), the knife (329), the piercer (323) and the retouched flakes may also be mid–late Neolithic in date. Beaker activity is indicated by 'thumbnail' scrapers (for example, 324 and 1884). A double ended awl (319) and three small, neatly retouched end-and-side scrapers (1892, 1800) may also be of Beaker date.

The debitage is dominated by hard-hammer struck flakes; hinge fractures and other accidents of debitage were recorded. Occasional soft-hammer struck flakes were recorded (for example 1800). Multi-platform flake cores dominate the assemblage but keeled (1740) and single platform (1759) examples were also recovered.

Possible Mesolithic activity is suggested by two retouched flakes, a truncated blade-like flake (1800), and a notch (1886), although there is nothing particularly diagnostic about these artefacts. A possible unfinished leaf-shaped arrowhead (1760) attests earlier Neolithic activity. This is supported by the recovery of a flake from a polished implement. The blade-like flakes and the occasional soft-hammer struck flakes (for example, 1800) could be either Mesolithic or earlier Neolithic in date. A fragment of a sandstone whetstone or hone of circular cross-section and pointed outline was also recovered. Numerous marks on the object can be interpreted as knife sharpening damage.

SO260607 (PRN 23349) A flake and a piece of miscellaneous retouch were recovered. The miscellaneous piece is a possible knife fragment with invasive retouch.

SO260646 (PRN 2204) In all, 181 pieces of worked flint and two pieces of burnt unworked flint were recovered from this grid reference. The flint is summarised below:

Flake	118
Utilised blade	1
Blade-like flake	1
Chip	25
Irregular waste	7
CRF	2
Polished flake	1
Core	2
Core fragment	4
Arrowhead	1
Scraper	6
Retouched flake	4
Piercer	3
Knife	2
Fabricator	1
Miscellaneous retouch	3
Burnt unworked	2
Total	183

Burning was recorded on 43 flakes, 2 core fragments, 13 chips, 1 piece of irregular waste, and a scraper. Diagnostic retouched forms include a leaf-shaped arrowhead (271) indicating some earlier Neolithic activity, a discoidal core (342) suggesting some mid to later Neolithic activity, a bilaterally scale-flaked knife (367), which is typical of later Neolithic or early Bronze Age flintworking, and a fabricator (357) which provides a more general

Bronze Age date. Two end scrapers (371, 379) on the ends of long flakes may possibly be Mesolithic in date. A single flake from a polished implement (427) and some of the other retouched forms, for example, some of the scrapers (356, 346), retouched flakes (334), and piercers (378) would be consistent with a Neolithic date. Three miscellaneous retouched pieces were recovered; these include a possible fragment from a chisel arrowhead (336) of mid to later Neolithic date, a possible arrowhead blank (339) of probable Neolithic or Bronze Age date, and a possible piercer (376). A steeply retouched scraper on a core tablet (340) is likely to be Bronze Age in date.

The debitage is dominated by hard-hammer struck flakes, and hinge fractures were fairly commonly noted. Some other accidents of knapping, for example *siret* fractures, were also recorded. Occasional soft-hammer struck flakes were recorded, although these are generally infrequent, and are probably related to the tentatively identified Mesolithic activity or the earlier Neolithic material. The single blade-like flake and utilised blade are probably of this date also. The cores recovered include a discoidal type (342) and a core on a flake (391). The latter was rejected because hinge fractures precluded further flaking. One of the core fragments has some evidence of platform preparation, perhaps indicating a relatively early date.

SO261613 (PRN 23350) Seven pieces of worked flint were recovered from this grid reference, including five flakes, a core fragment, and a piece of miscellaneous retouch. Three of the flakes and the miscellaneous retouch are burnt. The miscellaneous piece is probably a scraper.

SO261643 (PRN 19061) Three flakes were recovered from this grid reference. One of the flakes is burnt.

SO262597 (PRN 23348) Ten pieces of worked flint and a piece of burnt unworked flint were recovered, including eight flakes, a chip, and a retouched flake. The retouched flake is a broken blade-like flake with invasive retouch along its right-hand side and distal end.

SO262598 (PRN 3662) Two flakes and a piece of irregular waste were recovered from this grid reference.

SO262617 (PRN 19035) A single burnt flake was recovered.

SO262630 (PRN 19031) A spindlewhorl was recovered. It is likely to be Iron Age in date.

SO262639 (PRN 19062) A flake and a burnt piece of irregular waste were recovered from this grid reference.

SO262645 (PRN 19069) Eight pieces of worked flint were recovered, including four flakes, a flake from a polished implement, a core, a piece of irregular waste, and a piece of miscellaneous retouch. One flake and the miscellaneous retouched piece are burnt.

SO262647 (PRN 19070) A single serrated flake was recovered from this grid reference. It has been finely retouched along its left-hand side with approximately twelve serrations per 10mm. Edge gloss was recorded along this side, and the right hand side was much more coarsely serrated.

SO263614 (PRN 23351) Five flakes and a chip were recovered from this grid reference. One flake and the chip are burnt.

SO263629 (PRN 23347) Three pieces of worked flint and a piece of burnt unworked flint were recovered from this grid reference. The material consists of a flake and two pieces of miscellaneous retouch, one of which is burnt. The miscellaneous pieces are a possible scraper fragment and a possible unfinished arrowhead.

SO264630 (PRN 19030) A total of 31 pieces of worked flint and a single piece of worked stone were recovered from this grid reference. This material consists of 25 flakes, a bladelet, a chip, two pieces of irregular waste, a scraper, and a fragmentary leaf-shaped arrowhead. The piece of worked stone is an egg-shaped pebble with central depressions on both sides. However, the object appears to have been broken, possibly during manufacture, leaving only the very base of the second depression visible. Six flakes and one piece of irregular waste are burnt. The leaf-shaped arrowhead provides an earlier Neolithic date. The flakes are mostly hard-hammer struck.

SO264634 (PRN 19044) Two flakes, a retouched flake and an end-and-side scraper were recovered from this grid reference. The scraper is steeply retouched and may be of early Bronze Age date.

SO264645 (PRN 19072) Three flakes and two chips were recovered from this grid reference. Both of the chips and one flake are burnt.

SO264–6B (mistranscribed NGR, PRN unassigned) A single burnt flake was recovered from this location.

SO265629 (PRN 3532) A total of 153 pieces of worked flint and a single piece of burnt unworked flint were recovered from this grid reference. The flint is summarised below:

Flake	103
Blade	2
Blade-like flake	2
Chip	5
Irregular waste	5
CRF	3
Polished flake	1
Core	3
Core fragment	4
Scraper	7
Retouched flake	4
Awl	1
Knife	1
Notch	1
Fabricator	1
Miscellaneous retouch	10
Burnt unworked	1
Total	154

Burning was recorded on 38 flakes, 2 pieces of irregular waste, 2 chips, a polished flake, a core fragment, 3 scrapers and 3 pieces of miscellaneous retouch. No diagnostic retouched forms were recovered from this scatter to provide dating. However, some broad dates may be provided by less diagnostic pieces, for example a notch (186) which may be Mesolithic in date, the flake from a polished implement (35, earlier Neolithic), scrapers (for example 1046, 1047, 1048, 1049, ?early Bronze Age) which are all small, invasively retouched examples, and an awl (1039) which is probably Bronze Age in date. The fabricator fragment (1036) is also probably of Bronze Age date. The remaining retouched forms would not be out of place in a Neolithic or Bronze Age context. The numerous miscellaneous retouched pieces include a possible scraper fragment on a flake from a polished implement (1053), many broken retouched pieces (for example, 160, 1599), and a bifacially worked piece which would seem to be an arrowhead that has been broken during manufacture (1055).

The debitage consists mainly of hard-hammer struck flakes although some soft-hammer struck material was recorded (for example, 166, 168, 209). A core fragment (1627) has some blade-like scars. Two blades and two blade-like flakes were also recovered, and this material is probably Mesolithic or earlier Neolithic in date. The cores include two multi-platform types and a discoidal core, possibly of mid–late Neolithic date.

SO266613 (PRN 19076) Two flakes, a chip, and a probable rod or fabricator fragment were recovered from this grid reference. One of the flakes is burnt. The rod or fabricator fragment (297) is very steeply retouched and similar to find numbers 257 and 281. It is likely to be of early Bronze Age date.

SO266629 (PRN 13224) An assemblage of 108 pieces of worked flint and a single piece of burnt unworked flint was recovered from this grid reference. The flint is summarised below:

Flake	94
Blade-like flake	1
Chip	10
Core fragment	3
Burnt unworked flint	1
Total	109

Burning was recorded on 43 flakes, five chips and a core fragment. The flakes are mostly hard-hammer struck although the occasional soft-hammer struck flake was recorded. No diagnostic pieces were recovered but the predominance of hard-hammer struck flakes would suggest a later Neolithic/early Bronze Age date. However, any dating must be regarded as tentative given the lack of retouched forms.

SO266636 (PRN 23074) Twenty-one pieces of worked flint and a single piece of worked stone were recovered from this grid reference. The material consists of twelve flakes, a core, a core rejuvenation flake, a microlith, a barbed and tanged arrowhead, a retouched flake, a borer, three pieces of miscellaneous retouch, and a polisher. Burning was recorded on seven flakes, a core and four pieces of miscellaneous retouch. Diagnostic retouched forms include an obliquely blunted point (524) of early Mesolithic date. A barbed and tanged arrowhead (288) and a possible barb from a second arrowhead indicate Beaker activity. The polisher is a smoothed oval pebble.

SO26756027 (PRN 26311) Six flakes and two pieces of burnt unworked flint were recovered from this grid reference. Two of the flakes are burnt. PRN 26311.

SO267621 (PRN 23355) Five flakes, two of which are burnt, were recovered from this grid reference.

SO268612 (PRN 23352) A single flake was recovered from this grid reference.

SO268614 (PRN 23353) A single flake was recovered from this grid reference.

SO269599 (PRN 19050) A total of 65 pieces of worked flint and a single piece of rock crystal were recovered from this grid reference. The flint is summarised below:

Flake	51
Utilised flake	1
Chip	5
Irregular waste	1
Core	1
Scraper	1
Retouched flake	2
Miscellaneous retouch	3
Rock crystal	1
Total	66

Burning was recorded on nineteen flakes and two chips. No diagnostic retouched forms were found, however, the small end scraper may be of Mesolithic date and the discoidal core, possibly reused as a scraper, is probably mid to later Neolithic in date.

SO269617 (PRN 23354) A single flake was recovered from this grid reference.

SO270612 (PRN 23357) Fifteen pieces of worked flint were recovered from this grid reference. The material consists of ten flakes, a blade (115), a piercer, (84) a microlith (89) and two scrapers (87, 119). Burning was recorded on two of the flakes. The microlith is badly damaged but it would appear to be a minimally retouched rod type. A later Mesolithic date is indicated by this artefact. The blade, a soft-hammer struck flake (116), and a flake with blade scars on its dorsal face (82), may also be Mesolithic. The piercer has a long but minimally retouched point and may be of later Neolithic date.

SO270614 (PRN 19051) A single chip was recovered from this location.

SO271590 (PRN 13225) A flake, a blade-like flake, and a retouched flake were recovered from this location. The latter has fine, bifacial retouch and may be of early Bronze Age date.

SO271616 (PRN 23358) Two flakes and an end scraper were recovered from this grid reference. The scraper is a small, steeply retouched example on a thin, non-cortical blank, and an early Bronze Age date is probable.

SO271618 (PRN 23359) Seven pieces of worked flint were recovered from this grid reference. The material consists of four flakes, two core fragments, and a piece of miscellaneous retouch. One of the core fragments and three of the flakes are burnt. The miscellaneous retouched piece (1360) has steep, slightly curving retouch along one edge and may be an arrowhead fragment. However, not enough of the object survives to enable a more precise identification to be made. One of the flakes has been soft-hammer struck (1365).

SO272611 (PRN 23360) A single flake was recovered from this grid reference.

SO272613 (PRN 23361) Three flakes were recovered from this grid reference.

SO272619 (PRN 3531) An obliquely blunted point was recovered from this grid reference. An early Mesolithic date is indicated by this artefact.

SO273597 (PRN 13226) Three flakes and a burnt piece of irregular waste were recovered from this grid reference.

SO273615 (PRN 23362) A flake, a retouched flake, and a burnt polished flake were recovered from this grid reference.

SO273631 (PRN 19064) A burnt flake and a retouched flake were recovered from this grid reference.

SO274601 (PRN 19049) In all, 36 pieces of worked flint were recovered from this grid reference. The flint is summarised below:

Flake	30
Blade-like flake	1
Truncated blade	1
CRF	1
Core fragment	1
Retouched flake	1
Miscellaneous retouch	1
Total	36

Nine of the flakes are burnt. The truncated blade is probably Mesolithic in date; the blade-like flake may also be of this date. The miscellaneous retouched piece may be a scraper fragment.

SO274627 (PRN 13227) A leaf-shaped arrowhead and two barbed and tanged arrowheads were recovered from this grid reference. These arrowheads provide earlier Neolithic and Beaker dates respectively. All of the arrowheads are finely worked.

SO275636 (PRN 19032) Six pieces of worked flint were recovered from this grid reference. The material consists of two flakes, a blade-like flake, a chip and two pieces of miscellaneous retouch. The chip is burnt. The miscellaneous pieces are a possible fabricator fragment (1428) and a knife fragment (1790).

SO276629 (PRN 19040) A single flake was recovered from this grid reference.

SO277634 (PRN 19074) A flake, two scrapers, and a leaf-shaped arrowhead were recovered from this grid reference. One of the scrapers is burnt. The arrowhead provides an earlier Neolithic date. The scrapers are neatly retouched, one has invasive retouch (8), and these too may be Neolithic in date.

SO277636 (PRN 19073) Two scrapers and a core were recovered from this grid reference. The scrapers are both neatly retouched, one is an end-and-side scraper (1237), and the other is on an irregular flake (1238).

SO278633 (PRN 19045) A piece of miscellaneous retouch was recovered from this grid reference. The object is steeply retouched and may be a scraper fragment.

SO28216120 (PRN 26307) Two burnt flakes were recovered from this location.

SO291593 (PRN 13228) A flake and a burnt miscellaneous retouched piece were recovered from this grid reference. The miscellaneous piece is a bifacially worked object made on a flake from a polished implement.

SO295614 (PRN 13229) A flake, a backed knife, and a retouched flake were recovered from this grid reference. The flake is burnt.

SO349615 (PRN 13230) A single core was recovered from this grid reference.

Discussion

Flintwork of Mesolithic to Bronze Age date was recovered, although the collection included surprisingly little Mesolithic or earlier Neolithic material. This may reflect collection biases: microliths and other diagnostic pieces such as microburins are less visible than the larger retouched forms common to later periods. However, the recovery rate was extremely good, with small pieces of burnt unworked flint and chips measuring less than 10mm being retrieved. The period biases may therefore be real, with the bulk of the collection dating from the mid to later Neolithic through to the early Bronze Age. This would also coincide with the increase in monument building within the region.

Just over 11% of the collection is composed of retouched forms. This is a relatively high figure and may simply reflect collection biases. However, given the very high quality of recovery, collection biases would seem less likely. Wainwright (1972, 66) suggests a figure of 4–5% for retouched forms as being typical for the majority of settlement sites. However, certain specialised assemblages, such as those resulting from hide processing or funerary assemblages, would necessarily have a higher proportion of retouched forms than those resulting from everyday activities (cf Bradley 1994). The mixed nature of the collection will almost certainly have enhanced the percentage of retouched forms. The predominance of very fine retouched forms may be due to collection bias, although as noted above, this seems unlikely in this instance.

The collection is dominated by scrapers (approximately 28%), retouched and serrated flakes (23%), and miscellaneous retouched pieces (25%). These types are good indicators of domestic assemblages. Much of the miscellaneous category is composed of broken and unfinished artefacts such as scrapers, knives, piercers and arrowheads, but also includes some atypical forms. Certain artefact types indicate that activities such as hunting (the microliths and arrowheads), and knapping were occurring. A possible scraper retouch chip indicates that some maintenance of tools was occurring. No flint or stone hammerstones were recovered from the surface collection but the excavation at Upper Ninepence Field did produce some. Several of the cores from the surface collection exhibited areas of battering which may have resulted from use as hammerstones.

Many of the diagnostic retouched types have well documented ceramic associations elsewhere in Britain, for example, barbed and tanged arrowheads and 'thumbnail' scrapers are associated with a variety of Beaker ceramics; oblique, chisel, and *petit tranchet* arrowheads with Peterborough Ware and Grooved Ware; plano-convex knives with Collared Urns and other early Bronze Age pottery.

A wide range of raw materials were used, many of which are of very high quality. The use of high quality flint is of some interest, given the lack of readily available local raw materials. The use of imported flint has been reported at other sites, but has generally been reserved for grave goods (Healey 1993, 187). Stone and flint axes were reused once they were broken and they provided a source of very high quality raw materials. All stages of the reduction sequence were recovered; the presence of wholly and largely cortical flakes indicates that the raw materials were being reduced in the locality rather than at the source. The recovery of core rejuvenation flakes suggests that there was some concern for raw material conservation. The average core weight for the surface collection is 16.9g, which is very low in comparison with the excavated assemblage from Peterborough Ware and Grooved Ware contexts at Upper Ninepence, where the average weight is 26.3g. However, the high proportion of core fragments from the surface collection may have skewed the results. The low weight of the surface cores suggests more extensive working, perhaps more typical of domestic assemblages.

The cores from the pits at Upper Ninepence were not being worked to their full potential, perhaps suggesting that the deposition of valuable, high quality flint was an important part of the ritual process. This deposition may have been especially important in an area of few locally available sources of flint. These assemblages also showed a relatively low incidence of rejuvenation, again indicating that raw material conservation was not seen as important. At Barrow Hills, Radley, in Oxfordshire, cores from a series of Grooved Ware pits were also less extensively worked than cores from the surface collection (Bradley forthcoming). At the same site a series of intercutting pits contained flint assemblages with a higher percentage of retouched pieces, more extensively worked cores, and a very high proportion of broken pieces compared with the contemporary Grooved Ware pits. It has been suggested that these assemblages may represent domestic debris, whilst the material from the Grooved Ware pits seems to have had a more complex history and was certainly deposited in a formal manner, though perhaps also originating from domestic activities (Bradley forthcoming).

In general, the surface collection showed little sign of careful flintworking strategies, such as core preparation and maintenance. Soft hammers were used, for example, from grid references SO 250126136, SO250613, SO260646, SO265629 and SO270612, although hard hammers do dominate. Blade cores are relatively scarce in the collection (see Table 16) but the occurrence of flakes, blades and fragments from blade cores, including opposed platform types, suggests that the quantity of carefully flaked material might be higher than is suggested at present by the core types. Careful and controlled knapping strategies, using blade or single platform flake cores which are maintained and rejuvenated frequently, are indicative of the earlier periods of flintworking and although Mesolithic and earlier Neolithic artefacts were recovered, they tend to be scattered across the landscape. The lack of preparation and maintenance does not seem to have affected the overall quality of the flintworking; many fine later Neolithic and early Bronze Age artefacts are present in the collection. Preferred blank types continued to be produced, for example, blades were used for specific artefacts such as the plano-convex knives (Fig 42 nos 2 and 4; Fig 44 no 29, bags 3, 1856, 367). The frequency of keeled and Levallois cores is interesting (see Table 16), and it has been suggested that the latter provided blanks for transverse arrowheads. These types of cores required a degree of skill to produce consistent blanks suitable for subsequent retouching as arrowheads or other artefacts.

Many artefacts are finely worked; scale-flaked knives are well represented and many of the arrowheads are also particularly finely worked (Fig 43 nos 17 and 26; Fig 44 no 37, bags 325, 301, 300). The decline in the quality of flintworking through time, and the reduction in the number of retouched tools being produced, partly linked with the increased use of metal, is now well established (see for example Ford et al 1984, 167). However, the continued production of very fine artefacts, partly contemporary with this apparent decline in craftsmanship, indicates that the situation is complex. It seems likely that the emphasis changed to a more expedient everyday technology, with very skilful knapping

being reserved for particular artefact types or depositional episodes.

There is evidence that artefacts were used, for example, some of the arrowheads have impact fractures at their tips. Macroscopic edge gloss was recorded on serrated flakes (eg from grid reference SO244615, Fig 42 no 6, bag 1701), and scraping edges on many of the scrapers are worn (eg from grid reference SO246610, Fig 42 no 9, bag 304). Many of the retouched flakes and some of the awls and piercers also exhibit signs of use. In addition, some of the material from the Peterborough Ware and Grooved Ware pits at Upper Ninepence Field shows signs of being used, although some artefacts do not appear to have been used. One of the scrapers, a fairly small neatly retouched example from grid reference SO250613, seems to have been hafted as it has been provided with a tang (Fig 43 no 19, bag 1336).

Seventeen scatters consist of more than 100 pieces of worked flint (see above). Many of these scatters are dominated by debitage, for example, no retouched forms were recovered from grid reference SO266629. The majority of these scatters are multi-period with Neolithic and Bronze Age flintwork dominating. Some of the difficulties of dating surface collections have already been discussed, and it is apparent that the identification of early Bronze Age material – other than diagnostic forms such as 'thumbnail' scrapers, barbed and tanged arrowheads, or plano-convex knives – is particularly difficult. Distinguishing Mesolithic and earlier Neolithic debitage without the accompanying retouched forms is also difficult. The large surface scatter above the barrow at Upper Ninepence is of some interest, in that its composition in terms of forms and date range is very similar to the excavated assemblage from the site. Mesolithic and Bronze Age flintwork from the site is poorly represented. The bulk of the excavated assemblage is firmly mid to later Neolithic and contemporary flint was recovered from the surface scatter.

The evidence for Mesolithic activity in Wales has recently been reviewed (see for example, Jacobi 1980; David 1989; Berridge 1994). In general, earlier Mesolithic activity is very sparsely distributed, except to the south and west where there is much evidence for coastal exploitation (Jacobi 1980, 138; David 1989, 241; Berridge 1994, 130). Later Mesolithic activity is a little more widespread (Jacobi 1980, 169) and recent discoveries within the region of further Mesolithic sites and findspots continues (eg Barton et al 1995), enhancing our knowledge of hunter-gatherer communities.

Some comparable flint assemblages have been recovered from the immediate area, for example, at Trelystan, Powys (Healey 1982, 175), Four Crosses, Powys (Green 1986, 77–8) and material from the Welshpool cursus (Aldhouse-Green 1994, 177). At Clyro, Radnorshire a scalene triangle of the later Mesolithic and Neolithic to Bronze Age flintwork was recovered (Wainwright 1963, 101). The stratified assemblage from Upper Ninepence Field has obvious similarities with the flint scatter recovered from the area (see above) but its general characteristics can be paralleled at a number of other sites. Mesolithic to Bronze Age flintwork has been recovered from surface scatters in counties bordering Powys, particularly Herefordshire (Bradley 1988; Children and Nash 1994). Neolithic and Bronze Age activity within Wales was reviewed (Savory 1980; Lynch 1980; Burgess 1980), and showed that the distribution of finds and monuments is widespread across the south and north-west of the Principality and along the Marches (Savory 1980, 211, fig 5.2, 2.18, fig 5.4; Lynch 1980, 240, fig 6.4).

Catalogue of illustrated pieces (Dunn Collection) (Figs 42–46)

Catalogue entries are ordered as follows: grid reference, brief description, weight (cores only), bag number. Abbreviations are as follows: LHS – left hand side, RHS – right hand side. Broad dates have been given where possible: M – Mesolithic, LM – late Mesolithic, EN – early Neolithic, N – Neolithic, M–LN – middle to late Neolithic, LNEBA – later Neolithic/early Bronze Age, EBA – early Bronze Age, BA – Bronze Age, MBA – middle Bronze Age.

1 Unprovenanced. Levallois core on polished stone axe fragment. 50g. M–LN. Bag number 30.
2 SO2161 (Knowle Hill). Plano-convex knife. On blade-like blank, steep, scale-flaking covers much of the dorsal face. Proximal break. EBA. Bag number 3.
3 SO214617. Neatly retouched disc scraper on oval blank. Fine invasive retouch at base and part of RHS, LHS and the distal end are more steeply retouched. Scraping angle 45–65°. ?EBA. Bag number 318.
4 SO238615. Plano-convex knife. Scale-flaking restricted to edges, dorsal face has a large area of cortex remaining. Distal end broken and reworked, probably during manufacture. EBA. Bag number 1856.
5 SO243624. Multi-platform flake core, some blade-like scars. 14g. Bag number 1536.
6 SO244615. Serrated flake on a core rejuvenation flake (face/edge). Light grey chert. RHS serrated, 6 serrations per 10mm, ventral gloss. Bag number 1701.
7 SO244615. Scale-flaked knife, proximal break. LHS scale-flaked, cortex present RHS. There is additional steeper retouch upper RHS and lower RHS. ?EBA. Bag number 1567.
8 SO244615. Fabricator. On blade-like blank, steeply retouched LHS and RHS. Characteristic crushing occurs at the distal end. BA. Bag number 1577.
9 SO246610. End-and-side scraper. Neatly retouched, scraping angle 65–75°. Worn/damaged scraping edge. Break at proximal end has been re-flaked, probably broken during use. Pink flint, small area of worn cortex. Bag number 304.
10 SO246613. ?Rod microlith, on dark grey chert. Broken at both proximal and distal ends. Bag number 78.
11 SO246620. Bifacially worked object, rod-like piece. Proximal break. Extensively and finely retouched. Point or piercer?, very similar to bag number 257. ?EBA. Bag number 281.

12 SO249615. Flake from a polished stone implement. Fine-grained grey stone. Bag number 69.
13 SO249615. Chisel arrowhead, broken LHS. M–LN. Bag number 279.
14 SO249615. Double-ended awl. Dark grey chert, very neatly retouched. N or EBA. Bag number 522.
15 SO250608. Fabricator. Large, robustly retouched fabricator, characteristic crushing at distal end and along both edges. ?M. Bag number 249.
16 SO250608. Serrated flake. Proximal break. On an irregular flake with large hinge fracture on dorsal face. LHS very finely serrated, approximately 15 serrations per 10mm, RHS possibly used. Ventral gloss LHS. Bag number 1323.
17 SO250613. Leaf-shaped arrowhead. Very small, neatly retouched example; retouch extends over much of dorsal face but is confined to the edges of the ventral face. EN. Bag number 325.
18 SO250613. Retouched flake. Proximal and distal breaks, neatly retouched LHS with cortical backing RHS. Bag number 1335.
19 SO250613. End-and-side scraper. Small, neatly retouched scraper, scraping angle 55–65°. Retouch extends around much of the circumference of the object. The butt has not been removed thus forming a slight projection or tang. This may have been used to haft the artefact. ?EBA. Bag number 1336.
20 SO250613. 'Thumbnail' scraper. Small, neatly retouched example, lightly burnt. Steep retouch and area of smooth brown cortex RHS. Scraping angle 65–80°. LNEBA. Bag number 526.
21 SO250613. Backed knife. On a blade-like blank with invasive retouch LHS, slightly denticulate retouch RHS. Possibly also used as a piercer. LNEBA. Bag number 75.
22 SO250616. Microlith. LM. Bag number 519.
23 SO250616. Sub-triangular piece. Steeply retouched. ?M. Bag number 521.
24 SO250616. Chisel arrowhead, LHS slightly damaged. M–LN. Bag number 262.
25 SO250616. Piercer. Extensively retouched on a thick blank, worn point. LN. Bag number 1519.
26 SO250616. Barbed and tanged arrowhead, one barb broken. Very fine bifacial retouch. LNEBA. Bag number 301.
27 SO252609. Tanged arrowhead, damage to tip and tang. Retouched over much of both faces. MBA. Bag number 274.
28 SO252613. Truncated blade, proximal and distal breaks. Obliquely truncated RHS. M. Bag number 1641.
29 SO252613. Plano-convex knife. On blade-like blank, proximal break. Very finely scale-flaked example with rough polishing on ventral face. EBA. Bag number 267.
30 SO252613. 'Thumbnail' scraper. Small, very neatly worked example, retouched around its entire circumference. Scraping angle 55–75°. LNEBA. Bag number 264.
31 SO253616. Flaked and polished stone axe. Small axe, polishing confined to the higher arises, some plough damage. N. Bag number 1596.
32 SO253616. End scraper. On long blank with white, chalky cortex on dorsal face. Neatly retouched at distal end with additional retouch at proximal end, perhaps to aid hafting. Scraping angle 50–60°. ?EN. Bag number 1623.
33 SO254615. Piercer. On distal end of a blade-like blank, proximal break. Slender point, some wear to tip. ?M. Bag number 5.
34 SO254615. Backed knife. ?Derived flint. Shallow,

68

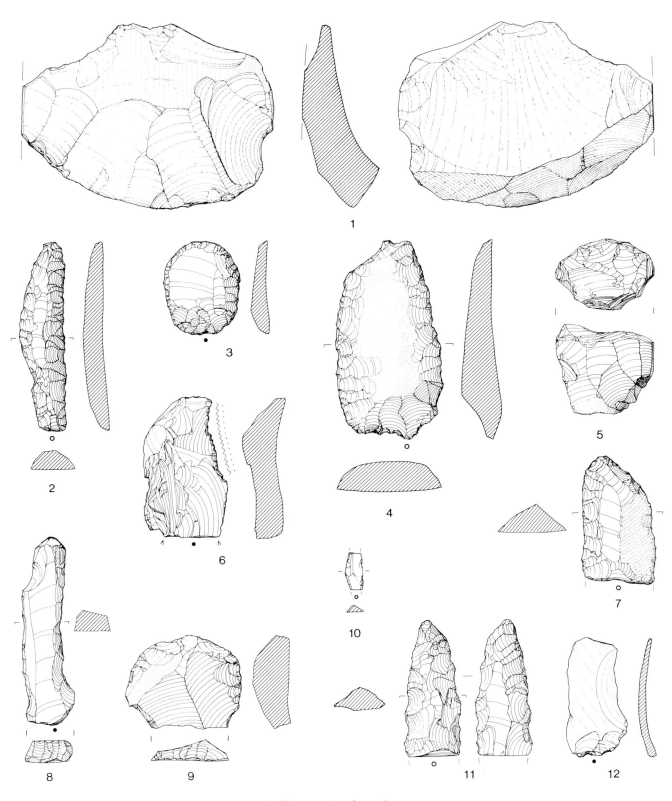

Figure 42   Flint and stone from the Dunn Collection (scale 1:1)

slightly invasive retouch LHS with cortical backing RHS. Bag number 1738.

35 SO254630. Awl with quite finely worked long point. Some wear at the tip. ?LN. Bag number 1739.

36 SO255617. Leaf-shaped arrowhead. Broken at tip. Quite a large example with retouch confined to the lower part of the arrowhead. Possibly broken during manufacture or abandoned unfinished. EN. Bag number 256.

37 SO257610. Chisel arrowhead. Extensively worked arrowhead with hooked LHS. Unusually, the cutting edge has also been retouched. M–LN. Bag number 300.

38 SO257614. Single platform flake core, rejected because of many hinge fractures. A small area of cortex remains on the base of the core. No platform preparation. 22g. Bag number 305.

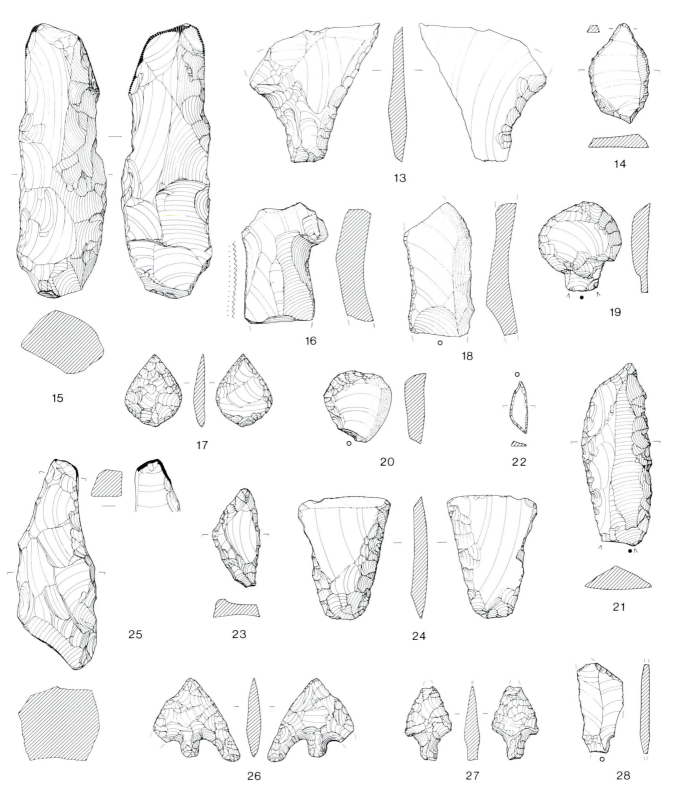

Figure 43 Flint and stone from the Dunn Collection (scale 1:1)

39 SO257614. Levallois core, small area of cortex remaining. 37g. M–LN. Bag number 1706.

40 SO257614. Awl, small, neatly retouched. ?EBA. Bag number 253.

41 SO258645. Small, neatly retouched example of *petit tranchet* derivative arrowhead with wide cutting edge. M–LN. Bag number 275.

42 SO258645. Unfinished barbed and tanged arrowhead. Broken during manufacture, small neat example

with large cherty inclusions which may have caused the breakage. LNEBA. Bag number 273.

43 SO259613. Bifacially worked piece, ?unfinished leaf-shaped arrowhead. Thick blank with bifacial retouch around edges. EN. Bag number 1760.

44 SO259613. Flake from a polished implement. Part of side facet remains, striations visible. Light brown flint. N. Bag number 1749.

45 SO259613. End scraper on blade-like blank, faceted

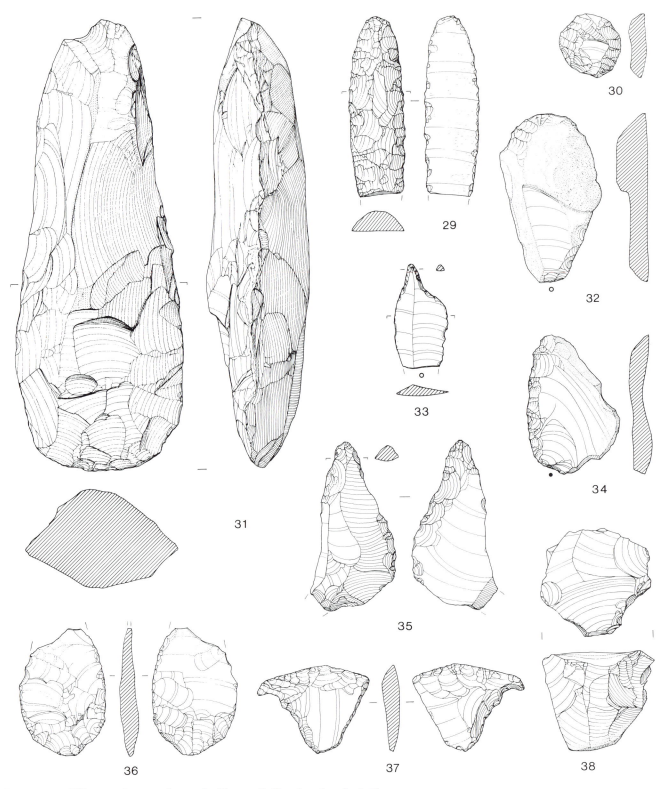

Figure 44 Flint and stone from the Dunn Collection (scale 1:1)

butt, scraping angle 75°. Some plough damage to edges. ?N. Bag number 317.

46 SO259613. Keeled core, flake removals, burnt. Many hinge fractures on the flaking faces may have led to the core's discard. 21g. No preparation. ?LN. Bag number 1740.

47 SO259613. Multi-platform flake core. Some cortex remaining. Areas of battering may indicate use as a hammerstone. Many hinge fractures may have led to the core's discard. 65g. No preparation. Bag number 13.

48 SO259613. 'Thumbnail' scraper. Small, neatly re-touched example, on a fairly thick blank. Retouched around the majority of it's circumference. Scraping angle 65–70°. LNEBA. Bag number 1884.

49 SO259613. Awl, double-ended with one worn point. LNEBA. Bag number 319.

50 SO260646. End scraper. Soft-hammer struck, neatly retouched. Scraping angle 65°. Bag number 356.

51 SO260646. End-and-side scraper, finely retouched. Some cortex remaining on dorsal face. Scraping angle 65–75°. Bag number 346.

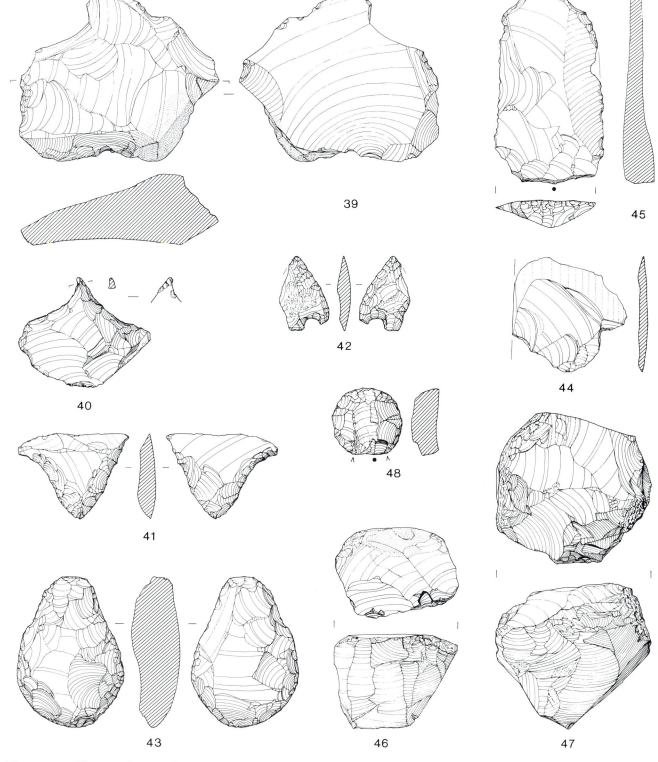

Figure 45 Flint and stone from the Dunn Collection (scale 1:1)

52 SO260646. Fabricator, made on a broken flake. Characteristic crushing at distal end and a smaller area at the proximal end. Steeply retouched lateral edges. ?BA. Bag number 357.

53 SO262647. Serrated flake, distal break. On a blade-like blank with opposed blade-like scars, soft-hammer struck. LHS very finely serrated, approximately 12 serrations per 10mm, RHS more coarsely serrated, worn. Ventral gloss recorded on both edges. Bag number 1190.

54 SO265629. Multi-platform flake core, some platform preparation. Small patch of cortex on base of core. 10g. Core rejected because of its small size and the many hinge fractures on most flaking faces precluded further reduction. Bag number 1052.

55 SO266636. Microlith. Obliquely blunted point on proximal end of a blade. LHS obliquely truncated, some additional retouch RHS, slight distal break. EM. Bag number 524.

56 SO266636. Bifacially worked piece on a blade-like flake. Distal break. Extensively retouched over bulbar

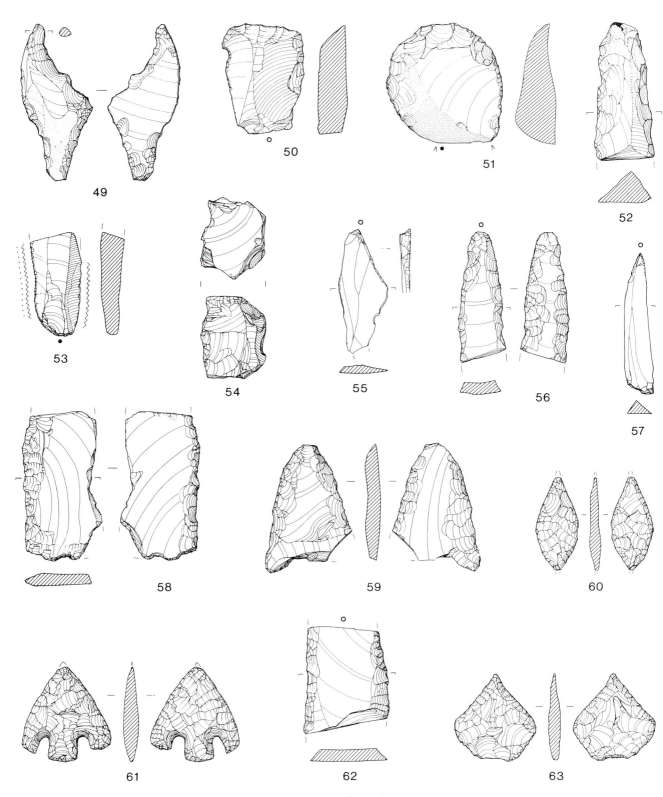

Figure 46 Flint and stone from the Dunn Collection (scale 1:1)

face with scale retouch. Retouch is confined to the edges on the dorsal face. ?Unfinished plano-convex knife or awl. EBA. Bag number 257.

57 SO272619. Microlith. Edge blunted point. On the distal end of a blade butt intact, LHS retouched with additional retouch RHS. M. Bag number 523.

58 SO271590. Scale-flaked knife, proximal and distal

breaks. Bifacial retouch along one edge. ?EBA. Bag number 1933.

59 SO274614. Oblique arrowhead, slight break to RHS. Finely retouched along edges of arrowhead. M–LN. Bag number 254.

60 SO274627. Leaf-shaped arrowhead. Small, neatly retouched example, retouch extending over much of both faces. Slight breaks to tip and base, ?impact fracture. EN. Bag number 322.

61 SO274627. Barbed and tanged arrowhead. Very finely retouched over both faces. Slight damage to tip, ?impact fracture. LNEBA. Bag number 320.

62 SO275636. ?Knife. Proximal and distal breaks. Blade-like blank with invasive retouch along both edges. ?EBA. Bag number 1790.

63 SO277634. Leaf-shaped arrowhead. Very squat but finely bifacially retouched example. EN. Bag number 6.

Excavated assemblages

Rough Close

Two flakes and a miscellaneous retouched piece were recovered from this site. The miscellaneous retouched piece is almost wholly cortical with some retouch and macroscopic edge gloss.

Walton cursus

Three flakes, an end-and-side scraper and a possible piercer were recovered from the top of the Walton cursus. The scraper has minimal retouch (c 60–70°), the possible piercer has a broken point and is worn.

Hindwell I

Two flakes were recovered from the upper fill of the enclosure. One flake has a hinge fracture and the other is broken.

Upper Ninepence

A large assemblage of 1540 pieces of worked flint and three pieces of burnt unworked flint was recovered from the excavations in Upper Ninepence Field. The assemblage is summarised in Tables 19–21, selected pieces are illustrated in Figures 47–48 and described in the catalogue.

Raw materials and condition

The flint is mostly mid to dark brown in colour with a buff or white cortex. Although frequent large cherty inclusions were noted, the flaking quality of the material is good. Cortication, where present is light to medium. The majority of the flint is relatively fresh with sharp edges and some of the material from the mound exhibits greater edge damage. Approximately 18.9% of the assemblage is burnt and 44.3% broken. Twelve pieces of Bullhead flint, seven pieces of grey chert and three pieces of worked quartzite (a flake and two chips) were also recovered. Three flakes from polished implements were recovered from the mound and unstratified contexts. One flake is possibly greenstone (L106) and the other two flakes are creamy white and grey flint respectively (L12 and L37). Several pieces of unworked rock crystal were found across the site and may have been

deliberately collected. No good quality raw material occurs on the site and the nearest sources would have been some distance; flint occurs within superficial deposits around the northern Cotswolds (Charlesworth 1957, 77; Tyler 1976, 4) and gravel deposits occur around Cardiff and in the Vale of Glamorgan (Dutton 1903, 111). Good quality flint is available further south on the Berkshire Downs and Chiltern Hills. Bullhead flint occurs in the south-east around Thanet (Rayner 1981, 357) but has also been recorded in the Reading area (Healy *et al* 1992, 48) and it is possible that this distinctive flint occurs in gravel deposits closer to the site. The creamy white flint may have come from the Louth area of Lincolnshire (J Humble pers comm).

Description

The flint assemblage was recovered from a series of pits, postholes, mound material, and layers associated with the mound. Approximately 1267 pieces of flint were recovered from the topsoil above the mound and form part of the Dunn collection. This material has been discussed above but a summary is included here. The material is dominated by debitage (Table 18) and in keeping with the excavated assemblage very little burnt unworked flint was recovered. Altogether approximately 40.6% of the collection is burnt, twice the figure for the excavated assemblage. The majority of the surface material would appear to be Neolithic in date, although an obliquely blunted point would indicate some Mesolithic activity. The few blade-like flakes and blades may belong to this earlier activity. Two 'thumbnail' scrapers, a plano-convex knife, a backed knife, an end scraper, and an awl indicate Beaker and early Bronze Age activity. The retouched forms include scrapers, retouched and serrated flakes, piercers and transverse arrowheads. The cores recovered include multi-platform and single platform types. A polished implement fragment had been reworked as a core and five polished flakes also indicate the re-working of broken polished implements. Four core rejuvenation flakes (two tablets and two face/edge flakes) were also recovered. This accords well with the range material recovered from the excavation.

The bulk of the stratified assemblage is of mid–late Neolithic date and is associated with Peterborough Ware and Grooved Ware (Table 21). However, a small quantity of earlier material included a possible microlith (Fig 48 no 16) from the mound, a few blades and blade-like flakes and a possible leaf-shaped arrowhead fragment which was found in topsoil (L24). The type of microlith, an obliquely blunted point, occurs throughout the period (Pitts and Jacobi 1979, 169, fig 5); so the dating of this piece cannot be refined. The blades and blade-like flakes may be of Mesolithic or earlier Neolithic date and the possible leaf-shaped arrowhead fragment provides an earlier Neolithic date. A small element of Beaker and early Bronze Age flintwork is represented by a single barbed and tanged arrowhead and three 'thumbnail' scrapers. Numerous other neatly retouched knives,

Table 19 Upper Ninepence: excavated assemblage: core typology

Context	Multi-platform	Keeled	Levallois	Fragments	Total
000	–	–	–	1	1
11	1	–	–	1	2
23	–	–	1	1	2
133	–	–	–	2	2
294	–	1	–	–	1
465	–	–	1	–	1
Topsoil/U/S	1	–	–	–	1
Mound	1	–	–	3	4
Subsoil	–	–	–	2	2
Total	3	1	2	10	16

Table 20 Upper Ninepence excavated assemblage: retouched forms

Context	Scrapers	Knives	Retouched serrated flakes	Arrow-heads	Polished flakes	Piercers	Misc retouch	Microlith	Total
09	–	–	–	–	–	–	1	–	1
11	2 end-and-side	–	–	2 chisel	–	–	2	–	6
13	–	–	–	–	–	–	1	–	1
17	–	–	1 serrated	–	–-	1	1	–	3
21	–	–	1 serrated	–	–	–	–	–	1
23	2 end 4 end-and-side 1 other	–	–	1 chisel	–	–	–	–	8
50	–	–	–	1 *petit tranchet*	–	–	–	–	1
76	–	–	1 serrated	–	–	–	–	–	1
133	1 end	–	–	–	–	–	3	–	4
155	1 end 1 end-and-side 2 other	1	2 retouched	–	–	–	1	–	8
289	–	–	1 retouched	–	–	–	2	–	3
291	1 end-and-side	–	–	–	–	–	1	–	2
292	–	–	–	–	–	–	1	–	1
294	–	–	–	–	–	–	1	–	1
topsoil u/s	1 thumb	–	–	1 chisel	1	1	8	–	12
mound	1 thumb 2 end 2 other	1	2 serrated	1 barbed and tanged 1 hollow	2	4	11	1	28
top of natural	1 thumb	–	–	–	–	–	–	–	1
palaeo-soil	3 end-and-side 1 end	–	–	–	–	1	6	–	11
Total	26	2	8	7	3	7	39	1	93

Table 21 Upper Ninepence: assemblage composition –
Peterborough Ware and Grooved Ware associated material

Ceramic assoc	Context	Flake	Blade	Chip	Core/core frag	Irreg waste	Retouched forms	Burnt un-worked	Total
Peterborough Ware	11	21	1	20	1 multi-platform core 1 core fragment	–	2 chisel arrowheads 2 end-and-side scrapers 2 misc retouch	–	50
	13	4	–	1	–	–	1 misc retouch	–	6
	17	3	2	12	–	–	1 serrated flake 1 piercer 1 misc retouch	–	20
	21	4	–	3	–	–	1 serrated flake	–	8
	66	1	–	7	–	–	–	–	8
	292	–	–	–	–	–	1 misc retouch	–	1
Grooved Ware	09	34	–	1	–	1	1 misc retouch	2	39
	23	17	1	11	1 levallois 1 core fragment	–	1 chisel arrowhead 2 end scrapers 4 end-and-side scrapers 1 misc scraper	–	39
	36	4	–	15	–	–	–	–	19
	56	–	–	4	–	–	–	–	4
	72	90	1	14	–	–	–	–	105
	86	3	–	6	–	–	–	–	9
	133	22	2	13	2 core fragments	–	1 end scraper 3 misc retouch	–	43
	137	1	–	7	–	–	–	–	8
	151	19	–	6	–	–	–	–	25
	155	30	–	8	–	–	2 retouched flakes 1 end-and-side scraper 1 end scraper 2 misc scrapers 1 knife 1 misc retouch	–	46
	199	10	1	5	–	–	–	–	16
	289	3	–	14	–	–	1 retouched flake 2 misc retouch	–	20
	291	–	–	4	–	–	1 end-and-side scraper 1 misc retouch	–	6
	298	7	–	–	–	–	–	–	7
Peterborough and Grooved Ware	201	1	–	1	–	–	–	–	2
	502	2	–	–	–	–	–	–	2

scrapers and piercers may also belong with this activity, as may some of the small, hard-hammer struck flakes recovered from the mound and un-stratified contexts.

However, the majority of the assemblage is of mid–late Neolithic date as indicated by the retouched forms present (see below) and confirmed by the ceramic associations. The debitage is characterised by relatively small, hard-hammer struck flakes.

Occasional soft-hammer struck flakes were recorded, examples are those from contexts 11, 17, 133 and unstratified contexts. Butts tend to be plain or cortical, with occasional faceted and dihedral butts (Tixier *et al* 1980) recorded, for example, from contexts 133, 155 and 291. Hinge fractures and other accidents of debitage were noted amongst the material. All elements of the reduction sequence are represented, although surprisingly few cores and pieces of irregular waste were recovered. The cores are mostly non-specific flake cores and core fragments dominate (Table 19); two Levallois cores may have been used to produce blanks for transverse arrowheads (eg Fig 47 no 10). The other core types present include a keeled core from context 294 and three multi-platform cores (eg Figs 47 no 3 and 48 no 17). Few of the cores show any evidence of preparation or maintenance during knapping. Only three core rejuvenation flakes were recovered (from contexts 72, 133, and the mound) indicating that carefully controlled knapping strategies were not of great significance. The cores are all well reduced; the average core weight for complete examples being 26.3g. The extensive working of the cores is as expected given the distance between the site and a good source of raw materials. It is a little surprising that more rejuvenation flakes were not recovered; it may be that the flint was easily obtained despite the distance from the nearest good source. The three flakes from polished implements indicate that once broken these tools were reused as cores and worked as valuable sources of high quality raw material.

Chips are well represented in the assemblage (271 or 17.6%) and are mostly micro-flakes or broken and burnt fragments. This reflects the general lack of core preparation and maintenance and the dominance of plain and cortical butts. Chips were recovered from both Peterborough Ware and Grooved Ware associated contexts but were perhaps more common in the latter (Table 21).

Apart from the probable obliquely blunted point, possible leaf-shaped arrowhead and the Beaker flintwork, the retouched forms are of mid to late Neolithic type (Table 20). Diagnostic forms include chisel arrowheads (eg Fig 47 nos 4, 9, and possibly 5; Fig 48 no 14), a *petit tranchet* arrowhead from context 50, a possible hollow-based arrowhead, knives, a variety of scrapers, piercers, and serrated and retouched flakes. Apart from miscellaneous retouched pieces and generally broken or unfinished tools, scrapers are the most numerous retouched form (Table 20). The dominance of scrapers is to be expected given the domestic nature of the assemblage. The scrapers tend to be small, neatly worked examples on thin non-cortical blanks (eg L80, L45, L14). End and end-and-side scrapers are the most frequent type (Table 20). Several examples exhibit edge gloss and some have worn scraping edges, such as L48 from context 23, L76 from context 133, L65 from context 155 and L142 from context 291. The true number of scrapers in the assemblage would perhaps have been higher as many of the miscellaneous retouched pieces are probably scraper fragments.

Serrated and retouched flakes are also well represented in the assemblage (Table 20). Many of the retouched flakes have sporadic retouch along one or more edges (eg Fig 48 no 15). In some instances the retouch may simply be use damage. The serrated flakes are mostly finely serrated (between seven and nine serrations per 10mm) and worn. One example

from the mound (L12) is very coarsely serrated with only four serrations per 10mm. Macroscopic edge gloss was recorded on three examples indicating use on silica-rich plant materials (Ungar-Hamilton 1988). Only two knives were recovered, one from context 155 (Fig 48 no 12) and one from the mound (Fig 48 no 18). Both examples are relatively large on oval or sub-oval flakes, cortex and/or retouch form the backing for these knives. The higher number of retouched and serrated flakes may explain the relative paucity of this implement type. Other broken or unfinished examples are also undoubtedly represented amongst the miscellaneous retouched class. The knives bear some similarities to discoidal types but they have not been polished and are not as extensively worked.

Seven piercers were recovered from context 17, the mound and other unstratified contexts. Most of the examples are minimally retouched and one or two show clear wear at their tips, for example, L10. Miscellaneous retouched pieces are the most common retouched form (Table 20) and include broken, unfinished and atypical pieces. Amongst the retouched forms there are ten possible scraper fragments, sixteen flakes with miscellaneous retouch, six arrowhead fragments and two fabricator fragments. The arrowhead fragments include a possible leaf-shaped example and two transverse ones; the remainder could not be assigned to type.

Discussion

When comparing pit groups with ceramic associations, there tend to be fewer flint artefacts from Peterborough Ware contexts (Table 21). The range of flint artefacts from both the Grooved Ware and Peterborough Ware associated contexts are similar, although the former tend to have greater numbers of retouched pieces (Table 21). Technologically, these two groups of material are similar, in that small, hard-hammer struck flakes predominate and there is little evidence for platform preparation. The quantity of chips would suggest that the collection of knapping debris rather than *in situ* knapping was occurring. However, this collection must have been partial as no long refitting sequences were found, although Dr Donahue identified two pairs of refitting artefacts (see Donahue, this report). Artefacts from these pits have used edges and macroscopic gloss was recorded on several pieces, notably the serrated flakes. Such edge gloss results from use on silica-rich plant materials (Ungar-Hamilton 1988). Artefacts within both Peterborough Ware and Grooved Ware contexts are frequently burnt, broken and have macroscopic use-damage. The flint assemblage suggests that several activities were occurring on the site, including knapping, the preparation of hides and foodstuffs, and hunting. The assemblage is therefore essentially domestic in character; the burning and breakage rates being consistent with this. The condition of the material, together with the predominance of domestic tools (notably scrapers, retouched and serrated flakes, and piercers) would indicate that this material is collected domestic debris. However, this does not necessarily imply that the deposits were made in a purely domestic context.

The use of good quality flint is of some interest given the lack of locally occurring raw materials. Cores were extensively worked down although there does not appear to have been much attempt at raw material conservation through core rejuvenation. The flakes from polished implements suggest that quite distant sources of flint were being exploited: the creamy white material from the mound, for example, perhaps coming from the Louth area of Lincolnshire (J Humble pers comm). The use of chert and quartzite may indicate that more local sources of stone of suitable flaking quality were also being exploited. The occurrence of Bullhead flint is of interest, since this material may have been available within superficial deposits locally, rather than being imported from the south-east. However, a more distant source for this material should not be ruled out, as it is good quality flint and has an attractive appearance. At Barrow Hills, Radley, Oxfordshire, Bullhead flint appears to have been especially selected for deposition within Grooved Ware pits (Bradley forthcoming). The Bullhead flint from Upper Ninepence does not appear to have any particular ceramic association as the majority of it was recovered from the mound and unstratified contexts. A burnt end-and-side scraper was recovered from context 11 (Fig 47 no 2) which is associated with Peterborough Ware, and a burnt flake was found in layer 72 which also produced Grooved Ware. A piercer made from Bullhead flint was recovered from context 2. Similarly, the chert was mainly recovered from the mound, although two flakes of dark grey chert were recovered from contexts 9 and 23, both of which also produced Grooved Ware.

The composition of the Peterborough Ware associated flint assemblages is typical of those from other parts of Britain (see, for example, Manby 1975). Apart from a few areas of the country, such as Yorkshire, Peterborough Ware associated flint industries are ill-understood, and are frequently small and largely composed of undiagnostic debitage. At Cam, Gloucestershire, for example, Fengate pottery, a fragmentary stone macehead, animal bone, daub, and flint were recovered from a pit (Smith 1968, 16–20). The flint was rather undistinguished, consisting of a core fragment, utilised flakes, and a flake from a polished implement (Smith 1968, 19). At Yarnton, Oxfordshire, small Peterborough Ware associated flint assemblages have been recovered from a series of pit deposits on the Thames floodplain (Bradley 1996). Typically these deposits contain a range of debitage and retouched pieces, including a *petit tranchet* arrowhead, scrapers, backed knives, and serrated and retouched flakes (Bradley 1996).

The retouched forms from the Grooved Ware associated contexts are also typical of those found nationally (Wainwright and Longworth 1971, 254–61). No 'fancy' items were recovered although some of the scrapers and arrowheads are very finely worked. There did not appear to be any difference in quality between the flintworking in the Grooved Ware and Peterborough Ware associated contexts.

Large well-stratified flint assemblages are relatively rare in Wales and little flintwork has been recovered in the immediate region. Comparable Grooved Ware associated flint was recovered from features beneath two barrows at Trelystan, Powys (Healey 1982, 175). A small flint assemblage, principally of late Neolithic and early Bronze Age date, was recovered from various features within the Welshpool cursus complex (Aldhouse-Green 1994, 177). Neolithic and Bronze Age flintwork was recovered from ring-ditches at Four Crosses, Powys (Green 1986, 77–8). A small, generally poorly stratified, assemblage of worked flint, including Mesolithic and Neolithic to Bronze Age pieces, was recovered from excavations in New Radnor (Aldhouse-Green forthcoming). Worked flint, including microliths, a leaf-shaped arrowhead, scrapers and debitage, were recovered as surface finds and from subsequent excavation at Fron Ddyrys (Pye 1975, 40). Peterborough Ware and a fragment of a polished stone axe were also recovered (*ibid*; A Gibson pers comm). At Clyro, Radnorshire, a later Mesolithic scalene triangle together with Neolithic and Bronze Age flintwork was recovered (Wainwright 1963, 101). The numerous flint scatters recovered from the Walton Basin by Christopher Dunn (see above), also provide evidence for contemporary Neolithic and Bronze Age activity. The slight evidence for Mesolithic activity recovered from both the surface collection and the excavations within the Walton Basin adds to the growing body of evidence for early occupation within Wales.

In a wider context comparable flint assemblages have been recovered from the surrounding counties, particularly Herefordshire (Children and Nash 1994, 14–16; Bradley 1988). This material mostly comes from surface collections, and concentrations of Neolithic and Bronze Age flintwork have been recorded from Dorstone Hill, Cefn Hill and the Golden Valley area (Children and Nash, 1994, 14–17; Bradley 1988, 30–1).

Catalogue of illustrated pieces (Figs 47–48)

Entries are ordered as follows: context number, brief description, weight (cores only) and bag number.

1 Context 11. End scraper, neatly retouched on a thick non-cortical blank. Scraping angle 60–70°. L257.
2 Context 11. End-and-side scraper, heavily burnt. Bullhead flint. Scraping angle 55–70°.
3 Context 11 (from sieving). Multi-platform flake core, 33g. Many hinge fractures on flaking faces, probably rejected because no further flakes could be removed.
4 Context 11. Chisel arrowhead. On a thick blank possibly unfinished. L259.
5 Context 13. Miscellaneous retouched piece, probably a transverse arrowhead. L182.
6 Context 23. Broken scraper, neatly retouched on a thin non-cortical blank. Scraping angle 30–65°. L80.

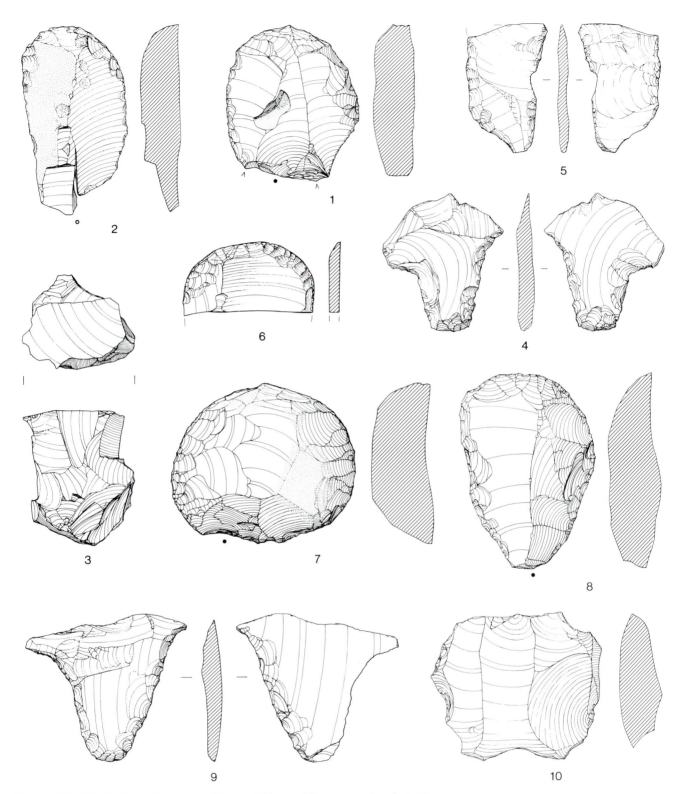

Figure 47 Flints from the excavations at Upper Ninepence (scale 1:1)

7 Context 23. Disc scraper, very finely worked around its circumference, invasive retouch. Scraping angle 40–50°. L45.

8 Context 23. End-and-side scraper. On a large blank with cherty inclusions, burnt. Scraping angle 45°. L44.

9 Context 23. Chisel arrowhead. L52.

10 Context 23. Discoidal core (22g). L53.

11 Context 133. Bifacially worked piece, possible fabricator fragment. Crushed and worn areas at tip. L73.

12 Context 155. Backed knife, on a large flake. Minimal retouch confined to edges. L86.

13 Context 155. End-and-side scraper. On a square flake, scraping angle 75–80°. L67.

14 Context 289. Bifacially worked piece with trimming at butt end, possibly an unfinished arrowhead. L148.

15 Context 289. Retouched flake. L164.

16 Context mound north-west quadrant. Unfinished /broken microlith. Probably an unfinished obliquely

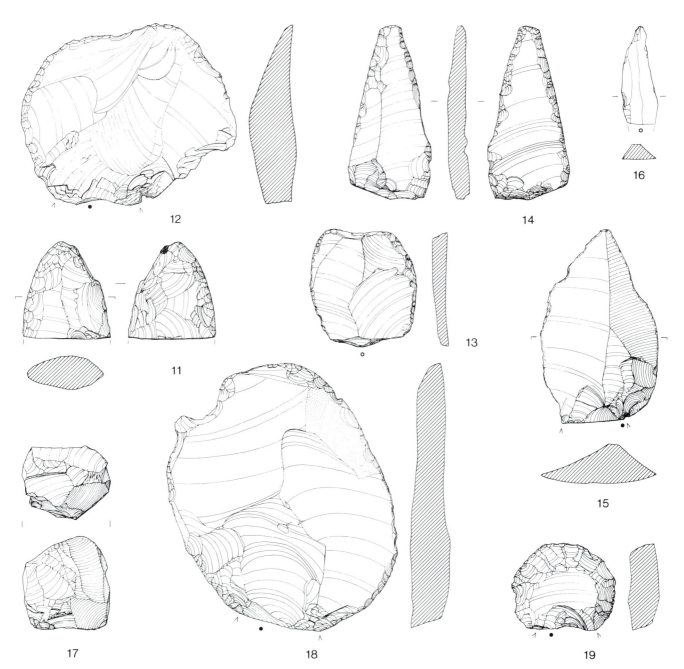

Figure 48   Flints from the excavations at Upper Ninepence (scale 1:1)

blunted point on the proximal end of a blade-like flake. L13.

17 Context mound south-east quadrant. Multi-platform flake core (14g). Greatly reduced. L111.

18 Context mound south-east quadrant. Backed knife on large oval flake with steep retouch. L105.

19 Context old ground surface north-east quadrant. End-and-side scraper. On a thick blank, steeply retouched, scraping angle 65–75°. L14.

Upper Ninepence II

Five pieces of worked flint and a single piece of worked stone were recovered from the excavations. The material consists of three flakes, a core rejuvenation flake (face/edge), a multi-platform flake core

and a cup-marked stone (see Table 15). The latter is relatively small, measuring 33mm long by 27mm wide, and it has a maximum thickness of 17mm. The maximum diameter of the depression is 13mm.

Hindwell Ash

A small assemblage of nine pieces of struck flint was recovered from the excavation of the barrow (Fig 49). Flakes were the most numerous category with a chip, a core fragment, a possible unfinished microlith and an oblique arrowhead also being recovered (for assemblage composition see Table 15). The oblique arrowhead is a very fine example made on a thin flake and is of later Neolithic date (Fig 49 no 1).

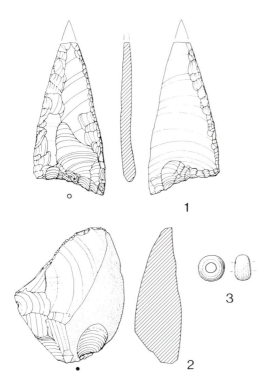

Figure 49 Finds from Hindwell Ash (scale 1:1)

The other stone artefacts from Upper Ninepence
(geological identifications by D Jenkins)

The following stone artefacts were recovered from the excavations at Upper Ninepence.

Catalogue

L56 (pit 22). Disc-shaped stone pounder averaging 65mm in diameter and 35mm thick. There are traces of polish on both surfaces and abrasion to the edge of the disc. The rock is a fine grained (0.5mm) well-sorted Carboniferous quartz sandstone containing abundant quartzodes and iron ore minerals. The rock is unlikely to be local and may be an imported artefact (Fig 50 no 4).

L72 (pit 22). Rounded oval pounder measuring 58mm by 50mm by 40mm thick. There are traces of abrasion on the rounded ends but one round-sectioned groove may be modern accidental damage. The rock is a weathered and river-rounded pebble of medium to coarse-grained igneous dolerite. The rock is not local (Fig 50 no 2).

L80 (pit 154). Irregular stone pounder measuring a maximum of 95mm by 65mm by 60mm thick. The utilised end is rounded and bears well-defined abrasion. The rock is a coarse well-sorted Old Red Sandstone with particles up to 10mm in size. Possibly Devonian and probably imported (Fig 50 no 3).

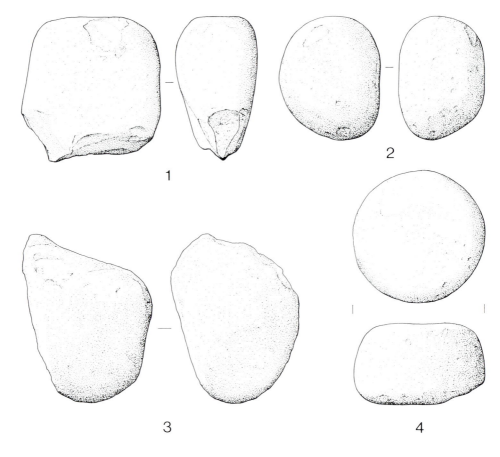

Figure 50 Worked stone from the excavations at Upper Ninepence (scale 1:2)

L97 (mound, south-east quadrant). A damaged pounder with impact spalls on one edge. The surviving fragment measures 67mm by 70mm by 40mm (max) thick. The rock is a local fine-grained, well-graded siltstone broken along well-defined bedding planes (Fig 50 no 1).

L106 (mound, south-east quadrant). A fragment of a polished stone axe in a fine-grained uniformly grey rock with a thin brown patina. The geology is uncertain though it appears to be from a silicified sedimentary rock.

Discussion

Of the five non-flint lithic artefacts, one represents an unprovenanced polished stone axe fragment while the other four are hammerstones or pounders. Of these, only one (L97) is local and the others are of foreign, and probably imported, materials. The stratified artefacts (L56, L72, L80) are all from Grooved Ware pits and accordingly are rare associations in Grooved Ware contexts generally. At Durrington Walls, for example, the only non-flint artefact was a single greenstone axe fragment, possibly of West Country origin (Wainwright and Longworth 1971, 183). At Marden no non-flint artefacts are recorded (Wainwright *et al* 1971) despite a comparatively large Grooved Ware assemblage, and at the Kennet Avenue settlement (Smith 1965) only sarsen fragments are associated in Grooved Ware contexts. Grooved Ware associated non-flint lithics are also apparently absent from the Cranborne Chase excavations (Barrett *et al* 1991) and from the other Grooved Ware sites in Wales; Capel Eithin, Anglesey (White 1981; Lynch 1991) and Hendre, Rhydymwyn, Flintshire (Brassil and Gibson forthcoming). L72 compares well in size with S1 from Trelystan, Powys (Britnell 1982), an oval quartzite pebble with end-and-side abrasion which comes from the buried surface below barrow 2. At Redgate Hill, Hunstanton, Norfolk, two simple, oval discoid quartzite hammerstones were recorded from Grooved Ware contexts (Bradley *et al* 1993), a pebble hammerstone was recovered from Puddlehill, Bedfordshire, pit 6 (Matthews 1976), two quartzite rubbers were associated with Grooved Ware at Harmondsworth, Greater London (inf J Cotton) and a quartzite hammerstone and rubber fragment were found in a pit group at Martlesham, Suffolk (inf R Cleal).

Grooved Ware associated non-flint lithics are, however, more common in northern England. A pot-boiler and jasper hammerstone were associated with Grooved Ware at Rudstone Wold, East Reservoir Field, site 3, a piece of polished haematite was recovered from East Reservoir Field, site 5, and a quartzite cobble anvil stone was recovered from Carnaby Top, site 12 (Manby 1974). A larger non-lithic assemblage was recovered from the North Carnaby Temple sites comprising three hammerstones and four rubbers; eight flint hammerstones were also recovered (Manby 1974). However, non-flint lithic associations in Grooved Ware contexts are comparatively rare.

Pottery from Hindwell Ash and Upper Ninepence

Hindwell Ash

Three sherds of pottery were recovered from pre-barrow gully 11 (one sherd) and the material of the turf mound (two sherds). These finds must all pre-date the construction of the primary barrow. One small sherd may be tentatively identified as Beaker pottery from its thin light brown fabric. The other two sherds have coarse fabrics with abundant angular crushed quartz inclusions. They may well be Neolithic but, in the absence of formal elements or decoration, this identification is tenuous in the extreme.

Upper Ninepence

Introduction

The prehistoric pottery from Upper Ninepence may be divided into three main groups, Peterborough Ware, Grooved Ware and early Bronze Age (Figs 51–58). The last named group is represented by two vessels, P89 and P90, both probably belonging to the Food Vessel Urn tradition. P89 comes from the mound material (context 2), while P90 comes from the OGS (context 72), though both contexts must be regarded as largely unstratified. The Peterborough Ware assemblage is represented by fragments of 20 vessels (P1–P20), and comes from both unstratified contexts in the mound material and the animal disturbed palaeosoil, as well as from pits in a generally restricted area below the north-west quadrant of the mound. The Grooved Ware assemblage is represented by fragments of 68 vessels (P21–P88), which generally come from stratified contexts within pits dug into the natural subsoil. The Grooved Ware pits and Peterborough pits seem to have a slightly different distribution on the site (see Fig 33) and the C14 evidence demonstrates that there is also a chronological difference between the two periods (Tables 9 and 12). The only instance of cross tradition association is a small Fengate sherd, P16, which comes from Grooved Ware pit 154. P16 is, however, badly abraded and may well be residual.

Peterborough Ware (Figs 51–52)

The Peterborough assemblage has been dated to *c* 3000 cal BC (see above, Table 9) in keeping with other assemblages from Wales (Gibson 1993a; 1995a) and comprises vessels largely in the Mortlake style with a small Fengate component. The Mortlake vessels are decorated with impressions made with whipped and twisted cord, fingernail, incision or birdbone. Whipped cord maggots are present on vessels P2 and P18, while twisted cord impressions are visible as multiple horizontal lines on P1 and P17, and as diagonal lines on P12 and P16.

Fingernail impressions are altogether much more commonly arranged in a pseudo-cord arrangement on P6 and P8, as herringbone motif on P7 and P15, as oblique impressions on P5, and as apparently random impressions on P9–P11 and P20. Incised decoration is restricted to P1 where it occurs as diagonal lines on the inside of the vessel and P3 where it similarly occurs internally in the form of cross-hatching. The instance of birdbone impressions is restricted to a single vessel, P3, where they are found on the top of the rim.

The Walton assemblage brings the total number of Peterborough Ware findspots in Wales to 33 (Gibson 1995a) with the bulk of the material coming from the Marches. In the adjacent counties, Peterborough assemblages have been found in Shropshire at Meole Brace, (Hughes and Woodward 1995), Belle Vue, Shrewsbury (inf H Hannaford), and Brompton (inf A Woodward). In Warwickshire, it has been found at Barford (Oswald 1969; Loveday 1989), Polesworth (Gibson 1993b), and Wasperton (Hughes and Crawford 1995). Peterborough Ware has been found in Worcestershire at Kemerton (Dinn and Evans 1990), and in Gloucestershire at Tewkesbury (Hannan 1993), Cam (Smith 1968), Gloucester (Hurst 1972), Salmonsbury (Dunning 1976), Barnwood (Clifford 1930), and Bourton on the Water (Dunning 1932), as well as in the blocking of some Cotswold-Severn tombs (eg Saville 1979).

This scarcity of birdbone impressions on the pottery from Walton may be remarkable in view of their frequency in other Welsh assemblages (Gibson 1995a, fig 3.4), and may suggest that the assemblage is better paralleled in England. Indeed, few direct parallels for the Walton material are to be found in the Welsh or the Marches material. The combination of birdbone impressions and incision on P3 may be paralleled at Sarn-y-bryn-caled, Powys (Gibson 1994, fig 25, P1), and Cefn Bryn, Glamorgan (Gibson 1995a, fig 3.7, no 9). The twisted cord and fingernail impressions on the Walton material find closer parallel in the assemblage from Windmill Hill, Wiltshire (Smith 1965) and Cherhill, Wiltshire (Evans and Smith 1983) where both techniques are common: the latter particularly on vessels of the Fengate style. The ribbed exterior and fingernail impressions found on P5 are closely paralleled at Heathrow, Middlesex (Grimes 1960, 189) where, like P5, the vessel was also incised on the interior of the rim and neck. At Cherhill, too, ribbed vessels are common (Evans and Smith 1983), though at this site twisted cord maggots tend to fill the depressions rather than fingernail impressions. P3 has an elaborate motif of closely set fine birdbone impressions resembling toothed comb. The rim is decorated with a multiple chevron arrangement and horizontal lines. A similar motif is present on some Grooved Ware sherds from Site I at Dorchester, Oxon (Atkinson *et al* 1951), but such 'busy' decoration is rare within the Peterborough tradition.

P11, P16, P18, and P20 may be identified as Fengate style from a combination of their collars (P16, P19), the dimples or stabs in the necks (P16), the trunconic form (P11, P20), and the flat bases (P11). P16 comes from pit 154, which is an otherwise predominantly Grooved Ware context with a C14 date of 4050+35 BP (BM–2969), but the sherd is very abraded and may well be residual. P11 comes from pit 20 and is associated with one serrated flake, four flakes and three flint chips. P18 and P20 are associated with pit 500, form a closed group, and have a C14 date in keeping with the rest of the Peterborough assemblage. This provides further evidence for the early appearance of Fengate Ware (Gibson and Kinnes 1997) in the middle Neolithic. Fengate sherds are rare in Wales but have been recognised at Brynderwen, Powys (Gibson and Musson 1990), Ogmore, Glamorgan (Gibson 1990), and Castell Bryn Gwyn, Anglesey (Wainwright 1962). At this last named site, the same short multiple fingernail impressions are used to decorate the vessel as they are at Walton (P11) and similar decoration has been found on a Fengate collar from the Horslip long barrow, Wiltshire (Ashbee *et al* 1979), Windmill Hill (Smith 1965), Downton, Wiltshire (Rahtz 1962), West Kennet chambered tomb, Wiltshire (Piggott 1962), Baston Manor, Kent (Philp 1973), and from the West Kennet avenue, Wiltshire (Smith 1965), though here the fingernail impressions are arranged in a filled triangle motif. The designation of P18 as Fengate Ware is wholly dependent on the beginnings of a markedly concave neck present at the very base of the sherd. It once more finds parallels at Windmill Hill (Smith 1965), and Downton, Wiltshire (Rahtz 1962).

Grooved Ware (Figs 52–58)

The Grooved Ware assemblage from Upper Ninepence is rich and varied and by far the largest assemblage from Wales. Grooved Ware has been found elsewhere in the Principality at Capel Eithin, Anglesey (White 1980; 1981; Lynch 1991), Coed-y-dinas and Sarn-y-bryn-caled, Powys (Gibson 1994), Trefignath, Anglesey (Smith and Lynch 1987) and Lligwy, Anglesey (Lynch 1970). At Trelystan, Powys, a Durrington Walls style assemblage was associated with two similar sub rectangular structures (Britnell 1982) and the vessels from Hendre, Rhydymwyn, Flintshire are probably also in the Durrington Walls style (Brassil and Gibson, forthcoming).

Barrel, bucket, bowl, and tub-shaped vessels are represented in a variety of fabrics. The presence of applied and raised cordons, geometric decoration, and the occasional use of twisted cord decoration, places the majority of the assemblage in Longworth's Durrington Walls style, though P62, P63 and P78 with their converging incisions and lozenge motifs may well belong to the Clacton style (Wainwright and Longworth 1971). It is also interesting to note the difference in fabric between these vessels and the rest of the assemblage; P62, P63 and P78 being in a soft, 'corky' and pitted fabric.

Of particular importance in the Upper Ninepence assemblage is the presence of three internally decorated vessels, P34, P67 and P68 (Fig 54) all in the fine and well-finished fabric 5. P67 is represented only by a few sherds but none of them exhibit external decoration. The internal incised motif appears to have been triangular with herringbone or oblique infill. P34 is decorated on the upper part of the outer surface with incised oblique lines, while the interior is decorated with incised triangular motifs (suitable for internal decoration as they narrow towards the base), with panels of fine whipped cord maggots between the triangles (Fig 58). P68 is decorated with similar oblique maggot impressions externally and internally. Longer lengths of this fine whipped material are arranged in zigzags on the internal bevel. Such fine whipped cord decoration, made with a thread rather than a cord, is found elsewhere on Grooved Ware vessels, particularly at Marden, Wiltshire (Wainwright *et al* 1971).

Internal decoration is of course paralleled in the assemblage from Durrington Walls (Wainwright and Longworth 1971, fig 58) where sherds from ten internally decorated vessels were found in a variety of fabrics. The triangular incised motifs of P34 and P67 are directly paralleled at Durrington Walls where fine whipped cord impressions are also found. Fine whipped cord maggots and twelve internally decorated vessels were recovered from Tye Field, Lawford, Essex (Shennan *et al* 1985) where once again internal triangular motifs predominate, including elongated triangles as in P34 at Walton. Decoration akin to P37 was also found on a bowl at Hengistbury Head (Cunliffe 1987), and at Willington, Derbyshire (Wheeler 1979) while broad triangular internal decoration is found at The Sanctuary, Wiltshire (Cunnington 1931), Wyke Down, Dorset (Barrett *et al* 1991; Barrett *et al* (eds) 1991) and at Woodhenge (Cunnington 1929). Profuse internal incised decoration in the form of triangular motifs is found on two vessels from Mercer's excavations at Grimes Graves, Norfolk (Mercer 1981) and include impressed in-filling, though not the fine whipped cord of the Walton sherds. The vessel from Puddlehill, Bedfordshire (Matthews 1976) differs from the other vessels of this type in that the interior appears to be decorated with a chequer pattern of incised filled rectangles. The motifs on the internally decorated vessel from Colchester, associated with large Durrington Walls style vessels (Crummy 1992), is indistinct due to the small size of the sherds but converging lines imply triangular or lozengic patterns. A vessel from Harmondsworth, Middlesex appears to resemble P34 in shape and is decorated internally with what appear to be filled, elongated lozenges, and externally with panelled filled lozenges in the Durrington Walls style (inf J Cotton).

These internally decorated vessels are united in their preference for internal triangular motifs,

their splayed open forms, often with inturned rims, and the general lack of decoration on the outer surface, with the exception of occasional decoration near the rim. Clearly, the form of the pots and the position of all the decoration indicate that they were intended to be seen and had a display function. This is reinforced by the fact that carbonaceous residues are absent from the inner surfaces of these pots and they have clearly not been used for cooking purposes.

P26 and P38 are from fine-walled closed vessels in a hard well-fired fabric containing grog. P26 is unusual in having a simple rounded rim with a single well-executed horizontal incised line on the inside. These sherds bear comparison with similar fine-fabric tub-shaped vessels recently designated Irish Grooved Ware and found *inter alia* at the Co Meath passage graves of Knowth (inf Helen Roche), Newgrange (Gibson 1982, 211–12, 465–8; O'Kelly *et al* 1983) and the timber complex at Ballynahatty, Co Down (Hartwell 1994 and pers comm). This Irish fine ware material seems to be a true regional style and it occurs in contexts with, to British eyes, more familiar Grooved Ware and Beaker ceramics (Gibson 1982, 180, 210–12). The knobbed vessel P48, in a soft sandy fabric, may be cited in this context. Once more such small circular knobs are found in Irish Grooved Ware contexts (O'Kelly *et al* 1983) but are hard to parallel in Britain. Wales may well provide a link between the classic British assemblages and the increasingly recognised Irish material. The Capel Eithin sherds, for example, have clear similarities with some of the coarser material from Newgrange, Knowth and the Lough Gur area.

The rest of the Grooved Ware assemblage from Walton has all the traits of classic Durrington Walls style Grooved Ware, especially the opposed filled triangle motif (P21, P31, P35, P46, P52, P56, P57). The large barrel-shaped P33 has well-defined horizontal and vertical cordons and is largely undecorated. One scalloped rim sherd hints at intermittent rim decoration however, suggestive of the rim 'knots' on vessels in the Woodlands style. P39 is similar to P33 (though less well-preserved) and exhibits scars where the applied vertical and diagonal cordons have separated from the body of the pot. These breaks are not always associated with a fabric colour change suggesting that at least some of these cordons may have broken off during the firing process.

Decorated cordons are rare but P28 has, in effect, a double cordon with oblique fingernail impressions. P70 also has a cordon, horizontal in this instance, with small oval impressions on its crest. An incised cordon, represented by two parallel incised lines acting as zonal separators, is visible on P35 and draws close comparison with P221 from Durrington Walls (Wainwright and Longworth 1971, 110). P59 has a wavy cordon formed by decorating the cordon with oval fingertip impressions.

The radiocarbon dates from Upper Ninepence are

entirely consistent with the current Grooved Ware chronology. Of the 80 or so Grooved Ware C14 dates, 85% lie within the third millennium Cal BC and 70% centre between 2800 and 2400 Cal BC.

Early Bronze Age (Fig 57)

P89 and P90 probably date to the early Bronze Age. P90, a narrow flat base in a thick well-fired fabric may be best assigned to a large vessel in the Urn tradition but further precision is difficult. P89 has twisted cord maggot decoration and a cavetto zone with vertical stop-ridges. The thickness of the fabric, the decoration and the formal traits suggest that the vessel may belong to the Food Vessel Urn tradition, similar in form to that from Brynford, Flintshire (Savory 1980, 345.1), or from Goatscrag, Northumberland (Burgess 1972).

Catalogue of pottery

The stratigraphic details and quantities of pottery, with information regarding residue analysis, thin sections, and associated dates, are given in Tables 22–25. The fabric range is discussed in the thin section report below.

Peterborough Ware

P1 Collar and neck sherd from a Mortlake bowl.
The fabric is dark grey-black, very crumbly with abundant inclusions up to 6mm across. There are carbon encrustations internally and traces of coil/ring-building visible in the breaks.

The collar is straight and everted and is decorated with seven horizontal lines of twisted cord decoration. The neck is concave and bears traces of two deep stabs, neither of which have completely pierced the fabric but which have both raised slight internal bosses. The body has slight traces of diagonal lines of twisted cord impressions. Internally, decoration comprises traces of two diagonal incised lines with a single horizontal line in the same technique corresponding to the collar base.

P2 Shoulder sherd from a Mortlake bowl.
The fabric is dark grey-black, 13mm thick, with abundant inclusions up to 10mm across. There are traces of ring breaks.

The shoulder is sharp and angular and has been decorated below with oblique to vertical coarse and closely spaced whipped cord maggots.

P3 Rim and neck sherd from a Mortlake bowl.
The fabric is crumbly, dark grey-black, 13mm thick, with abundant inclusions up to 10mm across. There are traces of ring breaks.

The top of the rim is rounded in section and decorated with closely spaced fine birdbone impressions, arranged in a multiple chevron motif on the inner edge, and in encircling lines on the outer half of the moulding. The inside lip of the rim has small vertically arranged nicks or fingernail impressions, and the inside of the neck is decorated with deeply incised lattice motif.

P4 Body sherds from a ?Mortlake bowl.
The fabric is dark grey-black, 13mm thick, with abundant inclusions up to 7mm across. The largest sherd has traces of a shoulder and internal carbon encrustations.

Decoration on one sherd comprises faint traces of diagonal twisted cord impressions.

P5 Shoulder and body sherds from a Mortlake bowl.
The fabric varies from light grey-brown to dark grey-black, is up to 16mm thick and has abundant inclusions up to 6mm across. There are traces of ring breaks.

The decoration comprises horizontal lines of regularly-spaced oblique fingernail impressions. Two rows are visible in the slightly concave neck above the shoulder and a total of four rows are visible on the two sherds representing the main belly of the vessel. Internally, a single row of the same type of fingernail impressions is visible in the neck and is bordered below with a single line of horizontal overlapping fingernail impressions.

P6 Rim sherd from a ?Mortlake bowl.
The fabric has light brown surfaces with a black, slightly porous core. It contains inclusions up to 6mm across and is 11mm thick.

The decoration on the top of the rim comprises traces of five horizontal lines of overlapping fingernail impressions resembling pseudo-cord. The inside lip of the rim is slightly concave and decorated with oblique fingernail impressions.

P7 Neck sherd from a ?Mortlake bowl.
The fabric is thin, hard and well-fired with a reddish-brown outer surface and grey-brown inner surface. It contains inclusions up to 12mm across yet the fabric is only 8mm thick.

The decoration comprises a finely incised herringbone motif on the convex surface of the neck interior. The outer surface is undecorated.

P8 Rim sherd plus body flakes from a Mortlake bowl.
The fabric is hard and well-fired, has brown to dark grey surfaces and a black core, and is up to 12mm thick.

The decoration comprises seven horizontal rows of overlapping fine fingernail impressions resembling pseudo-cord. On the internal lip of the rim is a herringbone arrangement in the same technique. One of the body flakes bears paired fingernail impressions arranged in a crowsfoot motif.

P9 Body sherd from a ?Mortlake bowl.
The fabric has a reddish-brown outer surface and a black inner surface and core. It is up to 13mm thick and contains inclusions up to 6mm across. Many of these inclusions break the inner surface but lie flush with it.

The outer surface bears a single pair of fingernail impressions arranged in a crowsfoot motif.

P10 Body sherds from a ?Mortlake bowl.
The fabric has grey to brown surfaces and a black core. It is quite friable and contains inclusions up to 9mm across. The fabric is up to 17mm thick.

The decoration on four of the sherds appears to comprise random fingernail impressions while a shoulder sherd appears to have the shoulder accentuated with closely-spaced diagonal fingernail impressions arranged in a kind of cable pattern.

P11 Body sherds from a ?Mortlake/Fengate bowl.
The fabric has light brown to grey surfaces and a grey core. All the sherds are abraded and some are quite friable. The fabric varies from 11mm to 22mm thick and contains inclusions up to 10mm across.

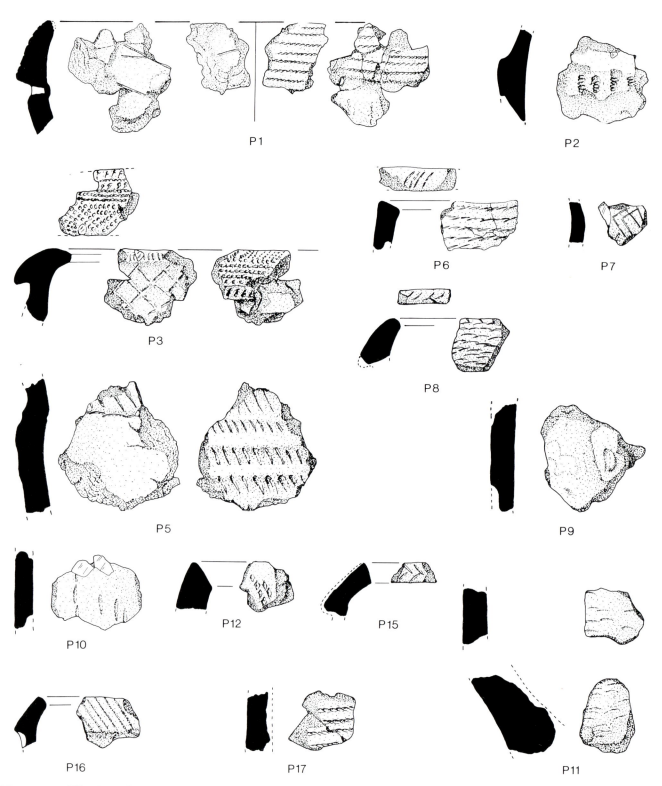

Figure 51   The Peterborough pottery from Upper Ninepence (scale 1:2)

The decoration comprises multiple randomly scattered and lightly impressed horizontal fingernail impressions. The profiles of the body sherds suggest a flaring profile and a thick, narrow base as if from a Fengate style pot. One neck sherd exhibits a deep circular stab resulting in a raised internal boss suggestive of Fengate decoration.

P12   Body and rim sherd from a ?Fengate bowl.

The fabric is coarse and heavy with black to brown surfaces and a black core. The sherds are up to 17mm thick and contain inclusions up to 7mm across.

One body sherd carries traces of random light fingernail impressions similar to P11 above. One rim sherd has a curved outer profile with an internal concave bevel and shows traces of diagonal twisted cord or pseudo-cord impressions on the outer surface.

P13 and P14   Both comprise crumbs of pottery in a fabric similar to the other Peterborough sherds above. None are decorated or exhibit formal traits. They may be residual and were recovered from the processed soil sample.

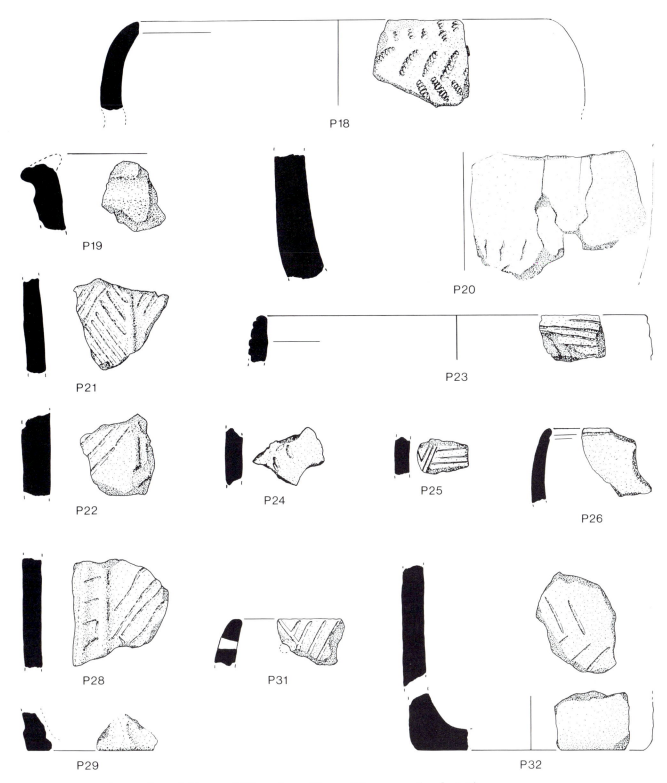

P18

P19

P20

P21

P23

P22

P24

P25

P26

P28

P31

P29

P32

Figure 52 Peterborough and Grooved Ware from Upper Ninepence (scale 1:2)

P15 Sherd from a rim and shoulder of a small Peterborough bowl. The fabric is reddish-brown externally, and grey internally. The surfaces are soft and friable and the fabric contains abundant angular stone inclusions up to 4mm across.

The rim has an external moulding decorated with incised or fingernail herringbone. The neck is largely undecorated, though there are traces of a possible fingernail impression. The sherd has broken near the shoulder. The vessel may best be placed loosely within the Ebbsfleet substyle of the Impressed Ware tradition.

P16 Sherd in a soft orange-brown sandy fabric, very abraded, with crazed surfaces.

The sherd is from a collar with fragments of the rim surviving and possibly with traces of a dimple below the collar. The collar itself is decorated with oblique incised lines. The sherd is best interpreted as Fengate Ware.

P17 Two sherds in a soft orange-brown fabric, very

abraded, with abundant inclusions up to 3mm across and including quartz. The fabric is 10mm thick.

Externally, the decoration comprises three horizontal lines composed of close-set fine 'birdbone' impressions. Probably Mortlake Ware.

P18 Sherd in a soapy-textured grey-brown fabric with large black inclusions up to 7mm across. The fabric is 10mm thick.

The rim sherd is from a vessel with a diameter of *c* 200mm. The rim is inturned and has a vertical internal bevel. There are slight traces of a neck at the base of the sherd. The decoration comprises two vertical lines of short whipped cord maggots at the top and below this a zone of herringbone motif in the same technique.

P19 Badly abraded rim sherd in a hard, well-fired fabric with abundant angular inclusions. The surfaces are light grey-brown and the core is black. The fabric averages 12mm thick.

The rim is strongly everted but badly damaged. Nevertheless, the form of the rim suggests a Mortlake bowl. There are faint traces of decoration on the body, possibly 'birdbone' though the sherd is too abraded to be certain.

P20 Sherds in a hard well-fired fabric, reaching up to 23mm thick, and with light brown surfaces and a black core. Inclusions up to 4mm across are abundant. The thickness of the sherds suggest that they come from the lower portion of a conical vessel, probably Fengate Ware.

The sherds are decorated with sparse vertical fingernail impressions.

Grooved Ware

P21 Sherds in a hard, well-fired pink/brown fabric with a black core and interior. The inner surface is coated with carbon encrustations and the fabric varies between 8mm and 13mm thick. The fabric is also voided and contains grog inclusions up to 6mm long.

The decoration consists of narrow raised vertical cordons with incised filled chevron motif in the resulting panels.

P22 Sherds in a soft friable sandy fabric with abundant well-crushed inclusions breaking both surfaces. The fabric varies between 10mm and 15mm thick, has an orange-brown outer surface and a dark grey inner surface and core.

The decoration comprises narrow, raised vertical cordons. Some sherds have incised diagonal lines in the resulting panels. One sherd has a small round applied pellet on the outer surface.

P23 Rim sherd from a barrel-shaped vessel in a porous, dark brown fabric with a black core and inner surface. There are internal carbon encrustations. The fabric contains inclusions up to 4mm long and reaches a thickness of 8mm. The rim is simple and rounded.

The decoration comprises four deeply incised horizontal lines on the outer surface.

P24 Sherd in a hard black fabric, well-fired and with smooth surfaces. The fabric has carbon encrustations externally and is 9mm thick.

The decoration comprises two oblique fingernail impressions on the outside.

P25 Sherd in a dark brown fabric, hard and well-fired with crisp fractures and smooth surfaces. It contains grog and sand and is 8mm thick.

The decoration comprises an arrangement of oblique finely incised lines, probably opposed diagonals separated by three verticals.

P26 Light sandy-brown fabric, hard and well-fired with crisp fractures and smooth surfaces. The fabric contains micaceous sand and is up to 7mm thick.

One sherd has a simple inturned rim with a single shallow internal scored line below, perhaps a result of finishing the rim.

P27 Light sandy-brown fabric, slightly crumbly texture. It contains sand inclusions plus pieces of angular stone up to 10mm across.

P28 Light brown, hard, and well-fired fabric with smooth, slightly sandy outer surface and a black, heavily carbon-encrusted inner surface. The fabric contains grog and sand inclusions.

The decoration comprises an undecorated vertical cordon with multiple diagonal incisions on either side.

P29 Base angle from a vessel in a light pink-brown fabric with abraded surfaces. The fabric contains grog inclusions.

The base of what appears to be a vertical finger-pinched cordon is visible on the outer surface.

P30 Single sherd from an inturned rim though the actual rim is missing. The fabric is soft and abraded with evidence of coil- or ring-building in the breaks. It is light brown in colour with a grey core and contains sand inclusions.

P31 Rim sherd from a barrel-shaped vessel in a dark grey fabric with finely crushed grog inclusions. The fabric is up to 12mm thick and there are traces of a drilled hole 13mm down from the rim. The rim has been drilled prior to firing.

The rim is simple and rounded. Externally the decoration comprises incised filled triangles.

P32 Sherds, including base, in a hard, well-fired fabric with pink-brown surfaces and a grey core and interior. The base in particular has heavy carbon encrustations. The fabric contains quartz and grog with occasional stone inclusions up to 11mm across. The fabric is up to 12mm across and traces of ring- or coil-building can be seen in the breaks.

The rim has had a diameter of approximately 120mm. The body sherd is decorated with opposed diagonal incised lines.

P33 Upper portion and one small base sherd from a large undecorated barrel-shaped vessel. The fabric is hard and well-fired with large inclusions up to 6mm across. It is grey-brown throughout and the inner surface has considerable carbonaceous build-up.

The rim is slightly inturned, has a sharp rounded top and vertical internal bevel. One sherd has a pie-crust effect on the rim suggesting that it may have been decorated at intervals on its circumference. A low, applied cordon encircles the vessel at the point of maximum diameter *c* 45mm below the rim, and vertical applied cordons run down from this.
The rim has had a diameter of *c* 300mm and the fabric averages some 12mm thick.

P34 Sherds in a hard and well-fired fabric with smooth, well finished grey-brown surfaces and a black core. The fabric contains finely crushed grog and sand.

The splayed bowl has had an inturned rim with a diameter of *c* 160mm. The base diameter is *c* 70mm. The fabric averages 7mm thick.

The vessel has been decorated internally and externally. Externally, the decoration appears to be restricted to the upper part of the vessel and comprises panels of

88

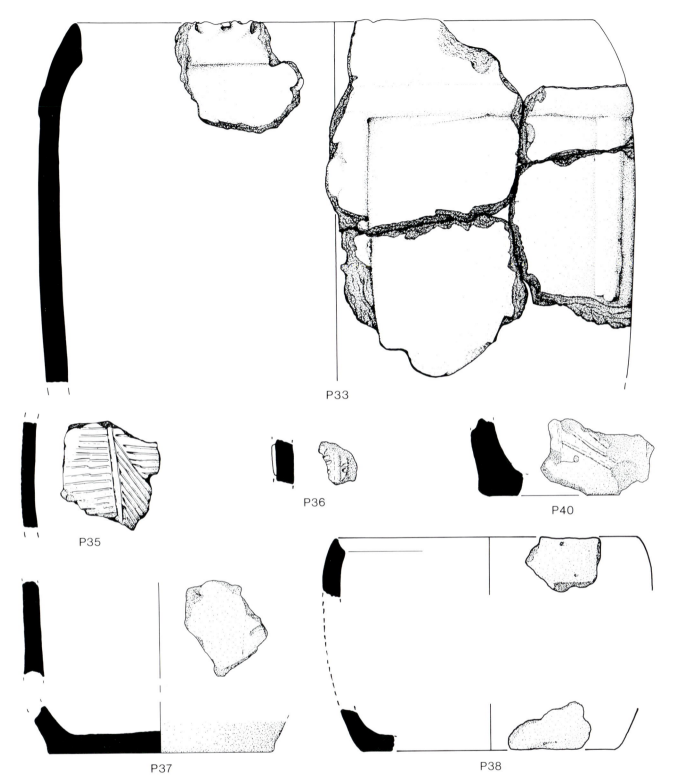

Figure 53 Grooved Ware from Upper Ninepence (scale 1:2)

multiple oblique incised lines. Internally the decoration comprises multiple lenticular stabs or impressions inside the rim with narrow panels of incised herringbone which narrow towards the base. The herringbone motif changes to oblique lines as the panels narrow. Between these elongated chevrons are panels of extremely fine twisted cord maggots.

P35 Sherds in a light brown to grey fabric, with a black core and internal surface, the latter being covered with carbon encrustations. The fabric is hard and well-fired,

7mm thick, and appears to contain grog and fine sand inclusions.

Decoration is restricted to the outer surface and appears to represent an incised vertical cordon, delineated by a double incised line, to the left of which is a panel of multiple horizontal incised lines. To the right, in the same technique, is a panel of oblique and horizontal lines.

P36 Sherd in a well-fired but coarse fabric similar to P33 above. The outer surface is light brown, the inner is

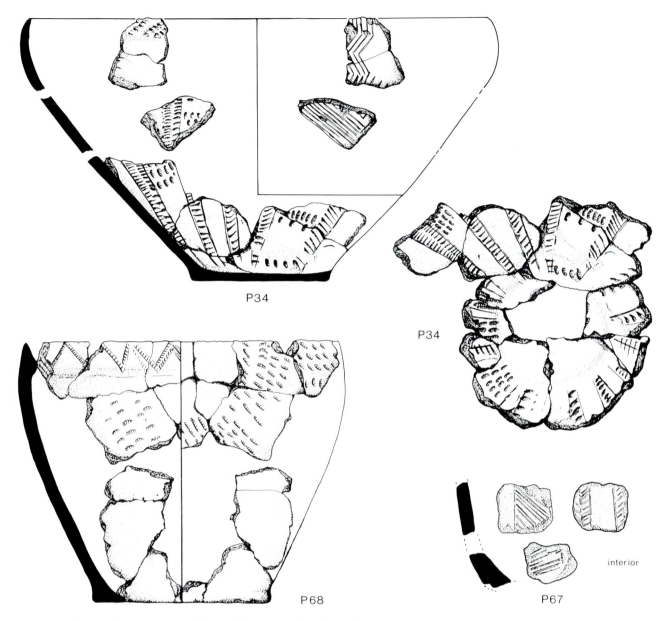

Figure 54   Grooved Ware from Upper Ninepence (scale 1:2)

black with a carbonaceous crust. The fabric is 9mm thick.

The external decoration comprises a narrow raised cordon, 5mm wide, with traces of either oval impressions or broad grooves on either side.

P37 Sherds from a straight-sided vessel in a soft, friable fabric with grog inclusions. The fabric is 9mm thick, orange-pink externally and black internally with heavy carbon encrustations.

The vessel has vertical applied cordons decorated with diagonal fingernail impressions. The flat base has had a diameter of 135mm.

P38 Sherds from a vessel in a fairly hard, well-fired fabric with a grey-brown outer surface, brown-black core and an inner surface varying from brown to black with patchy carbon encrustations. The fabric averages *c* 8mm thick and contains well-crushed inclusions.

The rim is slightly inturned, has a diameter of *c* 180mm and a vertical internal bevel 7mm deep. Sherds from the base angle of the vessel suggest a base diameter in the region of 130mm. The vessel is undecorated.

P39 Sherds from a large vessel in a fabric similar to P33

above but softer and with lighter brown surfaces. The fabric also appears to be less well-fired. The internal surface, particularly towards the base, is heavily carbon encrusted with the deposits reaching 5mm thick. The fabric averages 11mm thick.

The vessel is decorated with vertical and oblique applied cordons which have been imperfectly bonded and which, in many cases, have flaked off the surface. There appears to be no other decoration.

The base sherds suggest an estimated base diameter of *c* 160mm.

P40 Base and wall sherds with an estimated base diameter of 130mm. The fabric is coarse and friable with crazed surfaces through which erupt abundant inclusions up to 5mm across. The outer surface is light pink-brown. The fabric is 11mm thick and slightly laminated in texture.

The outer surfaces bears traces of three oblique, lightly incised lines. The inner surface is heavily carbon encrusted, up to 2mm thick in places.

P41 Sherd in a hard well-fired fabric with grog inclu-

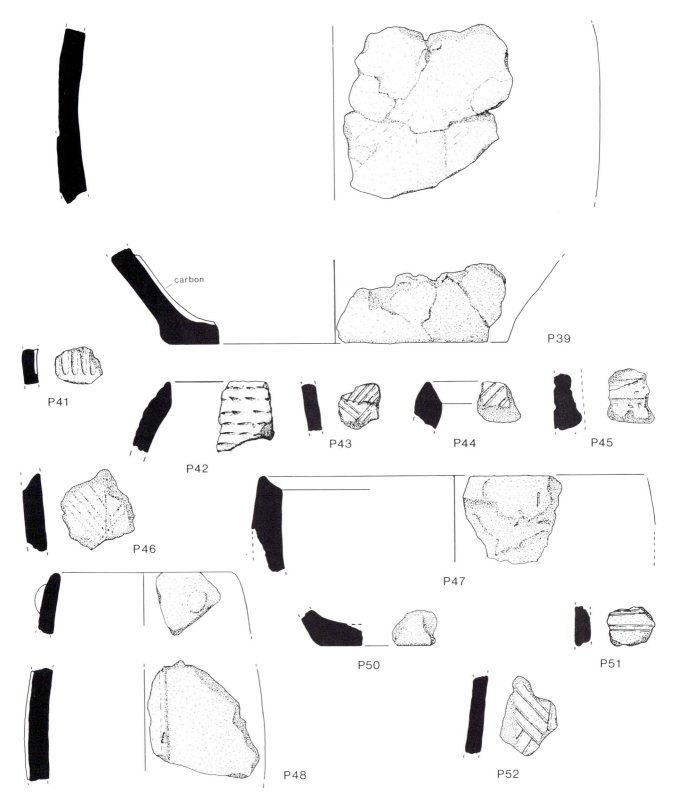

Figure 55 Grooved Ware from Upper Ninepence (scale 1:2)

sions and up to 8mm thick. The outer surface is dark brown; the inner is black.

The inner surface is decorated with traces of five vertical(?) broadly incised lines.

P42 Two sherds, including one rim, in a hard, well-fired, dark brown or grey-brown fabric with well-crushed inclusions and occasional voids. The rim sherd fabric averages 11mm thick, the body sherd, probably a base, has the inner surface missing.

The rim is pointed with an internal bevel and has an estimated diameter of 140mm. Externally, the profile is curved and the sherd is decorated with multiple lines of horizontal fingernail impressions arranged to resemble 'pseudo-cord'. Six lines are visible.

P43 One sherd in a hard, well-fired fabric, with light grey-brown outer surface and black inner surface. The inclusions are finely crushed and the fabric slightly porous. The fabric averages 8mm thick.

The decoration is incised and comprises a filled chevron motif.

P44 Four sherds in a hard, well-fired fabric, up to 15mm thick. The outer surface is light grey-brown to brown and the inner surface is grey with a dark grey core. The inclusions are finely crushed.

One rim sherd is pointed, apparently upright, and has two faintly incised diagonal lines on the internal bevel which is steeply angled and 12mm broad.

P45 Three sherds in a very soft porous fabric from near the base of the vessel. The fabric is dark grey to black throughout and the outer surface is pitted. The inner surface is missing.

P46 Single hard, well-fired sherd, with a light brown outer surface, a black inner surface and core. There are internal carbon encrustations. The fabric contains abundant inclusions, some of which break the inner surface, and averages 10mm thick.

External decoration comprises lightly incised lines arranged in a filled chevron motif.

P47 Rim sherd in a hard, well-fired and slightly porous fabric, 15mm thick, and with a light brown outer surface, grey-brown inner surface and core. The fabric contains grog and other inclusions up to 3mm across.

The rim is internally bevelled. The decoration comprises faint traces of fingernail impressions on the outer surface.

P48 Sherds in a soft friable sandy fabric with light brown surfaces and a grey core. Abundant sandy inclusions up to 3mm across break both surfaces and the fabric itself has a laminated appearance in section.

A rim sherd displays a simple rounded rim with, externally, a small applied pellet 10mm below it. Other sherds carry small, raised narrow cordons which appear to run vertically. Otherwise the vessel is undecorated.

P49 Sherds in a fairly well-fired fabric with light orange-brown outer surfaces and a black inner surface and core. The fabric averages 12mm thick. Undecorated.

P50 Abraded base sherd too small to allow an estimation of diameter. The fabric is soft but quite well-fired and has brown surfaces and a black core. It contains abundant finely crushed grog. Undecorated.

P51 Small sherd in a hard, well-fired fabric, with a smooth well-finished outer surface carrying traces of carbon encrustations. The outer surface is black-brown, the inner light brown and the core is black. The fabric averages 9mm thick and contains large angular inclusions up to 6mm across.

The decoration comprises four lightly incised lines divided into two parallel pairs.

P52 Sherds in a hard, well-fired fabric with grey-brown surfaces and a dark grey core. The fabric is well-finished, but abraded, and averages 8mm thick. It contains well-crushed grog.

The decoration comprises lightly incised lines in a filled chevron arrangement.

P53 Sherds in a soft abraded fabric with light brown surfaces and a black core. The fabric is porous, 10mm thick, and contains abundant crushed grog. Undecorated.

P54 Small abraded sherd in a light orange-brown fabric with micaceous inclusions up to 5mm across. Black inner surface, outer surface missing. Undecorated.

P55 Rim from a vessel with a diameter of *c* 160mm. The fabric is hard and well-fired with abundant angular inclusions up to 5mm across. Much of the outer surface is missing but the fabric has been grey throughout with a black carbon encrusted inner surface.

The rim is pointed with a steep internal bevel 10mm deep. Externally, the surviving decoration comprises two rows of short vertical incisions. Internally, below the bevel, are two rows of what appear to be vertically set 'birdbone' impressions, though the exact nature of these is masked by the carbon encrustations.

P56 Base and body sherds. The fabric is quite soft, but well-fired, and has light brown surfaces and a black core. The fabric contains finely crushed grog and averages 9mm thick at the walls, while the base is 17mm thick at the centre. The base diameter has been in the region of 80mm.

The decoration comprises zones of multiple diagonal incisions separated by applied converging cordons.

P57 Rim sherd in an extremely hard and well-fired fabric. The fabric is 17mm thick, and contains angular inclusions, including quartz, up to 10mm across. The fabric has light brown surfaces and a grey core. The curvature of the vessel suggests a barrel-shaped pot.

The rim is pointed with a steeply sloping internal bevel 18mm deep. The bevel is decorated with five horizontal lines of twisted cord impressions. On the outer surface, the decoration comprises lightly incised or scored lines arranged in a filled chevron motif.

P58 Sherds in a hard, well-fired fabric, abraded, and with angular inclusions up to 6mm across. The fabric appears grey throughout, though the outer surface is missing.

P59 Sherd in a hard but abraded well-fired grey fabric. It contains grog and averages 10mm thick.

The sherd is decorated with a wavy fingernail-dimpled cordon, to one side of which are multiple diagonal lines.

P60 Well-fired but abraded sherd, with brown surfaces and a black core. The fabric contains grog and is 7mm thick.

Two faint incised lines are visible on the outer surface.

P61 Single sherd in a hard sandy fabric. Very abraded with a brown outer surface and a black inner surface and core. The fabric is 10mm thick. Undecorated.

P62 Sherds from a soft, friable thin-walled vessel, with pitted fabric and generally abraded breaks. The outer surface is dark brown and the inner surface is generally grey-brown with a black core. The voids in the fabric and the pits on the surfaces indicate organic inclusions. The fabric averages 5mm thick.

The decoration is incised and comprises multiple horizontal and diagonal lines defining empty lozenges and/or elongated chevron panels.

P63 Sherds similar to the above, but in a harder and better-fired fabric, though still slightly pitted. The outer surface is brown and the inner surface is grey-brown with a black core. A rim sherd, by contrast, is black throughout. The fabric averages 8mm thick and the rim has had a diameter in the region of 140mm.

The decoration comprises multiple horizontal and diagonal lines with reserved lozenge and chevron panels. There appears to be a dot-filled border around at least one of the reserved lozenges. The rim sherd has an internal bevel decorated with a single encircling grooved line, giving a concave or stepped appearance.

P64 Sherds in a hard grey fabric with abundant coarsely crushed white inclusions up to 3mm across. The fabric is up to 10mm thick, and traces of join voids may be detected in the breaks. The rim diameter has been in the region of 120mm.

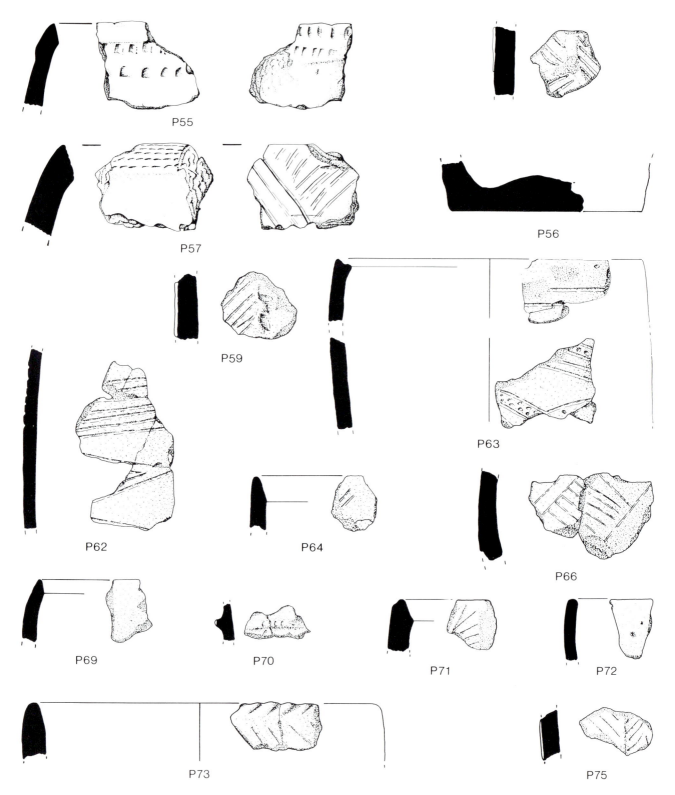

Figure 56   Grooved Ware from Upper Ninepence (scale 1:2)

The rim appears to have been slightly inturned. It is pointed with a narrow internal bevel. One of the rim sherds is decorated externally with a pair of finely incised diagonal lines.

P65 Undecorated sherds in a hard, well-fired fabric with light brown outer surfaces and black inner surfaces and core. The fabric has large coarse inclusions up to 7mm across, many of which break the otherwise smooth surfaces. The fabric exhibits many coil breaks and averages 10mm thick.

P66 Sherds from a coarse thick-walled vessel in a fairly soft fabric with a light brown to grey outer surface, light brown to black inner surface and a black core. The fabric averages some 15mm thick. Inclusions appear to comprise grog and angular stone up to 7mm across. One sherd from near the base of the vessel suggests a base diameter of *c* 120–40mm.

Three sherds are decorated with incised lines arranged apparently in a filled lozenge motif.

P67 Five sherds in a hard, well-fired grey fabric with

finely crushed grog inclusions. The fabric has smooth, well-finished surfaces and averages 7mm thick. One sherd from near the base of the vessel suggests a base diameter of *c* 100mm.

The decoration is internal comprising panels of multiple oblique lines and interrupted herringbone.

P68 Sherds in a fabric similar to P67 above. The fabric is grey throughout, slightly soapy in texture, and with apparently ferrous concretions on both surfaces. The rim diameter is 160mm and the base diameter in the region of 100mm. The estimated height of the vessel has been around 120mm.

The rim is rounded with a near vertical internal bevel or moulding. The decoration comprises small whipped cord maggots arranged in an irregular double chevron on the rim bevel, short evenly spaced oblique impressions on top of the rim and a rectilinear arrangement of multiple impressions on the outside. Internally, below the rim bevel, the same decorative technique is employed with multiple horizontal impressions arranged in broadly vertical zones converging towards the base. None of the base sherds are decorated either internally or externally suggesting that the decoration stopped short of the bottom of the pot.

P69 Small rim sherd in a soft and soapy textured fabric with finely crushed grog inclusions. The fabric is light brown throughout and averages 7mm thick.

The vessel appears to have had a slightly inturned rim with a near-vertical internal bevel. There are faint traces of slight dimples on this bevel indicating abraded decoration.

P70 Sherds in an extremely soft and friable fabric with pitted grey-brown surfaces and a voided black core. There are traces of incised lines on some sherds and a raised cordon decorated with oval impressions, probably fingernail 'nicks'.

P71 Rim sherd in a hard, well-fired fabric with brown surfaces and a black core. The fabric averages 10mm thick and contains finely crushed grog as well as stone inclusions up to 10mm across. The rim is pointed and has a steeply angled internal bevel.

Externally the sherd is decorated with five parallel diagonal lines.

P72 Two undecorated rim sherds in a soft soapy-textured fabric with a patchy brown outer surface and a black inner surface and core. The fabric is 7mm thick and contains grog. The outer surface is slightly pitted. The rim is rounded and slightly inturned.

P73 Rim sherd with an estimated diameter of 180mm. The fabric is brown externally, black internally and has a black core. It is up to 12mm thick and contains grog. It has a slight internal bevel and the laminated texture of the sherd indicates that this bevel has been applied.

The decoration comprises deep oblique impressions on the top of the rim giving a cabled effect to the top of the vessel. Below this are multiple parallel incised lines.

P74 Sherds in a soft and friable fabric varying between 10 and 18mm thick. The surfaces are brown and the core black.

One sherd is decorated with multiple lightly incised diagonal lines.

P75 Sherd in a fairly well-fired fabric with a brown outer surface and a black inner surface and core. The fabric is 8mm thick and contains finely crushed inclusions.

The decoration comprises a zone of incised herring-bone motif separated from a zone of multiple parallel diagonal incisions by a narrow raised cordon.

P76 Sherds in a soft fabric with a brown outer surface, and a black inner surface and core. The surfaces are frequently crazed and/or pitted and the sherds are generally abraded. There are carbon encrustations on the inner surface and the fabric is generally 10mm thick. Two base sherds suggest an estimated diameter of 100mm.

P77 Sherds in a hard well-fired fabric, 9mm thick, and with a dark brown outer surface and a black inner surface and core. Inclusions up to 4mm across seem sparse. One sherd, with a crescentic fracture, may be a firing waster.

Decoration comprises a narrow horizontal raised cordon, below which are multiple oblique lines of conjoined fingernail impressions, probably arranged in a filled triangle or similar motif.

P78 Sherd in a fairly hard fabric with a pink-brown outer surface, a black core and a grey-brown inner surface. The fabric averages 7mm thick and is pitted and porous from the leaching out of calcitic inclusions. Coil breaks are visible in both the upper and lower sections.

The decoration comprises four broad incised horizontal lines with a multiple chevron motif in the same technique below. The left arm of this multiple chevron motif comprises five rows of incisions, with four on the right arm.

The curvature at the base of the sherd is strongly suggestive of the beginnings of a base angle.

P79 Sherd in a hard and well-fired fabric which is grey throughout. The fabric has good surfaces but is abraded. It averages 11mm thick.

The rim sherd thinned internally resulting in a slight internal bevel. Externally the decoration comprises a roughly horizontal fingernail impression.

P80 Sherd in a hard and well-fired but abraded fabric with a brown outer surface and a grey inner surface and core. The fabric contains finely crushed grog and averages 14mm thick.

The decoration is very abraded and comprises linear arrangements of fingernail impressions.

P81 Undecorated sherd in a hard and well-fired fabric with a brown outer surface and a black core and inner surface, the latter being covered with carbon encrustations. The fabric is 12mm thick and contains white stone inclusions up to 5mm across.

P82 Sherd from a thinned but rounded rim, in a hard well-fired fabric reaching 7mm thick and containing finely crushed grog inclusions. The curvature of the sherd suggests that it may be from a barrel-shaped vessel or closed bowl.

There is a single external incised line below the rim.

P83 Abraded sherds in a well-fired fabric with a light brown outer surface and a black core and inner surface. The fabric contains grog and averages 13mm thick.

Decoration comprises multiple incised diagonal lines with raised cordons.

P84 Small black rim sherd in a hard and well-fired fabric with smooth well-finished surfaces. The rim is simple and rounded. Probably Grooved Ware.

P85 Sherd in a hard and well-fired fabric with a dark grey outer surface, black carbon encrusted inner surface and a black core. The fabric contains grog and measures 12mm in thickness.

The decoration comprises two rows of sub-triangular impressions.

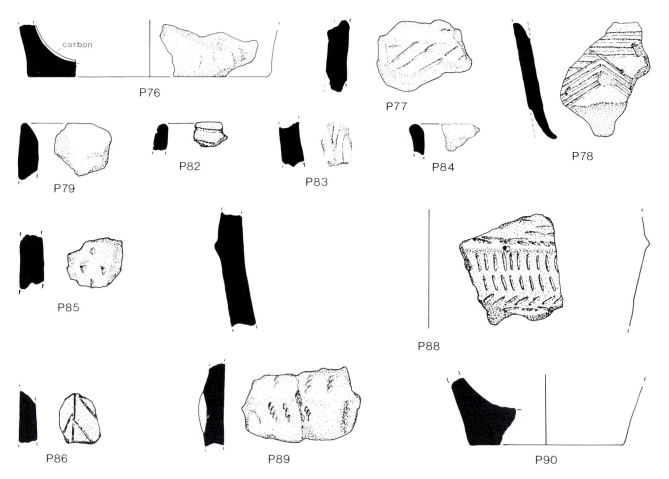

Figure 57 Grooved Ware and early Bronze Age ceramics from Upper Ninepence (scale 1:2)

Figure 58 Photograph of the internally decorated vessel P34

Table 22 Stratigraphy and quantities of the Peterborough Ware from Upper Ninepence

Pot no	Feature (context)	No of sherds	Residue analysis (yes/no)	Thin section (yes/no)	C14 date
1	Pit 12 (13)	17 +	Y	Y	
2	Pit 65 (66)	1	N	N	4470 ± 80 (SWAN-23)
3	Mound (2)	5 +	Y	N	
4	Mound (2)	6	N	N	
5	Pit 16 (17)	9	Y	N	4440 ± 50 (BM-2967)
6	Pit 16 (17)	1	N	N	4440 ± 50 (BM-2967)
7	Pit 16 (17)	1	N	N	4440 ± 50 (BM-2967)
8	Pit 10 (11)	1 +	N	N	
9	Pit 37 (38)	1	N	N	
10	Pit 6 (7)	15	Y	Y	
11	Pit 20 (21)	11 +	N	Y	4410 ± 35 (BM-2966)
12	Mound (2)	7	N	N	
13	Stakehole 47 (48)	crumbs	N	N	
14	Stakehole 325 (326)	crumbs	N	N	
15	Pit 200 (201)	1	N	N	4590 ± 60 (BM-3071)
16	Pit 154 (155)	1	N	N	4050 ± 35 (BM-2969) residual
17	U/S	2	N	N	
18	Pit 500 (502)	5	N	N	4590 ± 60 (BM-3071)
19	Pit 200 (201)	1	N	N	4590 ± 60 (BM-3071)
20	Pit 500 (502)	3	N	N	4490 ± 60 (BM-3070)

P86 Abraded fragments in a hard well-fired fabric with a reddish-brown to brown outer surface, a black core and a grey inner surface. The fabric averages 8mm thick and contains finely crushed grog inclusions up to 3mm across.

Some sherds are decorated with diagonal incisions suggesting a filled (lozenge ?) motif.

P87 Wall and base sherds in a soft, porous fabric with a brown outer surface, a dark brown inner surface and a grey-black core. The fabric contains grog. Undecorated.

P88 Single sherd with a dark brown outer surface, dark grey-brown inner surface and a black core. The fabric is hard and well-fired, 9mm thick, and with inclusions up to 3mm across.

The decoration comprises horizontal fingernail impressions above a raised cordon. Below this cordon is a zone of oblique, regularly-spaced fingernail impressions, a zone of herringbone motif in the same technique, and traces of a line of horizontal fingernail impressions at the base of the sherd.

Early Bronze Age

P89 Two sherds in a hard well-fired, if slightly abraded, fabric. It has a dark brown outer surface, a brown inner surface and a black core. The fabric contains grog and finely crushed stones and measures 10mm thick.

The decoration comprises vertical twisted cord impressions above a cavetto formed by two raised cordons. Within the cavetto is a row of short diagonal twisted cord impressions with attendant fingernail impressions towards the top. Vertical stop ridges fill the cavetto at intervals.

Probably from the upper portion of a Food Vessel Urn.

P90 Sherd in a hard and well-fired but grog-filled fabric. The fabric has good quality surfaces, brown externally and internally and with a black core. Grog inclusions break both surfaces but lie flush with them. The fabric is 10mm thick at the wall and 17mm thick at the base. The base has had a diameter of *c* 80mm. Probably from a Collared Urn or Food Vessel Urn.

Ceramic crumbs/undecorated sherds from context sample residues

The contexts in Table 25 produced small crumbs of pottery from processed environmental samples.

Daub/fired clay

Two pieces of fired clay were recovered from context 199. Both pieces are very porous having contained abundant organic inclusions.

Table 23 Stratigraphy and quantities of the Grooved Ware from Upper Ninepence

Pot no	Feature (context)	No of sherds	Residue analysis (yes/no)	Thin section (yes/no)	C14 date
21	Pit 198 (289)	7	Y	N	
22	Pit 198 (289)	15	N	Y	
23	Pit 198 (289)	3	N	N	
24	Pit 198 (289)	1	N	N	
25	Pit 198 (289)	1	N	N	
26	Pit 198 (289)	4	N	Y	
27	Pit 198 (289)	1	N	N	
28	Pit 198 (289)	2	Y	N	
29	Pit 198 (289)	1	N	N	
30	Pit 198 (289)	1	N	N	
31	Pit 198 (289)	1	N	N	
32	Pit 55 (56)	2	N	N	
33	Pit 154 (155)	35	Y	N	4050 ± 35 (BM-2969)
34	Pit 154 (155)	30	Y	Y	4050 ± 35 (BM-2969)
35	Pit 154 (155)	2	N	N	4050 ± 35 (BM-2969)
36	Pit 154 (155)	1	N	N	4050 ± 35 (BM-2969)
37	Pit 198 (199, 289) Pit 188 (191)	15	Y	Y	
38	Pit 154 (155)	45	Y	N	4050 ± 35 (BM-2969)
39	Pit 154 (155)	75	Y	Y	4050 ± 35 (BM-2969)
40	Pit 154 (155)	1	N	N	4050 ± 35 (BM-2969)
41	Pit 154 (155)	1	N	N	4050 ± 35 (BM-2969)
42	Stakehole 297 (298)	2	N	N	
43	Stakehole 297 (298)	2	N	N	
44	Stakehole 297 (298)	4	N	N	
45	Stakehole 297 (298) & U/S	4	N	N	
46	Stakehole 422 (423)	1	N	N	
47	Pit 198 (291)	1	N	N	
48	Pit 198 (199, 289)	10	Y	Y	
49	Pit 136 (137)	2	N	N	
50	Pit 150 (151) & U/S	3	N	N	
51	OGS (72)	1	N	N	
52	Pit 99 (100)	9	N	N	
53	Mound (2)	5	N	N	
54	U/S (9)	1	N	N	
55	Pit 180 (181)	1	N	N	
56	Pit 35 (36)	5	N	N	
57	Pit 146 (147)	1	N	N	
58	Pit 136 (137)	2	N	N	
59	Pit 136 (137)	1	N	N	
60	Pit 43 (44)	1	N	N	
61	U/S (9)	1	N	N	
62	Pit 85 (86/7)	12	Y	Y	4060 ± 40 (BM-3069)

Table 23 Stratigraphy and quantities of the Grooved Ware from Upper Ninepence (*cont.*)

Table 23 Stratigraphy and quantities of the Grooved Ware from Upper Ninepence (*cont.*)

Pot no	Feature (context)	No of sherds	Residue analysis (yes/no)	Thin section (yes/no)	C14 date
63	Pit 85 (86/7)		N	N	
64	Pit 293 (294)	14	N	N	
65	Pit 293 (294)	14	Y	N	
66	Pit 132 (133)	30	Y	N	4160 ± 35 (BM-2968)
67	Pit 132 (133)	5	N	N	4160 ± 35 (BM-2968)
68	Pit 132 (133)	78 +	Y	Y	4160 ± 35 (BM-2968)
69	Pit 132 (133)	1	N	N	4160 ± 35 (BM-2968)
70	Pit 22 (23)	7	N	N	
71	Pit 55 (56)	1	N	N	
72	Pit 55 (56)	2	N	N	
73	Pit 55 (56)	2	N	N	
74	Pit 55 (56)	13	N	Y	
75	Pit 55 (56)	1	N	N	
76	Pit 55 (56)	13	N	Y	
77	Pit 198 (289)	6	N	N	
78	Pit 85 (86)	1	N	Y	4060 ± 40 (BM-3069)
79	OGS (72)	1	N	N	
80	OGS (72)	1	N	N	
81	OGS (72)	5	N	N	
82	Posthole 478 (479)	1	N	N	
83	Mound (2)	7	N	N	
84	Mound (2)	1	N	N	
85	Mound (2)	1	N	N	
86	Pit 299 (300)	12	N	N	
87	Stakehole (278)	9	N	N	
88	Pit 198 (292)	1	N	N	

Table 24 Stratigraphy and quantities of the early Bronze Age ceramics from Upper Ninepence

Pot no	Feature (context)	No of sherds	Residue analysis (yes/no)	Thin section (yes/no)
89	Mound (2)	2	N	N
90	OGS (72)	1	N	N

A single piece of fired clay was recovered from context 147 (fill of pit 146). The fabric is quite dense.

The Iron Age pottery from Hindwell I

Description

Fragments of four vessels were recovered from the upper silts (context 502) of the enclosure ditch in site A and a single sherd was recovered from the uppermost silts (context 101) of the ditch in site B. This latter material comprises an undecorated wall sherd in a gritty textured, slightly laminated fabric. The fabric contains abundant quartz sand and is slightly micaceous.

The sherds from site A are in two similar but different fabrics. Vessels IA1, 3 and 4 (Fig 59) are in a well-fired fabric which contains finely crushed sandstone and organic and calcitic inclusions which have both burnt out and leached out of the fabric leaving pitted surfaces. Vessel IA2 is also in a well-fired, grog-filled fabric and has slight traces of

Table 25 Quantification of ceramic crumbs from sampled contexts

Feature (context)	Pottery ID	C14 Date
Mound (2)	Grooved Ware ?	
OGS (72)	Grooved Ware ?	
Pit 22 (23)		
Hearth 28 (29)	Grooved Ware ?	4240 ± 70 (SWAN-24)
Pit 33 (34)	Grooved Ware ?	
Pit 35 (36)		
Pit 55 (56)		
Pit 65 (66)		4470 ± 80 (SWAN-23)
Pit 146 (147)		
Pit 152 (153)	Grooved Ware ?	
Pit 200 (201)	Peterborough ?	4590 ± 60 (BM-3071)
Pit 188 (289)		
Pit 188 (291)	Grooved Ware ?	
Pit 293 (294)	Grooved Ware ?	
Pit 313 (314)		
Pit 370 (371)		
Posthole 440 (441)		
Stakehole 448 (449)	Grooved Ware ?	
Pit 500 (502)	as P20 ?	4490 ± 60 (BM-3070)

mica visible in the surfaces. The outer surfaces of all the vessels are well-finished and burnished, and vary in colour from black to grey. The inner surfaces are also generally well-finished though lack the burnishing, and vary from purplish-grey to brown in colour. Vessel IA4 has extensive carbonaceous deposits in the interior. Macroscopically, the fabric corresponds to Peacock's (1968) fabric group C which is sandstone (as opposed to limestone) based and which can be sourced to the area west of the Malverns.

Vessel IA2 is decorated with a zone of diagonal incisions between an upper and lower horizontal scored line. Vessel IA4 exhibits a fire-spall on the outer surface indicating that it was damaged during firing, or possibly as a result of its subsequent use as a cooking pot (though this is less likely). The spall, therefore, though damaging the vessel, was not sufficient to warrant its discard.

Vessels IA1, 3 and 4 all have slightly everted rims and appear to have had bulbous or at least slightly sinuous profiles. Pot IA2 differs in having a slightly thickened and angular rim and is more straight-sided, though the walls are still slightly convex. Only IA1 appears to be from a closed vessel, though it must be stressed that so little survives of this pot that the rim angle is not unequivocal.

The vessels belong firmly to the Saucepan Pot tradition of the middle Iron Age; the distribution of which covers central southern England and extends into the southwestern counties, South Wales and the Marches (Cunliffe 1991, 79–82). The simple scored or incised linear decoration below the rim of IA2 places the vessels in Cunliffe's Croft Ambury-Bredon Hill style which clusters around Herefordshire and the Cotswolds (Cunliffe 1991, 81) though the 'duck-stamped' elements of this style are absent from the present assemblage. Savory (1976, 111) illustrates a parallel for IA1 from Llanmelin and close parallels from Bredon Hill are illustrated by Peacock (1968, fig 3, 19–20). Dating of these styles in southern England suggests a currency from c 400–100 BC, though their currency in Wales and the Marches may well have continued until the Roman occupation.

Catalogue

IA1 Closed jar with a bulbous body and everted rim. The rim itself is rounded and slightly thickened. The diameter of the rim is 220mm.

IA2 Slightly convex-sided vessel with angular rim and external decoration. Rim diameter 160mm.

IA3 Open vessel with a slightly everted rounded rim with slight internal flattening. Rim diameter 140mm.

IA4 Convex-sided vessel with everted rim which is flattened internally to provide an internal bevel. Characteristic traces of a substantial firing spall on the outer surface. Rim diameter 160mm.

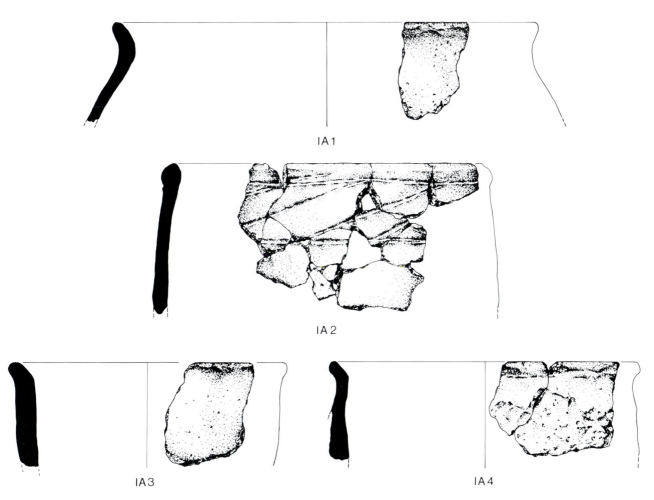

Figure 59   The Iron Age pottery from Hindwell I (scale 1:2)

The glass bead from Hindwell Ash

The glass bead (see Fig 49 no 3) measures 7mm in diameter overall with a near-central perforation measuring 2.5mm in diameter. The bead is circular with a slightly flattened section up to 4mm thick. There are traces of wear on both sides indicating that the bead has been strung as one of a group. The glass is a uniform royal blue in colour and the surfaces appear to be slightly pitted with small ?air bubbles. An analysis of the bead is presented below, the results of which suggest a middle Iron Age date.

The slag from Hindwell I
M Walters

A total of 245g of slag was recovered from context 501, the uppermost fill, of the ditch terminal at Hindwell I. It comprises ferrous secondary smithing slags which are generally black or grey-black in colour, light and vesicular, and with a high silica content probably derived from the melting of hearth wall clays. Some fragments have occasional traces of grey clay hearth lining adhering to them. One fragment has a plano-convex base with traces of remnant charcoal fuel ash.

3 Scientific analysis of the artefacts

Microwear analysis of the flint artefacts from Upper Ninepence
Randolph E Donahue

Introduction

The poor preservation of faunal and floral remains at a prehistoric site, such as occurs at Upper Ninepence, can seriously impede an archaeologist's ability to make economic inferences. The application of lithic microwear analysis, when the quality and condition of the lithic material is appropriate, can partly compensate for such limitations. The recovery of lithic artefacts from pits associated with specific wares at the culturally mixed Neolithic site of Upper Ninepence provides an opportunity not only to reconstruct economic activities at a prehistoric site, but also to examine similarities and differences between the site economies of the inhabitants who used Peterborough Ware pottery, and those who used Grooved Ware pottery some centuries later.

Background

Lithic microwear analysis is the microscopic examination of surface wear and fracture scars that form along the edges of fine-grain siliceous stone such as flint and chert. Experimental studies demonstrate that microscopic wear and fracture scar characteristics result from tool use and vary systematically according to the worked material (eg, hide, wood, meat, bone) and to the applied forces and motions (eg, cutting, scraping, wedging, etc). The development of principles regarding these relationships permits microwear analysts to infer the past use or uses of lithic artefacts with a greater degree of precision and accuracy than through reliance on either macroscopic attribute analysis or ethnographic analogues of tool form. Natural processes also produce systematic microwear features which can often make inferences about tool use more difficult (Keeley 1980; Levi-Sala 1986a, 1986b), but can aid in the understanding of site formation processes (Donahue 1994).

Method

The entire assemblage of lithic artefacts collected from Upper Ninepence was made available for microwear analysis. Artefacts were sampled from pits and other features that were securely associated with an occupational period, although by accident a few artefacts were studied which could not be culturally affiliated with one particular period. All lithic artefacts from the appropriate contexts were visually examined for possible selection. The sample included all retouched artefacts, and all non-patinated artefacts larger than 20mm in length with at least one 'usable' edge. Because the Peterborough Ware sample was small, a few artefacts less than 20mm in length were included to enlarge the sample. The sample includes 35 artefacts from Peterborough Ware contexts, 74 from Grooved Ware contexts, and five from unaffiliated contexts for a total sample size of 114 artefacts. This is not a random sample, yet, given that the smallest artefacts analysed appear to be unused, virtually all used artefacts from the selected contexts have been sampled. Importantly, the degree to which the artefacts in the pits are representative of the entire site is not known.

The sampled artefacts were bathed for 10 minutes in a 10% solution of HCl, and thoroughly rinsed and bathed in water for 20 minutes. The artefacts were viewed with an Olympus KL-BHM metallurgical microscope principally at 200× magnification. Microwear characteristics were recorded, categorised following Donahue (1994), and interpreted.

Results

Of the 114 artefacts examined, 28 have microscopic wear on their edges that can be attributed to some category of use, and 30 artefacts are interpreted as unused. The microwear analysis did not provide adequate information to infer use of the remaining 56 artefacts as a result of one or more confounding factors. Table 26 lists those artefacts which have one or more identifiable uses and Table 27 summarises the results for all artefacts examined.

Hide working is the most common form of tool use evident at the site with thirteen artefacts (44.8% of identified uses) displaying such wear patterns (see below for brief descriptions of wear characteristics from use). Most of these artefacts were used for scraping dry hides, but also evident is the cutting of dry hide and possibly the working of fresh hide. Meat cutting or butchering is evident on seven artefacts (24.1%). This use often occurs on both lateral edges of blades, and on flakes and side scrapers. Many of these flakes are broken or fragments.

Often one finds numerous tools used for cutting siliceous grasses and cereals at Neolithic sites. And although gloss is reported on a number of artefacts, only one artefact from the site has microwear indicative of such use. The artefact, L172, is a large

Table 26 Flint artefacts with identifiable use

Artefact	Period	Context	Type	Edge	Material	Action
L014F	U	2	end scraper	front	dry hide	scraping
L172	P	11	flake	l	sil. plant	slicing
L173	P	11	flake	l	meat	butchering
L173	P	11	flake	bit	bone	graving
L176	P	11	msc ret flake	distal end	hard (wood?)	shaving
L259F	P	11	chisl arrwhd	transverse	unknown	impact
R902	P	11	flake midsect	l	dry hide	scraping
R904	P	11	blade midsect	l&r	meat/hide	butchering
R905	P	11	piercer	transverse	hide	haft??
L033	P	13	msc ret flake	l	hard (wood?)	shaving
L182F	P	13	knife?	rt notch	wood	shaving
L183	P	17	denticulate	l&r	dry hide	working
L188	P	21	flake midsect	lat	meat/hide	butchering
L045F	G	23	end scraper	front	hide	scraping
L048	G	23	end scraper	front & l	hide	scraping
L080F	G	23	end scraper	front	dry hide	scraping
L076	G	133	end scraper	front	dry hide	scraping
L202	G	133	flake midsect	r&l	meat?	butchering
L065	G	155	end scraper	front	dry hide	scraping
L066	G	155	end scraper	front	dry hide	uncertain
L067F	G	155	dbl truncatn	r&l	dry hide	working
L083	G	155	end scraper	front	fresh hide	scraping
R912/L079	G	155	splinter flake	r	unknown	impact
L147	G	199	side scraper	r&l	meat/hide	butchering
L236	G	199	blade	l&r	wood	whittling
L133	G	289	flake frag	l&r	meat?	butchering
L241	G	289	side scraper	r&l	dry hide?	working
L142	G	291	end scraper	front	dry hide	scraping
L164F	G	291	blase/flake	r&l(distal)	wood	shaving
L149	U	292	blade	r	meat	cutting

and relatively ovate flake (Fig 60 no 1), and clearly not the kind of flake normally associated with sickle blades. The edge is well rounded and the surfaces near the edge are extremely smooth and bright. The surface is not brilliantly polished as one expects with sickle gloss; it appears that the surface texture has been slightly roughened by post-depositional processes as to reduce the typical brightness. The surface contains numerous small pits of which many are comet-shaped; a feature noted only from plant use and results from the direction of rubbing against the plant silica. There are numerous striations parallel to the edge indicating a slicing motion. It should be noted that sickle blades usually have striations oblique to the edge, and this may suggest a different use of the tool or a different way of manipulating it; however, there is no doubt that it was used intensively on soft siliceous plant fibre.

Five artefacts were used for working wood, principally with a whittling or shaving motion. The wear is often found in a notch or along a concave edge. Wear from wood is similar to that from plant fibre, but limited to the edge and its immediate adjoining surfaces.

The working of bone is another use observed just once, on the broken flake L173 (Fig 60 no 2). The wear is located on the bit of the burin as might be expected, but it is very limited in its distribution. The bit

Table 27 Catalogue of artefacts examined for lithic microwear analysis

Artefact	Type	Edge	Material	Action	Ridge	Comments	Context	Period
L013F	piercer	tip & lat	unknown		1.0	Both edges?	2	U
L105F	backed knife	r	unknown		4.0	PDM	2	U
L111F	multi platform flake core		unused			Abrasion tracks from flake production	2	U
L014F	end-and-side scraper	front	dry hide	scraping	1.5		72	U
L149	misc retouch	r	meat	cutting	0.1	Uncertain	292	U
L172	flake	l	sil. plant	slicing	0.2	Uncertain right edge	11	P
L173	broken flake	l	meat	butchering	0.1	1 of 2 uses	11	P
L173	broken flake	bit	bone	graving	0.1	2 of 2 uses	11	P
L174	blade-like flake	l&r	unknown		1.0	PDM	11	P
L175	flake (burnt)	l&r	unused			Thin	11	P
L176	msc ret flake	distal end	hard; wood?	shaving	0.1	Concave edge	11	P
L177	core frag	r	unused		0.1		11	P
L178	flake	notch	unknown			PDM	11	P
L179	flake	r	unused		0.1	Thin	11	P
L180	flake frag	l&r	unused			Thin	11	P
L181	flake (burnt)	all	unused		0.1	Small & thin	11	P
L257F	end scraper	l&front	unknown		2.5	Probably dry hide	11	P
L258	flake	r&l	unknown		0.3		11	P
L259F	chisel arrowhead	transverse	unknown	impact	0.2	Projectile point?	11	P
L260F	end-and-side scraper	front	unknown		11.0	PDM & fire	11	P
L401F	core		unknown			Poor quality material	11	P
R902	flake midsect	l	dry hide	scraping	0.1	Visible @10×	11	P
R904	blade midsect	l&r	meat/hide	butchering	0.1	Heat altered?	11	P
R905	piercer	transverse	hide?	haft?		Undetermined if point was used	11	P
R907	broken flake	r	unused			Fire	11	P
L033	msc ret flake	l	hard; wood?	shaving		Concave edge	13	P
L182F	misc retouch-arrowhead frag ?	rt notch	wood	shaving	2.0	Rt edge: PDM or hide cutting	13	P
R908	irreg flake or spall?	all	unused				13	P
L042	ser. flake	l	unknown		0.1	Post-depositonal modification (PDM)	17	P
L183	misc retouch blade ?	l&r	dry hide	working	0.3		17	P
L184	flake frag				0.3	Damaged from fire	17	P
L185	piercer		unused			Minimal wear	17	P
L186	flake	l			0.1	PDM	17	P
L187	flake		unused				17	P
L188	ser flake (burnt)	lat	meat/hide	butchering	0.1	Left, possibly right	21	P
L189	flake (burnt)		unknown			Damage from fire	21	P
R906	flake frag	l&r	unknown			Fire & PDM (recent)	21	P
L160	flake frag	r	unknown			Thin	201	P

Table 27 Catalogue of artefacts examined for lithic microwear analysis (*cont.*)

Artefact	Type	Edge	Material	Action	Ridge	Comments	Context	Period
R903	broken flake	r	unknown		0.1		201	P
L157	broken flake	l&r	unused		0.1		502	P
L254	flake	r&l	unknown			PDM	502	P
L132	flake	all	unused			Thin retouch flake	9	G
L137	blade frag	r&l	unknown			PDM	9	G
R917	flake frag	l	unknown		0.3	PDM	9	G
R918	flake, srrtd?	r	unknown		0.2	Poor quality material	9	G
R919	broken flake	l	unknown			PDM	9	G
R920	MRF	l	unknown		0.1	Rt also unused	9	G
R921	flake	all	unused			Retouch flake	9	G
R922	broken blade	l	unknown			PDM; poor quality	9	G
R923	flake	distal	unused		0.2		9	G
L044F	end-and-side scraper	front	unknown		4.0	Possibly dry hide	23	G
L045F	end-and-side scraper	front	hide	scraping	1.0	(Circular scraper)	23	G
L046	core frag	front	unknown			Heat spalled; refits R924	23	G
L048	end-and-side scraper	front & l	hide	scraping	0.4	Poor quality material	23	G
L049	end scraper	front & l	unknown		4.0	Dry hide?	23	G
L050	end-and-side scraper	front	unknown		0.2	PDM	23	G
L051	end scraper	front	unknown			Dry hide?	23	G
L052F	chisel arrowhead	transverse	unknown		2.5	Much edge rounding	23	G
L053F	lev. core	all	unused		0.6	Probably unused	23	G
L054	heat spall	all	unknown			PDM	23	G
L080F	end-and-side scraper or disc scraper	front	dry hide	scraping	2.0	Also PDM; refits L190	23	G
L190	broken flake	r&l	unknown		3.0	Hide/meat/PDM? refits L080	23	G
L191	flake	r	unknown		1.2	PDM	23	G
L193	flake frag	all	unknown		5.0	Edges missing	23	G
L194	flake	l/distal	unused				23	G
L196	flake	all	unknown		0.1	Not visible	23	G
L197	blade-like flake	r&l	unused		0.1	Minimal use; meat?	23	G
L198	flake	l	unknown		0.2	PDM; Fire damage	23	G
L272	flake frag	l	unknown		2.0	PDM? fire	23	G
L273	heat spall	all	unused			No original edge	23	G
R924	heat spall	front	unknown			PDM; refits L046	23	G
L073F	fabricator frag	l&r	unknown		1.5	Too battered!	133	G
L076	end scraper	front	dry hide	scraping	0.1	Unused lateral edges?	133	G
L088	msc ret flake	all	unused				133	G
L201	flake	r & distal	unused		0.1		133	G
L202	blade-like flake	r&l	meat?	butchering	0.1	Serrated edge? PDM	133	G
L204	flake	all	unused				133	G

Table 27 Catalogue of artefacts examined for lithic microwear analysis (*cont.*)

Artefact	Type	Edge	Material	Action	Ridge	Comments	Context	Period
L207	flake	r	unused		0.3		133	G
R909/	broken blade	l&r	unused		0.1	Possibly used	133	G
L065	scraper frag	front	dry hide	scraping	0.1	Broken	155	G
L066	end scraper	front	dry hide	uncertain	0.1		155	G
L067F	end-and-side scraper	r&l	dry hide	working	1.0	Sidescraper	155	G
L082	ret flake	left	unknown		1.0	PDM	155	G
L083	scraper end ?	front	fresh hide	scraping	0.1		155	G
L086F	backed knife		unknown			Poor quality	155	G
L219	flake	all	unknown			Poor quality	155	G
L221	broken flake	all	unused		0.3		155	G
L222	flake	all	unknown		0.2	PDM	155	G
L223	flake frag	bit	unused		0.5		155	G
L229	flake	distal	unused		0.1		155	G
R910	flake	l & distal	unknown			PDM	155	G
R911	flake frag	all	unknown			PDM; snapped edges	155	G
R912/ L079	splinter flake	r	unknown	impact	0.8	Much PDM	155	G
R913	blade; MRF?	r	unknown		0.1	PDM	155	G
R914	end scraper	front	unknown		5.0	PDM; broken	155	G
R915	flake frag	A	unknown			All snapped	155	G
R916	MRF frag	ret edge	unknown		0.8	PDM	155	G
L147	flake	r&l	meat/hide	butchering	0.2		199	G
L234	flake frag	r&l	unknown		0.4	PDM	199	G
L235	flake frag	all	unknown			All edges snapped	199	G
L236	blade-like flake	l&r	wood	whittling	0.1		199	G
L239	flake	r & l	unused		0.1	Small	199	G
L133	flake frag	r&l	meat?	butchering	0.1	PDM?	289	G
L148F	misc retouch - unfinished arrowhead ?	l&r	unknown		0.2	PDM?	289	G
L241	misc retouch – bifacially worked flake	r&l	dry hide?	working	0.2	PDM?	289	G
L142	end-and-side scraper	front	dry hide	scraping	0.6	All edges; PDM?	291	G
L143	ser flake	all	unknown			Fire	291	G
L164F	retouched flake	r&l(distal)	wood	shaving	2.0		291	G
L242	flake	r	unknown			Thin edge; PDM	294	G
L246	flake	r	unused				294	G
L247	flake frag	r&l	unknown		0.8	PDM	294	G
L248	opposed platform core bipolar core		unused		0.4	Wedge?	294	G
L138	flake	r	unknown		0.4	PDM	298	G
L171	flake	r&l	unknown		0.2	PDM	298	G
L252	flake frag	all	unused				298	G

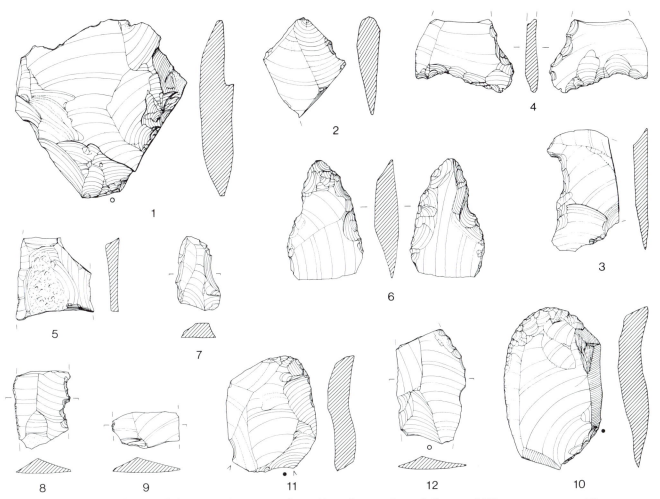

Figure 60   Flint artefacts exhibiting microwear from Peterborough and Grooved Ware contexts at Upper Ninepence (scale 1:1)

displays severe fracture damage which might explain, in part, the limited amount of wear. The edge was not stable but fractured away continually under the applied force. This flake is also the only tool to be identified as having been independently used on two materials; bone on the portion used as a borer and meat along a lateral edge. As a result this tool is listed twice in the tables.

The only other tool uses identified are those which have impact damage. Two tools are identified as having impact damage which is unlikely to have resulted from bipolar knapping (uncertain in other examples). Of these two tools, one is a chisel arrowhead and the fracture damage on its transverse end would support the hypothesis that it is a projectile point (see Fischer 1989; Fischer *et al* 1984; Odell and Cowan 1986). The other artefact is a flake and its impact damage is more typical of wedging where numerous blows are struck on one edge while the opposite edge receives much less damage. It was not possible to identify the material which was being wedged.

Many flakes show no evidence of use, and are categorised as unused. A few may have some wear or damage that results from post-depositional processes, but never so much as to obliterate evidence of use

if it had been there. The remaining 56 artefacts display a variety of different kinds of wear that result from non-use processes, and have the potential to remove traces of use or modify use-wear to the extent that one cannot differentiate the kind of use. All such artefacts are categorised as 'undetermined.' These artefacts and the modifications associated with them can contribute to our understanding of the site.

Microscopic surface modifications not related to use

Artefacts with post-depositional modification have generally been omitted from use-wear analysis as they are unable to provide useful information. Research by Donahue (eg 1994) shows that such wear can provide valuable insights into the formation of archaeological sites and should not be simply ignored. With this in mind there follows a brief discussion of the post-depositional surface modifications observed on the artefacts, what processes may have produced them, and the degree to which they may have influenced the use-wear interpretations. Six different wear and fracture damage patterns have been identified that are not

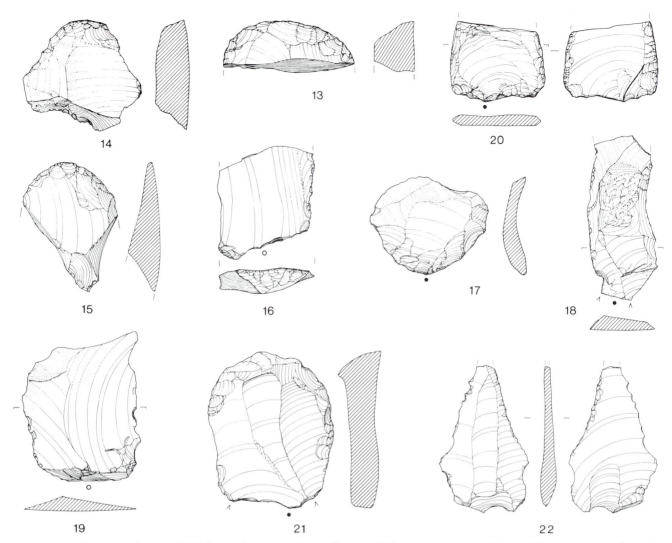

Figure 61 Flint artefacts exhibiting microwear from Grooved Ware contexts at Upper Ninepence (scale 1:1)

related to tool use. They are presented in no particular order.

Metal residue

Observed occasionally on protruding surfaces of the flint are very small, extremely bright, silver-colour patches that correspond to contact with metal (most likely steel) according to experimental studies. The metal residue is likely produced during excavation when contact with trowels or other digging equipment occurs, or as a result of contact with metal callipers when being measured in the laboratory. The limited size of these residue patches and their distinctive characteristics mean that they have little effect on the interpretation of tool use.

Plastic deformation

This form of surface modification is characterised by a flat and bright surface. Often the surface will have deep or shallow abrasion tracks of various widths running across the surface. It occurs as patches on the flint surface, often near an edge. The patches can occur well over 5mm in diameter and be observed without magnification as an area of 'gloss.' As such it is sometimes confused with 'gloss' observed on flints used for cutting opal-rich (siliceous) soft plant fibre. This form of surface modification results from pressure applied to the artefact surface by an object of greater hardness. Plastic deformation rarely impedes ones ability to interpret use-wear, but when observed on an artefact it requires substantial caution in the interpretation of tool use because other kinds of surface wear, and particularly edge fracture damage, have likely resulted from associated post-depositional processes.

Silica edge polishing

This form of wear is very common in this particular assemblage. It consists of a brightly polished surface that tends to be extremely localised to protruding surfaces, and is often observed as a bright line of surface polishing located directly on the edge of an artefact. It is very smooth and is occasionally associated with narrow striations that are almost always aligned perpendicular to the edge or ridge. It is very similar to wear produced during the early stage of wood working, and virtually duplicates the brightly polished edge sometimes observed associated with wear produced by meat cutting and butchering, when it results from incidental contact with flint or other hard material. It develops from rubbing against flint particles that are derived from the flint surface itself. In all these cases the principal mechanism is the same, contact with small silica particulate or mild, incidental contact with larger pieces of flint. Within the assemblage many of the artefacts not originally bagged separately display some of the more extensive examples of this wear, but many artefacts known to have been bagged separately at the excavation also display it. Because of its similarities to wear produced by tool use, extreme caution is required when this pattern of wear is encountered. As a result, some artefacts with possible use-wear from wood working or butchering may have been categorised as undetermined.

Non-polishing edge rounding

This form of surface modification proves to be the most common, most extensive, and most problematic for use interpretation at the site. It generally mimics the wear produced by dry hide, but produces a greater surface sheen with a much more rough rather than matt texture. The other major distinction is that it lacks the wide striations and linear depressions typical of working dry hide. Interestingly, and not fully understood, this form of wear can occur with no striations or with a multitude of narrow, multiple-direction striations. This suggests that there may be two mechanisms involved in the production of this kind of wear (and explains the vagueness of the labelling). It probably results from movement within the sediment matrix, but it may also include some form of chemical dissolution. Experimental research is currently investigating the underlying mechanisms that produce this wear. Because of the aggressive nature of the edge rounding, it is thought that it can remove virtually all traces of any form of wear produced from tool use with the possible exception of wear from intensive siliceous plant cutting. Because it mimics hide working, extreme caution has been exercised when considering such interpretations.

The potential impact of this form of post-depositional wear meant that it would prove useful if its impact on individual artefacts could be discerned. One cannot measure edge rounding directly since tools that were used will also have rounded edges. Instead, a technique has been applied that permits measurement of the rounding of dorsal ridges. This variable is a measure of the width of intense light reflected back during observation of a section of the dorsal ridge at a magnification of 200×. With no rounding the intersecting surfaces produce such a sharp ridgeline that it is almost invisible, often with no

measurable width of bright light being reflected. The minimum measurable level is approximately 0.1 units (about 7.1µm). Experimental research in progress is indicating that dorsal ridge rounding measuring as low as 0.5 units is already impacting upon use-wear. It is suggested that artefacts with ridge rounding of 1.0 unit and greater must have very clear evidence of use-wear and one must be capable of explaining why such wear has survived. For example, the knife L182F with ridge rounding measuring 2.0 units, maintains evidence of having worked wood because the use-wear is located in a relatively protective notch. With this in mind it is interesting to note that ridge rounding has been measured up to 11.0 units (an extreme example that was affected by thermal alteration, patina formation, and post-depositional wear. As can be seen from this last example, dorsal ridge rounding is affected by other factors besides soil abrasion.

Fire (thermal alteration) and its effects

Numerous artefacts were severely damaged by thermal alteration. This can be a direct effect such as with heat spalls (potlids) and thermal surface cracking, but it also can be indirect as in promoting much more rapid formation of white patina on an artefact surface. While thermal alteration may not obliterate use-wear patterns, the early stage development of white patina will cloud the artefact surface making it difficult to identify use-wear characteristics. In later stages, it leads to complete loss of the original surface characteristics.

Other post-depositional processes

Many artefacts have fracture scars along their edges that, to various degrees, mimic fracture scars produced by tool use and can even mimic retouch. In addition, and rather surprisingly, I regularly observed large snap fractures on thin edges, but also on relatively large and thick flakes. In a few cases virtually all original edges are snapped. Such fracture damage results from sudden high load forces being applied to the artefacts approximately perpendicular to the ventral surface plane. It is thought that this may have occurred when the flint artefacts were deposited in the pits. Alternatively, this damage may have resulted from trampling following the original discard and prior to discard into the pits. This issue will be considered later.

Discussion

The relationship between artefact use and type

Because of the expense of microwear analysis, sample sizes tend to be relatively small. For this reason, it becomes a very valuable exercise to

Table 28 Association between tool use and occupational periods

Category	% Peterborough Ware	% Grooved Ware	Peterborough Ware	Grooved Ware	Unknown	Total	% All	% Use
Hide	18.2	62.5	2	10	1	13	11.3	44.8
Meat	27.3	18.8	3	3	1	7	6.1	24.1
Plant	9.1	0.0	1	0		1	0.9	3.4
Wood	27.3	12.5	3	2		5	4.3	17.2
Bone	9.1	0.0	1	0		1	0.9	3.4
Impact	9.1	6.3	1	1		2	1.7	6.9
Unused			10	19	1	30	26.1	
Undet.			15	39	2	56	48.7	
Total	100.1	100.1	36	74	5	115	100.0	99.8

determine if there are any specific relationships between tool types and use. Such associations can then be used to generalise more widely about economic activities at the site. Some types do appear to be associated with certain kinds of use (eg, notched/concave edges with wood shaving), but the low number of interpreted artefacts does not warrant conclusions to be drawn. The one tool form that does conform to use expectations in adequate numbers is the end scraper. Some 21 end scrapers were examined. Of these, nine display wear characteristics of hide scraping while the remainder are not interpretable. No other use is associated with the end scraper fronts. This relationship will be very important for understanding economic differences of the two cultural units that occupied the site of Upper Ninepence.

The association between pits (contexts) and artefact use

The sample size taken from each pit limits the investigation into the spatial organisation or contextual associations of activities at the site. For example, from pit 12 (context 13) two of the three artefacts microscopically examined were interpreted as having worked wood. Some pits do have adequate sample sizes and produced interesting results. The results for pit 10 (context 11) indicate use on a variety of materials, and it would appear very much that it contained debris from a domestic setting where maintenance as well as food processing activities had occurred. However, pits 22 and 154 (contexts 23 and 155, respectively), show very strong associations with hide working activities. At C23, of the 21 artefacts examined, all five with use identified were used for scraping hide. In addition, of the sixteen artefacts with use not identified, five are end scrapers. The same pattern occurs at context 155, where of the eighteen artefacts examined, hide working is identified on all four interpreted artefacts. One uninterpreted end scraper occurs here also. These two pits seem to contain lithic artefacts primarily coming from special activity (hide working) areas. It

has been suggested that, although they are rather specialised sub-assemblages, they still represent domestic (household) deposits.

Economic differences between Grooved Ware and Peterborough Ware contexts

Comparison of the microwear results between the two cultural units shows that there is a significant difference in economic activities (Table 28; Fig 62). Hide working is much more evident (62.5% of tool uses) during the Grooved Ware occupation phase than during the earlier Peterborough Ware occupation phase (18.2% of tool uses). In addition, it has been observed that while there is a broad spectrum of activities well represented during the Peterborough Ware phase, one gets the impression of a much more specialised economy during the Grooved Ware phase. The frequency distribution of end scrapers reported from the two sub-assemblages supports this hypothesis. A total of sixteen end scrapers are identified from the culturally identifiable pits. Fourteen end scrapers representing 28.6% of retouched tools are associated with Grooved Ware contexts while only two end scrapers (18.2% of retouched tools) are associated with Peterborough Ware contexts. This interpretation assumes that the tools from these pits are representative of the activities performed during each phase at the site, and that they have been redeposited in the pits from similar contexts.

Association of contexts with particular post-depositional processes

As previously mentioned, the microscopically examined artefacts display wear and fracture scars identified as having resulted from various post-depositional processes. Further study of these post-depositional modifications, particularly their intensity, interaction, sequence of formation, and context can provide valuable additional information regarding site for-

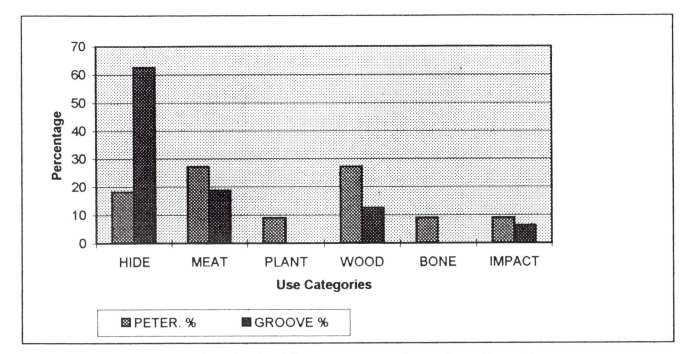

Figure 62   Distributions of tool use for the different occupational episodes at Upper Ninepence

Pit 22 (Context 23) Artefact Dorsal Ridge Rounding Values

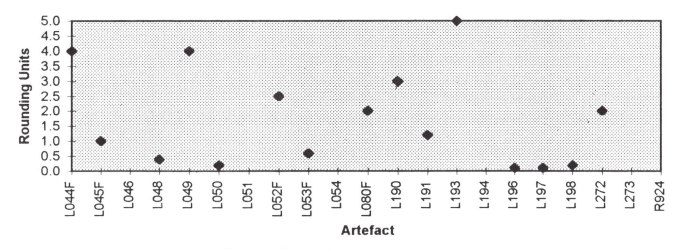

Figure 63   Pit 22: artefact dorsal ridge rounding values

mation processes. It should be understood from the outset that the strengths of the interpretations that follow are limited because non-random samples of artefacts from the pits were examined.

Among the post-depositional processes that have affected the artefacts found within the pits, non-polishing edge rounding occurs most often and alters surfaces more than any other form of wear. The intensity of this form of wear needs explaining. Of great importance is the need to determine if this wear formed principally while the artefacts were in the pits, or if it occurred prior to deposition. One way to test this is to examine the relationship of the intensity of this wear, as measured by dorsal ridge rounding, and the context of the artefacts. If the variability of ridge rounding within each pit is high

then we would expect that the principal cause of modification occurred prior to deposition, whereas if the within pit variation is low and there is much variation between pits, then we would expect that the wear is principally caused by mechanisms within each pit. Examination of the results of the analysis (see Table 29) indicates that there is substantial variation in dorsal ridge rounding within and between pits (Figs 63–64). This leads us to conclude that a major part of this wear is caused by processes prior to deposition in the pits.

The internal variability of artefact modification produced by post-depositional processes can best be explained as resulting principally from processes that preceded deposition in the pits. I suggest that this wear results from soil abrasion during tram-

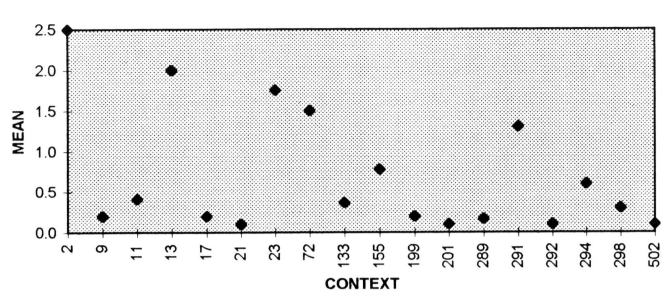

Figure 64 Mean dorsal ridge rounding values for various contexts

Table 29 Summary statistics for dorsal ridge rounding of artefacts for each context (pit)

Context	Mean ridge rounding	St dev ridge rounding	Count
2	2.5	2.12	2
9	0.2	0.1	4
11	0.4	0.7	12
13	2.0		1
17	0.2	0.1	4
21	0.1		1
23	1.8	1.6	15
72	1.5		1
133	0.4	0.6	6
155	0.8	1.3	13
199	0.2	0.1	4
201	0.1		1
289	0.2	0.1	3
291	1.3	1.0	2
292	0.1		1
294	0.6	0.3	2
298	0.3	0.1	2
502	0.1		1

pling. Such a situation is most likely to occur in the areas of domestic activities, such as around hearths within, and possibly in front of, dwellings. The scenario suggested is that some artefacts used in domestic and maintenance activities in this locality would be discarded or lost there, or possibly tossed into the hearth. Other stone artefacts, as part of compound tools, would be returned to the domestic work area for repair or replacement and would also be discarded here. Some of these artefacts would

undergo burning and develop thermal fractures or even heat spalls. Other artefacts would be trampled causing edge fracturing, snapping, plastic deformation and soil abrasion. The degree of damage would vary because the position where they were discarded would be differentially susceptible to trampling. Many artefacts can be expected to have received little modification. At various times the domestic area would be swept and along with ashes and other hearth debris the lithic artefacts would be discarded away from the occupation or, if available, tossed into a nearby disused pit. Ethnoarchaeologically, large pits such as these would be used for storage, and would normally be emptied during winter or early spring. This would suggest that such pits were used for dumping domestic debris during late winter or spring. The pits probably contained much organic material that decomposed and caused long term settling. One could also expect quite different geochemical conditions in the pits. Such conditions may have accelerated modification of the artefact surfaces, and led to increased rounding of edges and ridges.

Because the pit contents are derived from domestic settings, one would expect artefacts to represent domestic and tool maintenance activities. It would be unexpected to find a large proportion of flint debris, since the occupants would want to limit the amount of sharp flint flakes around the domestic area. When such debris is produced, much of it is likely to be discarded into the hearth. Most of the pits, when adequate artefact numbers are represented, have a variety of activities indicated by use-wear (eg pit 10). The two pits mentioned earlier do not display such a pattern, but instead indicate a single principal activity of hide working. This could be the result of sampling error or disposal of hide working materials from the domestic area. Although possible, it is unlikely to result from the direct discard from a hide working area because the burnt flints, including a thermal fractured end scraper, a refitted, heat-spalled end scraper, and a broken refitted end scraper, from these pits are left unexplained in such a model.

Conclusion

The lithic microwear analysis of the Upper Ninepence Neolithic site led to the interpretation of tool-use for only a few artefacts. Nonetheless, a number of tentative conclusions about the site can be drawn. It would appear that the pits were filled principally with domestic debris. There is no need to suggest ritual roles for the pits or that they were used for disposing the debris from special activity areas. Although an extremely small sample, the Peterborough Ware results would indicate a relatively balanced set of domestic and maintenance activities were being performed. The Grooved Ware sample would indicate that a more specialised set of activities were performed which centred around the processing of hides. This may relate to a more pastoral economy, seasonal differences of deposition (hide working would likely be an important indoor activity during winter), or one of many other explanations.

A brief description of wear characteristics

Wear caused by dry hide is characteristically matt in texture and relatively dull in appearance. The edges are generally very rounded, particularly when used for scraping when a sharp edge is not required for a functional tool. Fracture scars tend to be relatively scarce while striations tend to be common and consist of various forms including narrow, wide, and what Keeley (1981) describes as linear depressions, all of which will be aligned parallel to the direction the tool was used. Along the edge there will occur occasionally large circular pits of about 50 microns in diameter. These pits appear like small heat spall scars, and it has been suggested that they may be the result of localised high temperatures produced during use on dry hide which has a very high friction coefficient (Keeley 1981).

Tools used for cutting meat will have a very distinctive sheen along the faces near the edge and may have a rough texture, often with a bright line of surface polishing directly on the edge. Edge rounding is minimal. Fracture scars consist of point initiations and feather terminations, and are often slightly oblique rather than perpendicular to the edge. Striations are rare, but will be parallel or oblique to the edge.

Microwear characteristics of working siliceous soft plant fibre include a well rounded edge and extremely smooth and very bright surfaces near the edge. The one artefact with sickle gloss at the site is not brilliantly polished as would be expected. It appears that the surface texture has been slightly roughened, probably by post-depositional processes, which is the cause for the reduced brightness. The surface contains numerous small pits of which many are comet-shaped; a feature noted only of plant use and resulting from the direction of rubbing against the plant silica. There are also numerous striations that run parallel to the direction in which the tool was used.

Wear from wood is similar to that of plant fibre, but limited to the edge and its immediate adjoining surfaces. The polished surface does not lead to a levelling of the surface through abrasion but tends to abrade the higher surfaces so that brightly polished mounds are visible. The size of these mounds will vary according to the amount of use and the original topography and texture of the surface. Fracture scars are mostly point initiation and feather termination. Striations are infrequent. They are generally narrow and can be deep or very shallow. The working of bone produces wear that is bright, but very limited in its distribution with many small pits and a few narrow striations. There is a clear division between the polished surface and the unmodified surface.

Illustrated artefacts exhibiting microwear

Fig 60

1 L172 (context 11 – Peterborough phase). Flake used for slicing plant fibre.
2 L173 (context 11 – Peterborough phase). Flake used for boring and butchering.

3 L176 (context 11 – Peterborough phase). Retouched flake used for wood shaving.

4 R902 (context 11 – Peterborough phase). Flake used for dry hide scraping.

5 R904 (context 11 – Peterborough phase). Blade fragment used for butchering.

6 R905 (context 11 – Peterborough phase). Piercer used for boring hide.

7 L33 (context 13 – Peterborough phase). Retouched flake used for wood shaving.

8 L183 (context 17 – Peterborough phase). Denticulate used for dry hide working.

9 L188 (context 21 – Peterborough phase). Flake fragment used for butchering.

10 L48 (context 23 – Grooved Ware phase). End scraper used for dry hide scraping.

11 L76 (context 133 – Grooved Ware phase). End scraper used for dry hide scraping.

12 L202 (context 133 – Grooved Ware phase). Flake fragment used for butchering.

Fig 61

13 L65 (context 155 – Grooved Ware phase). End scraper used for dry hide scraping.

14 L66 (context 155 – Grooved Ware phase). End scraper used for dry hide scraping.

15 L83 (context 155 – Grooved Ware phase). End scraper used for fresh hide scraping.

16 L79 (context 155 – Grooved Ware phase). Splinter flake with impact fracture.

17 L147 (context 199 – Grooved Ware phase). Side scraper used for butchering.

18 L236 (context 199 – Grooved Ware phase). Blade used for wood whittling.

19 L133 (context 289 – Grooved Ware phase). Flake fragment used for butchering.

20 L241 (context 289 – Grooved Ware phase). Side scraper used for dry hide working.

21 L142 (context 291 – Grooved Ware phase. End scraper used for dry hide scraping.

22 L149 (context 292 – unphased). Blade used for meat cutting.

The organic residue analysis of the Neolithic pottery
Stephanie N Dudd and Richard P Evershed

Aims

The overall aim of the study was to determine the presence or absence of organic residues in the Walton sherds and to identify the nature of the lipid moieties observed. Conclusions were drawn based on comparisons with reference materials and data accumulated from investigations carried out on other assemblages in the Bristol laboratory. The objective was ultimately to suggest modes of vessel use and dietary habits, information which it is not possible to gain solely by making observations of vessel form and burial context etc. Furthermore, a new analytical approach was used to study degraded animal fats,

namely stable carbon isotope ratios, which was recorded for individual fatty acids and used to provide additional information concerning the origins of the fats.

Introduction

The study of amorphous organic residues is a relatively recent approach to pottery analysis in archaeology and is becoming increasingly incorporated into post excavation schemes. Organic residues occur in two forms, as surface deposits, occuring relatively infrequently, and organic matter absorbed into the vessel wall during use. While proteinaceous components have been detected in archaeological ceramics, the study of lipids, ie fats and waxes, is a significantly more developed area. Preservation of lipids, and indeed any other organic components, is facilitated by their entrapment in the clay matrix of the vessel. The hydrophobic nature of lipids further enhances their chances of survival, however in soils of high pH, or extreme conditions (such as cycles of wetting and drying), the potential for chemical degradation and dissolution is expected to be enhanced.

The study of the lipid components of organic residues has been improved by the development of modern analytical techniques including gas chromatography (GC) and gas chromatography-mass spectrometry (GC-MS). The use of high-temperature gas chromatography (HT-GC) in particular allows complex lipid extracts to be studied with only the minimum of wet chemical treatments, with the use of immobilised apolar stationary phases enabling very detailed compositional information to be obtained in a single analytical run (Evershed et al 1990). The identification of foodstuffs, or other material likely to have come into contact with the ancient vessels during their use, relies on matching the chemical compositions of the organic residues with those of contemporary plant or animal products likely to have been exploited in antiquity.

Commodities which have been identified from analyses of lipid components of potsherds, include *Brassica* vegetables (Evershed et al 1991), beeswax (Charters et al 1995), and numerous fatty residues including dairy products, adipose fats and tallow (Evershed et al 1992). In addition, the study of an adhesive used to repair an Ecton ware jar recovered from the Roman sediments of the river Nene provided the first unambiguous identification of birch bark tar from an archaeological site in the UK (Charters et al 1993a). However identification of specific commodities is not straightforward since autoxidation, hydrolysis, etc, alter the original composition of the lipid 'fingerprints' during use, and diagenetically during burial.

A further major area of investigation is concerned with the determination of vessel use based on organic residue data. Progress has been made in classifying vessel use by the identification of sites of accumulation of lipid in specific parts of vessels, for example base, body and rim (Charters *et al* 1993b). Interpretations drawn from chemical analyses of the archaeological ceramics are currently being tested in experimental simulations of vessel use, such as cooking (using replica vessels), followed by parallel organic residue analyses. Sherds from these replica vessels are being used in experiments to examine the effects of decay on the organic residue content (Evershed and Charters 1995).

Animal fats, although appearing to be quite severely degraded in ancient buried materials or artefacts, are relatively easily recognised by their characteristic distribution of mono-, di-, triacylglycerols and free fatty acids dominated by a high abundance of saturated C_{16} and C_{18} moieties. Animal fats are the most common residues which we encounter and hence the ability to obtain more detailed information, concerning in particular the species of animal from which the fats originated, would be invaluable, particularly where direct information from bone evidence is unavailable. Previous workers (Matter *et al* 1989; Matter 1992; Thornton *et al* 1970) have considered the distributions of saturated, monounsaturated and branched chain fatty acids, however, this approach is not well suited to the analysis of ancient fats which may have been exposed to chemical and/or microbial alteration during burial over millennia.

However, recent work (Evershed *et al* 1997) showed that distinctions could be drawn between degraded fat extracts from medieval lamps and dripping dishes on the basis of the positional isomers of the monounsaturated fatty acids. Further work by Mottram (1995) has shown that the natural variation in $^{13}C/^{12}C$ isotope ratios of animal fat components can been utilised to differentiate between fats, allowing distinctions to be made between a marine or terrestrial source, and further, to identify a ruminant or non-ruminant origin for the fat. De Niro and Epstein (1978) reported that the isotopic composition of the whole body of an animal reflects the isotopic composition of its diet, but that the animals studied were on average enriched in $d^{13}C$ by about 1‰ relative to the diet. Variation in the isotopic composition of animals is also thought to be determined by the isotopic fractionation which occurs during metabolism (Nier and Gulbransen, 1939). To date, however, limited isotopic work has been carried out which considers how species, sex and age of the animal affect the isotopic composition of fat and fundamental differences in the diet of different species of animals.

Samples

The sample set supplied by the Clwyd-Powys Archaeological Trust comprised seventeen sherds from Walton. Carbonised residues were found on seven sherds from the assemblage, namely, P1, P21, P28, P33, P38, P39 and P68. The residues were removed by gentle scraping with a scalpel and analysed separately from the absorbed residues.

Method

Solvent extraction of archaeological potsherds

Lipid analyses have been performed using our established protocol whereby approximately 2g samples were taken and their surfaces cleaned using a modelling drill to remove any contaminants (eg soil or finger lipids resulting from handling). The samples were then ground to a fine powder, accurately weighed, and a known amount (20mg) of internal standard (*n*-tetratriacontane) added. The lipids were extracted with a mixture of chloroform and methanol (2:1 v/v). Following separation from the ground potsherd, the solvent was evaporated to obtain the total lipid extract (TLE).

Preparation of trimethylsilyl derivatives

Portions of the TLE were derivatised using *N*, O-bis(trimethylsilyl) trifluoroacetamide (20μl; 60°C; 20mins) and analysed by gas chromatography (GC) and gas chromatography-mass spectometry (GC-MS).

Preparation of fatty acid methyl esters (FAME)

Selected TLEs have been saponified to break the ester linkages in the acylglycerols releasing the fatty carboxylic acids. Methanolic sodium hydroxide (5%v.v) was added to the TLE and heated at 70°C for one hour. After neutralisation, lipids were extracted into diethyl ether and the solvent reduced by rotary evaporation. FAME were prepared by reaction with BF_3-methanol (14% w/v; 2ml) at 70°C for one hour. The methyl esters were extracted with diethyl ether and the solvent removed under nitrogen. The FAME were redissolved into hexane for analysis by GC and gas chromatography-combustion-isotope ratio mass spectometry (GC-C-IRMS).

High temperature gas chromatography (HTGC)

The GC analyses were performed on a Hewlett Packard 5890 gas chromatograph coupled to an Opus V PC using HP Chemstation software which provided instrument control, data acquisition and post-run data processing facilities. Samples were introduced by on-column injection into a 15m × 0.32mm i.d. fused silica capillary, coated with HP1 stationary phase (immobilised dimethyl polysiloxane, 0.1μm film thickness). The temperature programme consisted of a two-minute isothermal hold at 50°C followed by a ramp from 50 to 350°C at

Table 30 Results of organic residue analyses on the Walton vessels

Pot no./ context	Analysts description	Pot ID	Sample weight (g)	Lipid content ($\mu g\ g^{-1}$)	Lipid components
P1(a)/13	Potsherd 5	P	2.17	120	FA ($C_{18:0}$ predominates over $C_{16:0}$; odd carbon number and branched chain moieties), mid-chain ketones, TAGs degraded
P1/13	Carbonised residue 5	P	0.08	Trace	
P1(b)/13	Potsherd 10	P	2.05	104	FFA ($C_{18:0}$ predominates over $C_{16:0}$; odd carbon number and branched chain moieties), mid-chain ketones, MAG, DAG, well preserved TAGs (C_{44}–C_{52})
P3/2	Potsherd 4	P	2.04	338	FFA (odd carbon number and branched chain moieties), MAG, DAG, TAG (C_{44}–C_{54})
P5/17	Potsherd 6	P	2.04	210	FA ($C_{18:0}$ predominates over $C_{16:0}$), mid-chain ketones, TAGs degraded
P10/7	Potsherd 11	P	2.00	13	FFA, DAG, TAG (C_{48}–C_{50})
P21/289	Potsherd 13	GW	2.19	Trace	
P21/289	Carbonised residue 13	GW	0.10	Trace	
P28/199	Potsherd 14	GW	2.57	0	
P28/199	Carbonised residue 14	GW	0.16	0	
P33/155	Potsherd 2	GW	2.09	13	MAG, DAG, TAG
P33/155	Carbonised residue 2	GW	0.27	434	FFA, MAG, DAG, TAG(C_{42}–C_{54}), TAGs well preserved
P34/155	Potsherd 7	GW	1.92	0	
P37/199/ 289/291	Potsherd 15	GW	2.56	Trace	
P38/155	Potsherd 16	GW	2.39	12	FFA, MAG, DAG, TAG (C_{44}–C_{54})
P38/155	Carbonised residue 16	GW	0.23	314	FFA (odd carbon number and branched chain moieties), MAG, DAG, TAG (C_{42}–C_{54})
P39/155	Potsherd 1	GW	2.05	7	Free fatty acids (FFA), diacylglycerols (DAG), triacylglycerols (TAG)
P39/155	Carbonised residue 1	GW	0.28	669	FFA (odd carbon number and branched chain moieties), monoacylglycerols (MAG), DAG, TAG (C_{40}–C_{52})
P48/199/289	Potsherd 17	GW	1.64	Trace	
P62/87	Potsherd 9	GW	0.71	Trace	Unresolved complex mixture (UCM), odd MAG
P65/294	Potsherd 8	GW	2.04	Trace	
P66/133	Potsherd 12	GW	2.00	118	FFA (odd carbon number and branched chain moieties), MAG, DAG, TAG (C_{48}–C_{54})
P68/133	Potsherd 3	GW	2.08	247	FFA (odd carbon number and branched chain moieties), DAG, TAG, (C_{48}–C_{54})
P68/133	Carbonised residue 3	GW	0.10	279	FFA, DAG, TAG (C_{48}–C_{54})

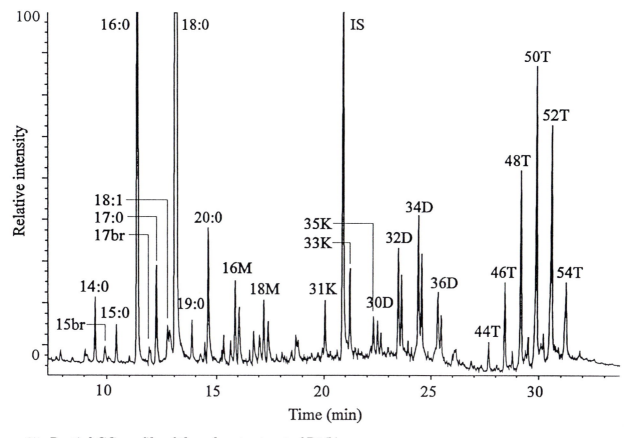

Figure 65   Partial GC profile of the solvent extract of P1(b).

The analysis was performed on a 15m × 0.32mm i.d. fused silica capillary column coated with a DB1 stationary phase (immobilised dimethyl polysiloxane, 0.32μm flm thickness). Following on-column injection at 50°C, the oven was programmed to remain at 50°C for 2 minutes and then to rise to 350°C at 10°C min $^{-1}$ and remain at 350°C for 10 minutes. Peak identities: 14:0–20:0, free fatty acids containing 14–20 carbons, respectivly, 14:0 = tetradecanoic acid ($C_{14:0}$); C15:0 = pentadecanoic acid ($C_{15:0}$); 16:0 = hexadecanoic acid ($C_{16:0}$); 17:0 = heptadecanoic acid ($C_{17:0}$); C18:0 = octadecanoic acid ($C_{18:0}$); 19:0 = nonadecanoic acid ($C_{19:0}$); 20:0 = eicosanoic acid ($C_{20:0}$); 15br = branched chain pentadecanoic acid ($C_{15:0}$br); 17br = branched chain heptadecanoic acid ($C_{17:0}$br); 16M, 18M, monoacylglycerols containing 16 and 18 acyl carbons, respectively, 16M = monopalmitoyl glycerol (C_{16}); 18M = monostearoyl glycerol (C_{18}). 31K–35K, mid-chain ketones, containing 31, 33 and 35 carbons, respectively, 31K = hentriacontan –16- one (C_{31}); 33K = tritriacontan-16-one (C_{33}); 35K = pentriacontan–18-one (C_{35}); IS, internal standard, n-tetratriacontane (C_{34}); 32D–36D, diacylglycerols, containing 32–36 acyl carbons, respectively, 32D = dipalmitoyl glycerol (C_{32}); 34D = palmitoylstearoyl glycerol (C_{34}); 36D = distearoyl glycerol (C_{36}); 44T–54T, triglycerols containing 44–54 acyl carbons, of various combinations of myristic ($C_{14:0}$), palmitic ($C_{16:0}$) and stearic ($C_{18:0}$) acids.

10°Cmin^{-1}. The temperature was then held at 350°C for ten minutes; hydrogen was used as a carrier gas. Flame ionisation detection was used to monitor the column effluent.

Gas chromatography-mass spectrometry (GC-MS)

GC-MS analyses were performed using a Finnigan 4500 quadrupole mass spectrometer directly coupled to a Carlo Erba 5160 Mega series gas chromatograph with on-column injection. Operating conditions were as follows: ion source, 170°C; emission current, 400mA and electron energy, 70 eV. The GC-MS interface was maintained at a temperature of 350°C. Spectra were recorded over the range m/z 50–750 every 1.5s. Data were acquired and processed using an INCOS data system. The GC operating conditions were the same as those described above except that helium was used as the carrier gas.

Gas chromatography-combustion-isotope ratio mass spectrometry (GC-C-IRMS)

Analyses were carried out using a Varian 3400 gas chromatograph attached to a Finnigan MAT Delta-S isotope ratio monitoring mass spectrometer via a modified Finnigan MAT combustion interface. The GC column used was a 25m × 0.32mm i.d. WCOT fused silica capillary coated with CP-Wax–52 CB stationary phase (polar polyethylene glycol, 0.2μm film thickness). The temperature programme consisted of three ramps from 40–150°C at 15°C min^{-1}, from 15–220°C at 4°C min^{-1} and from 220–240°C at 15°C min^{-1} remaining at 240°C for 15 minutes. Helium was used as the carrier gas. The Cu/Ni/Pt reactor temperature was maintained at 860°C and the mass spectrometer source pressure was 6×10^{-6} mbar. Samples were injected via a septum equipped temperature programmable injector (SPI). Carbon isotope ratios were expressed relative to the PDB standard (*Belemnitella americana*),

$$d^{13}C(‰) = 1000 [(R_{sample} - R_{standard})/R_{standard}],$$

where R is $^{13}C/^{12}C$.

Results

Gas chromatography analyses were performed for all samples. Preliminary observations have been made by reference to the GC profiles and identifications of individual lipids have been made on the basis of their retention times. Four samples were submitted to combined gas chromatography-mass spectrometry (GC-MS) for identification of components not recognised by GC alone. In addition eight extracts were submitted to analysis by GC-C-IRMS. The quantitative and qualitative data for all the samples studied are summarised in Table 30.

GC and GC-MS analyses

The total lipid extract of the fabric of P39 contained traces of palmitic ($C_{16:0}$) and stearic ($C_{18:0}$) acids, mono-, di- and triacylglycerols, together amounting to no more than 7 mg g^{-1} of lipid. The carbonised residue scraped from the surface of P39 contained 669 mg g^{-1} of lipid, which comprised a distinctive series of triacylglycerols ranging from C_{40} to C_{54} (denotes the total number of carbon atoms comprising the acyl groups in the acylglycerol). Diacylglycerols ranged in carbon number from C_{30} to C_{36}, monoacylglycerols ranged in carbon number from C_{14} to C_{18}, and free fatty carboxylic acids were present in the range $C_{14:0}$ to $C_{26:0}$, including odd carbon number ($C_{15:0}$ and $C_{17:0}$), monounsaturated C_{18} and branched chain components. This distribution of lipid components is consistent with the presence of degraded animal fats. The free fatty carboxylic acids, mono- and diacylglycerols are produced as a result of the hydrolysis of intact triacylglycerols either during use or burial (Fig 65). The extract from P33 and the associated carbonised residue contained 13 mg g^{-1} and 434 mg g^{-1} of lipid respectively, consisting of palmitic and stearic acids and di- and triacylglycerols. The analysis yielded a similar lipid distribution as seen in the carbonised residue of P39, however, the triacylglycerols appear less well preserved with only C_{44}–C_{52} components being identified. P3 contained 338 mg g^{-1} of degraded animal fat with analogous characteristics as seen in extracts from P39 and P33.

P68 yielded 247mg g^{-1} of lipid exhibiting a somewhat different lipid distribution to that seen above. The distributions of di- and triacylglycerols displayed narrower carbon number ranges, with only C_{32} to C_{36} diacylglycerols and C_{48} to C_{54} triacylglycerols being present. An analogous distribution of lipid components was found in the carbonised residue associated with P68, although the lipid was less well preserved than the other carbonised residues examined.

Lipid extracted from P1(a) appeared to be significantly more degraded than the residues discussed above. Although free fatty acids were detected, the residue lacked mono-, di- and triacylglycerols. The presence of a series of mid-chain ketones (also found in trace amounts in the carbonised residue associated with P1(a)) is indicative of high temperatures, probably greater than 400°C, being achieved during the use of the vessel in processing animal products. The degraded animal fat of P1(b) has the same characteristics as residues P39, P33 and P3 discussed previously. Again the presence of mid-chain ketones may indicate high heating during vessel use. Vessel P5 yielded 210 mg g^{-1} of lipid comprising free fatty acids and trace amounts of the same mid-chain ketones. The free fatty acids comprised $C_{16:0}$, $C_{17:0}$ and $C_{18:0}$ homologues with the latter being the most predominant component.

P10 and P66 contained 13 mg g^{-1} and 118 mg g^{-1} respectively, of degraded animal fat residues containing C_{32} to C_{36} diacylglycerols and C_{48} to C_{54} triacylglycerols, with a distribution analogous to that obtained from P68. The lipid extracts of the fabric from P38 and the carbonised residue from the same vessel contained 12 mg g^{-1} and 314 mg g^{-1} respectively, comprising C_{40} to C_{54} triacylglycerols, C_{30} to C_{36} diacylglycerols and $C_{14:0}$, $C_{16:0}$, $C_{17:0}$, $C_{18:1}$ and $C_{18:0}$ free fatty acids. The distributions are characteristic of degraded animal fats and analogous to those seen in P1, P3, P33 and P39.

There was no detectable lipid associated with P21 and only trace amounts of free fatty acids were revealed in the carbonised residue scraped from this sample. P28, the carbonised residue from P28 and P34, P37, P48, P62 and P65 all contained negligible amounts of lipid.

Stable isotope studies

Results of GC-C-IRMS analyses of individual fatty acids from the lipid extracts are plotted in Fig 66. The modern reference fats separate into two distinct clusters which correspond to ruminant and non-ruminant animals. The carbon isotope ratios of reference pig adipose fats fall within −25.59 ± 0.17 for $d^{13}C_{16:0}$ (‰) and −24.28 ± 0.15 for $d^{13}C_{18:0}$ (‰). In contrast, the isotope values for both cattle and lamb fat are significantly more depleted in ^{13}C. Hence, this criteria alone is not sufficient to distinguish unambiguously between fats from different species of ruminant animals, although the separation of the ruminant and non-ruminant animals is significant.

Extracts from five potsherds and two carbonised residues were selected for GC-C-IRMS analysis, since these extracts contained the quantities of lipid required for stable isotope analysis. The results showed that a clear distinction could be drawn between the extracts from P66 and P68 and those of P1(b), P3 and P5. The values obtained for extracts

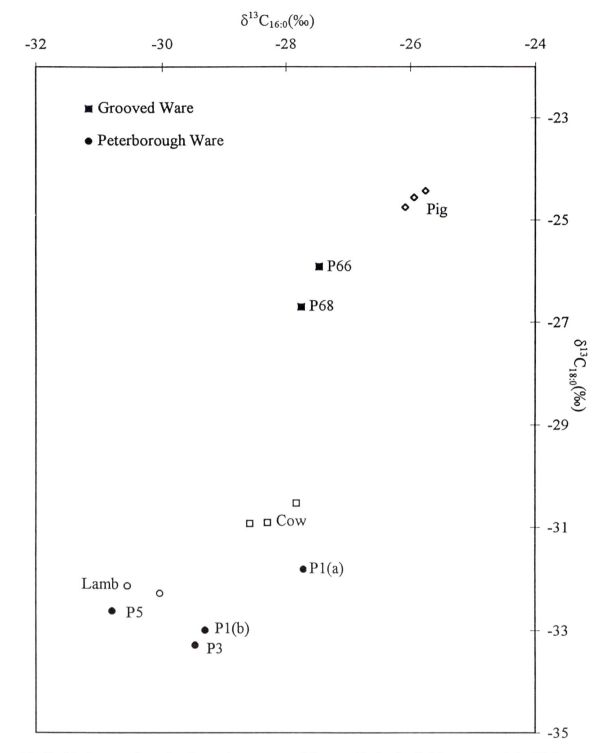

Figure 66 Stable isotope data for the major saturated fatty acids in the lipid extracts of the Walton vessels (plotted with data from modern reference fats)

from P66 and P68 indicate a non-ruminant origin such as pig, while those for P3, P5 and P1(b), appear to derive from ruminant animals, tending to plot closer to the reference lamb fat and cattle fat. The values obtained for the carbonised residues are somewhat more depleted in ^{13}C compared with the absorbed lipids from the same vessels (Table 31). One explanation for this is that lipid components of the carbonised residues adhering to the exterior of the vessel are more susceptible to microbial degradation

and/or alteration than lipid which has been entrapped in the porous microstructure of the pot wall.

It is interesting to note that P66 and P68, containing degraded lipids which are isotopically similar to those of the non-ruminant animals, both originate from the same site context (113) and exhibit very similar distributions of triacylglycerol components. Furthermore, extracts from P1(b), P3 and P5, which are isotopically similar to the ruminant fats, differ from P66 and P68 in their triacylglycerol distribu-

Table 31 Listing of $d^{13}C$ measurements (corrected) for both modern and ancient animal fats

Sample	$d^{13}C_{16:0}$ (‰)	$d^{13}C_{18:0}$ (‰)
Standard animal fats		
Cow (i)	−28.24	−30.63
Cow (ii)	−27.49	−30.23
Cow (iii)	−27.96	−30.61
Lamb (i)	−30.23	−31.85
Lamb (ii)	−29.72	−31.99
Ewe	−29.01	−30.76
Pig (i)	−25.43	−24.13
Pig (ii)	−25.74	−24.45
Pig (iii)	−25.60	−24.26
Ancient fats from potsherds		
Carbonised residue 1 (P39)	−30.18	−35.98
Carbonised residue 16 (P38)	−28.83	−33.82
Potsherd 3 (P68)	−27.42	−26.41
Potsherd 4 (P3)	−29.14	−32.99
Potsherd 5 (P1)	−27.38	−31.52
Potsherd 6 (P5)	−30.47	−31.20
Potsherd 10 (P1)	−28.98	−32.70
Potsherd 12 (P66)	−27.11	−25.62

tions. The wider carbon number envelope they exhibit derives from the presence of the shorter chain $C_{14:0}$ acyl moiety and is analogous to that seen in the intact triacylglycerols of ruminant fats. The extracts of P39, P33, P34 and P38, all from context 155, exhibit analogous characteristics to the reference ruminant fats. Hence, the distributional data supports the evidence obtained from the isotopic analyses.

Discussion

Lipid residues were recovered from ten of the seventeen potsherds examined. All the lipids were identified as degraded animal fats, characterised by the occurrence of acyl lipids, including free fatty acids, mono-, di- and triacylglycerols. The extent of degradation of the original animal fat differed between sherds. The extracts of P1(a) and P5 appeared to be the most severely degraded where free fatty acids predominated and intact acyl lipids were lacking. In contrast, triacylglycerols were relatively well preserved in P1(b), P3 and P68.

Saturated long-chain ketones with carbon numbers ranging from 31 to 35 were identified in extracts from three of the potsherds: P1(a), P1(b) and P5. The origin of long-chain ketones in organic residues has

recently been assigned to a condensation reaction involving long-chain carboxylic acids from animal fats (Evershed *et al* 1995). The reaction is catalysed by minerals in the pot fabric and occurs at temperatures in excess of 300°C. Thus the ketones are probably formed in the pot wall during heating either while cooking or through catastrophic failure of vessels.

The presence of carbonised residues associated with P21 and P28 would suggest that at some stage these vessels had been used for food preparation. However, the absence of lipid components in both the carbonised residues and pot walls indicates that either the commodities being processed contained little lipid or the burial conditions were not conducive to their survival. Since there are no carbonised residues associated with P65 and P37 and negligible absorbed residues in the sherds analysed, these pots may have had uses other than for cooking, for example as storage containers for grain, water, and so on.

P1(a) and P1(b) were analysed separately and subsequently found to have originated from the same vessel. The isotopic data is similar for extracts from the two sherds (−27.7 ‰ and −29.3 ‰ for $C_{16:0}$ and −31.8 ‰ and −33.0 ‰ for $C_{18:0}$, for P1(a) and P1(b) respectively) however, the distribution of lipid components is different. P1(a) contains no intact triacylglycerols, compared to P1(b) which contains an homologous series of triacylglycerols, and other acylglycerols, characteristic of degraded animal fat. It is not completely clear from which point on the vessel profile the two sherds originate. However, the state of preservation of the lipid in the two sherds may be significant in this respect. For instance, the extract from P1(a) contains only free fatty acids and mid-chain ketones, which appear to be characteristic of residues extracted from sherds that have experienced high heating, leading to thermal degradation of lipid. Intuitively we would expect sherds in the region of the vessel in direct contact with a fire to be most likely to exhibit evidence of thermally altered lipids. The presence of mid-chain ketones in these sherds is specific evidence for the vessel having been subjected to high temperatures (>400°C).

Substantial amounts of lipid absorbed in several of the Walton potsherds, including particularly P68, P4 and P1(b) (>210 mg g^{-1}) is direct evidence to suggest their use as cooking pots, since the action of heat is especially conducive to the absorption of lipid into the pot wall, compared with the use of vessels to store dry foodstuffs.

Conclusions

The preservation of organic material is remarkable considering the age of the vessels.

The measurement of $^{12}C/^{13}C$ isotope ratios for individual components for the first time in prehistoric pottery has been shown to be a particularly robust means of distinguishing between ruminant

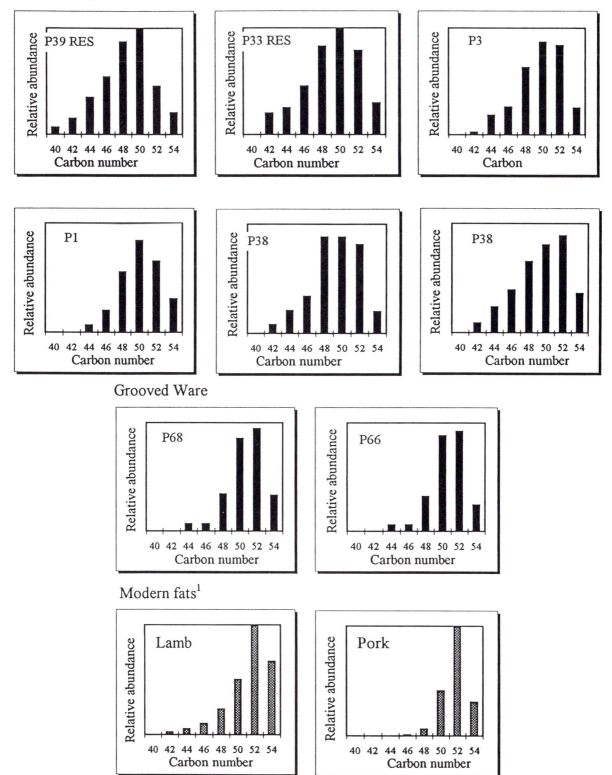

Figure 67 Distribution of intact triacylglycerols in Walton extracts. Triacylglycerol distributions in degraded modern reference fats are shown for comparison.

[1] Differences between triacylglycerol distributions in the modern and ancient fats are due to higher relative abundances of the $C_{18:1}$ component in the modern fats which are seen to be much depleted in the ancient fats

and non-ruminant fats. The isotopic data are supported by the corresponding triacylglycerol compositions of the remnant fats.

The results indicate that probably both pigs and sheep and/or cattle constituted the major part of the diet and no evidence was obtained to suggest that leafy vegetables had been processed in the vessels. The lack of leaf wax components is unlikely to result from their preferential degradation during burial since they are relatively much more resistant to degradation than acyl lipid such as the triacylglycerols that comprise animal fats.

There is little to suggest mixing of animal fats from ruminant and non-ruminant sources in the Walton vessels (Fig 67).

Thin section analysis of the pottery from Upper Ninepence
D Jenkins and J Williams

Introduction

Thirteen pottery sherds and one soil sediment from the Walton Basin were received for petrographic examination. The analysis of these samples aimed to characterise the fabric and mineralogical composition of the sherds, to establish the petrography of the coarse sand fraction in the sediment sample and to consider the results in terms of both grouping evident amongst the sherds, and also of provenance of the materials used in fabricating the pottery.

Preparation and analysis of thin sections

Thin sections of pottery sherds were prepared using the standard procedures developed at the University of Wales, Bangor. The size and colour of the selected sherds (c 25 × 20mm) were recorded, and the samples then halved, and one half ignited overnight at 500°C. The two halves were then impregnated side-by-side with a polystyrene resin system (Crystic + 1.25% Q17447 catalyst) diluted 1:1 with acetone to facilitate penetration. A slice (c 5mm thick) was cut from the impregnated block, and one side polished with 6–1μm diamond paste, and bonded to a glass slide. Excess sherd material (ie >1mm) was removed using a Logitech CS10 saw and the sample ground to 30μm thickness using a Logitech LP3 Lapping machine. This was again polished with diamond paste on a Kent polisher, and a cover slip attached with Epotek resin to provide adjacent thin-sections of the sherd both in its original and re-oxidised condition. The former preserved organic components in the sherd, whilst the latter clarified any dark/opaque unoxidised cores. It was found that such controlled re-oxidation greatly facilitates the identification of matrix components and, in particular, of grog.

Reference samples were also prepared from a local sediment (W296). The 2.0–0.6mm fraction was impregnated with resin and thin-sectioned to provide

an indication of the petrography of 'clast' material that would have been available locally. Similarly, the 'heavy mineral' fraction (ie SG > 2.95) of the fine sand (200–63m) was separated by centrifugation in tetrabromoethane and analysed to indicate which of the 'grains' identified in the sherds could be accounted for locally.

The composition (vol %) of the pottery sections was established quantitatively in terms of matrix, grains, grog, voids, and clasts, using a Swift Automatic Point Counter. The distinction between matrix, grains and clasts tends to be arbitrary but the guidelines used were <0.06mm for the matrix (ie silt + clay), 0.06–0.2mm for the grains (ie fine sand), and >0.2mm for the clasts which were further subdivided by their petrology. A visual assessment of matrix texture, orientation, grain mineralogy and the presence of bioliths was also recorded. These data form the basis for the quantitative assessments which lead to the classification and interpretation of the pottery fabrics.

Analytical results

Matrix

Matrix texture is dependent on the particle size distribution in the clay body and was assessed visually: degree of clay mineral orientation is also manifested in 'aggregate birefringence' which has been assessed as 'absent' (0), 'weak' (1), 'moderate' (2), 'strong' (3), or 'very strong' (4). Three matrices are evident:

(i) a silt-rich matrix is characterised by abundant quartz and felspar, occasional muscovite, and rare biotite. In the re-oxidised fabrics the clay fraction shows a moderately strong aggregate birefringence, whilst this is masked in the original unoxidised samples. Weakly variegated textural bands are present in P48 only.

(ii) a clay-rich matrix in which the birefringence of the clay minerals is very strong; parts remarkably producing first order interference colours (P1). Sparse detrital silt-sized quartz/felspar and rare muscovite/biotite are present.

(iii) a matrix characterised by its voids (P62, see below).

Grains

Although a silt fraction is common to abundant in most of the fabrics examined, fine sand grains (>60 – <200μm) are sparse. In ten fabrics such grains account for less than 5.5% of the total volumetric constituents, whilst in the remaining three fabrics (P11, P37, P76) they vary between 7.6% to 8.6%. The grains replicate the mineralogy of the silt fraction and consist of angular/sub-angular quartz/felspar and muscovite/biotite flakes. Less common minerals

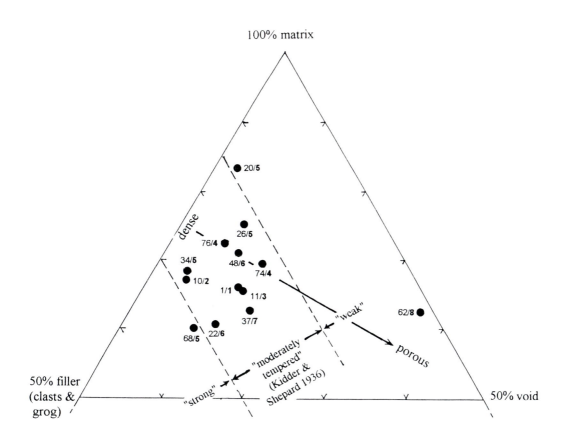

Triangular plot of fabric components

Figure 68 Triangular plot of fabric components in the pottery from Upper Ninepence

include angular plagioclase, clinopyroxene, amphibole, clinozoisite, and garnet. The last four heavy minerals were also recorded in the sediment sample (W296), together with zircon, tourmaline, rutile and (?) anatase.

Voids

Many voids are by-products of manufacture but others represent original components lost from the matrix. Voids may also be artefacts of slide preparation, and where such cases can be identified the resultant voids have not been included in the analytical data. In the fabrics examined, with one exception, the void contents vary from 2.8–12.4% (Fig 68). Inclusions are consistently margined by a void whilst small amorphous cavities with sharply defined outlines may occur in the matrix. Such features may reflect the poor wedging and preparation of the raw materials, and shrinkage strain caused by dehydration during firing.

In contrast, the high void count of 35.8% in P62 has resulted from the removal of a constituent from the matrix. The voids have distinctive shapes, some being long and narrow (0.1–2.0mm), but most are angular, oblate forms (0.5–0.8mm wide) with straight and/or stepped edges: the former are consistent with shell fragments and the latter with calcite

cleavage fragments. This very high void content results in a highly porous fabric with a distinctive vesicular ('corky') appearance.

Grog

Grog is especially revealing in that it mirrors the range of redundant pottery fabrics that were reused. However, it does not have the same sensitivity as rock clasts for defining potential provenance. Grog particles are present in all the fabrics examined, occurring as a minor component (0.8–5.0%) in three fabrics (P26, P37, P62), as a common component (5–12%) in six fabrics, and as an abundant component (>20%) in four fabrics (P1, P10, P22, P48). Particles can generally be identified by their angularity and vary in size from <0.5mm to 2mm. Most contrast with their host fabrics by colour, texture and birefringence, but some tend to merge leading to the underestimation of content. Two (eg P20), and rarely, three generations of grog may be identified within a single section. One grog particle in P20 contains an inclusion that may represent a sliver of burnt bone. Grog particles with the following matrix characteristics can be identified:

(i) a silt-rich matrix of similar composition to that of the host sherd

(ii) a clay-rich fabric forming light orange to reddish-brown grog particles. The fabric is slightly vesicular due to small (20μm) linear voids, and has not been encountered in the vessels analysed

(iii) vesicular grog showing the same void outlines as in sherd P62 (see above, ie P10)

(iv) a dark brown fabric not identified in the sherd samples which is characterised by sharply defined textural zones and dark/light banding. There are abundant triangular and elongated rectangular voids, many containing dark carbonaceous matter, suggesting removal of an organic component at the time of firing of the original vessel

(v) a vesicular grog characterised by regular circular voids in a dark coloured matrix. This type is again not present in the sherds studied (P20 & P34)

Rock clast fragments

Clasts of identifiable rocks are present in all the fabrics, with the exception of the vesicular vessel P62 where the original clast constituent has been lost. Content varies from very low (0.8%–5.0%), to moderate (5.0%–10%) to abundant (10%–22%). The majority of clasts are characterised by their angularity and the freshness of fracture, and in some fabrics very large (>2mm) clasts are present at the expense of smaller fragments and detached mineral grains, giving rise to a low grain content. The size of the larger fragments raises the question of representativeness in quantitative analysis.

The rock types identified fall into sedimentary, metamorphic and igneous groups.

Sedimentary rock clasts include the following types:

(i) a micaceous quartzose siltstone, occasionally showing foliation. Clasts vary from sub-angular to sub-rounded, and some are heavily masked with iron oxide

(ii) sub-angular clasts of a fine textured argillite

(iii) a distinctive coarse lithic sandstone (eg P1) consisting of rounded/sub-angular sand grains of monocrystalline and polycrystalline quartz, often displaying undulose extinction, altered orthoclase and plagioclase, and lithic clasts including a pseudomorphed mafic igneous rock(?), rhyolite and rhyolitic tuff (eg P1) quartz/muscovite schist, and a quartz siltstone with a birefringent matrix. There is an unidentified opaque cement associated with granular sphene(?)

(iv) an even textured arenite composed of well sorted, rounded quartz grains

Metamorphic rock clasts comprise angular fragments of a quartzite/mica schist.

Igneous rock clasts include the following types:

(i) a highly altered, coarse mafic igneous rock consisting of fibrous amphibole pseudomorphs of pyroxene phenocrysts, slightly pleochroic (dark green to greenish-yellow), and chloritised felspar (plagioclase?)

(ii) an ill-defined mafic igneous rock (dolerite?) represented by only two small clasts, one of which contains small granular olivine crystals showing slight marginal alteration and surrounded by fresh felspar, the second containing a pseudo-morphed pyroxene(?) crystal in direct association with epidotised felspar

(iii) a felted dolerite

Discussion

Although the various fabrics recognised are individually distinctive, it is difficult to define groups since, with one notable exception, they belong to a continuum of clast/grog constituents and also by common matrix characteristics. Four principal clast/grog constituents are recognised – grog, siltstone, lithic sandstone and mafic igneous rock fragments. Individually, grog-dominated (P26, P34, P37, P76), clast-dominated (P1, P10, P22, P48) and mixed assemblage (P11, P20, P68, P74) fabrics occur, but the variable distribution of the lithic constituents within these fabrics may reflect individual choice by the potter, or alternatively may reflect poor reproducibility where large clast fragments occur in the thin sections. Although poorly distinguishable, the thin-sections will be discussed under these headings.

Grog dominated fabrics

Grog has been identified in all the fabrics examined, but its contribution varies from <1.0 to four sherds (P26, P34, P37, P76) where it is >15%. In P26 all the particles are of similar composition to the host fabric, but in P37 and P76 the fragments are more heterogeneous in matrix composition, although in the latter two, banding and textural gradations in the matrix makes it difficult to record grog quantitatively and so the values may be mis-represented. Particles containing more than one generation of grog are common in all the sections. Rare small clasts of a fine siltstone are also present and one such clast is contained in a grog fragment; mafic igneous clasts are present in P34.

Clast dominated fabrics

These fabrics contain a clast component of >15% whilst grog is of secondary importance, varying from insignificant (P1, 0.8%) to common (P10, 8.4%). Four sherds are involved but each have differing clast petrologies:

Siltstone rich (P48) – abundant large (1–4mm) angular clasts of siltstone; common large (4mm) angular fragments of lithic sandstone, and rare small (0.9mm) angular gabbro clasts.

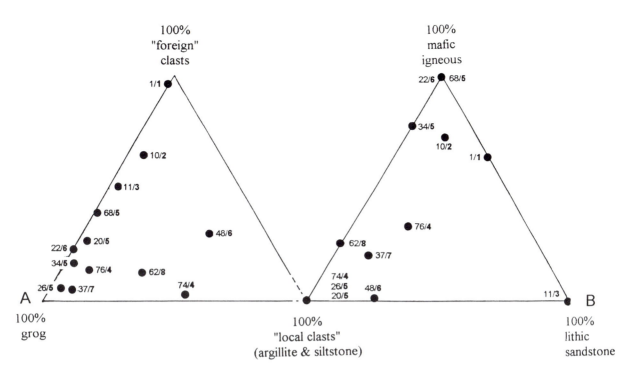

Plot of filler composition   **Plot of clast composition**

Figure 69   Plot of A – filler composition, and B – clast composition in the pottery from Upper Ninepence

Gabbro rich (P10) – the same rock types appear but in reverse order of frequency: abundant large (1–5mm) clasts of gabbro, common smaller (0.5–2.0mm) sub-angular/sub-rounded fragments of siltstone, but only rare small (0.5–1.5mm) angular clasts of lithic sandstone. Clasts belonging to two other rock types can be identified, angular fragments of quartzite/mica schist, and medium-sized (2–3mm) angular fragments of a fine grained, intergranular, amphibolitised dolerite.

Gabbro dominated fabric (P22) – abundant fragments (0.2–3.0mm) of gabbro and derived angular fragments, together with rare, small (0.4mm), sub-rounded clasts of siltstone.

Gabbro / lithic sandstone dominated fabric (P1) – angular clasts of lithic sandstone are abundant but the section is dominated by a single large (6mm) gabbro fragment. The lithic sandstone clasts contain siltstone and possibly also orthoquartzite clasts. Angular clasts of quartzite/mica schist (and rhyolite ?) might also derive from the lithic sandstone although their relatively large size (2mm) could also imply a primary origin.

Mixed assemblage fabrics

These (P20, P68) comprise fabrics with the most varied grog types present, and the most varied assemblage of rock clasts – detached quartz/felspar mono/poly-minerallic clasts (P20), mafic igneous

fragments (P68), argillite/siltstone (P74), and lithic sandstone (P11).

Vesicular fabric

This unique fabric type is represented by a single example (P62). It has been noted previously that in its original condition the fabric would have contained a calcite/shell filler that has been totally removed by dissolution subsequent to the burial of the pot. Only one small rock clast <0.25mm can be identified and this belongs to the siltstone group.

Conclusion

The results of this petrographic analysis of thirteen sherds from Walton can be interpreted in terms of both the provenance of the materials used in their manufacture and also in terms of affinities as a group and in relation to their suggested typology.

Provenance

The clasts recognised have been described above and include argillites, lithic sandstone, dolerite/gabbro and rare schists. Of these, the argillite is local to the Walton Basin (Silurian/Ludlovian), as is evident from its dominance in the 2–0.6mm fraction of the sediment sample (W296). There are also potential sources nearby for the mafic igneous rocks

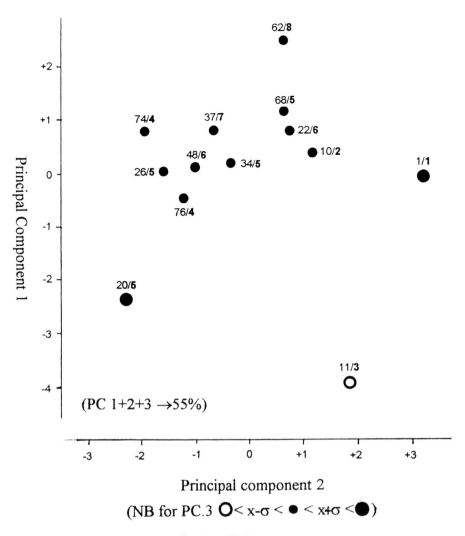

Figure 70 Plot of principal components 1 and 2 for all data

(dolerite/gabbro) in the Ordovician inlier some 10km to the west at Llandrindod, and also in the Old Radnor inlier a few kilometres to the south-east (Pocock and Whitehead 1953): material from the former might have been transported to the site by glacial action, as suggested by traces in the sediment sample, but that from the latter would not have been available on site. It is possible that the lithic sandstone could also derive from the Longmyndian rocks exposed at Old Radnor, but there are no immediate sources for the schistose rocks, the nearest possible being the Precambrian of the Wrekin, Malverns or Rushton, (Malvernian/Uriconian), unless – as suggested above – they were originally components of the secondary lithic sandstone.

In contrast, the analytical data relating to the matrix does not give any indication of sources other than the local material, and the absence of bioliths implies a sterile source deposit, such as glacial till or periglacial head, rather than a biologically active soil or fluvial/lacustrine sediment.

It is therefore concluded that the dominant clast materials used in the manufacture of the pots examined probably were derived from nearby sources (<10km); however, sources for the schist (Peterborough Ware vessels P1, P10 and ?P20) lie farther afield

(c 50km) unless present (together with rhyolites) in secondary rocks such as the lithic sandstone. The material for the matrices could be accounted for locally. With a detailed comparative study of the local petrography (Old Radnor, Llandrindod) it might be possible to identify the sources for the distinctive gabbro and lithic sandstone with greater precision.

Grouping

Sherds may be grouped by their fabric and their clast petrography, or by other microscopic features, as well as by their 'macro' typology. The fabric of the thirteen sherds can be presented in general terms through the proportions of matrix (including grains), filler (ie clasts and grog) and voids (Fig 68) to reflect the mode of manufacture. From this it can be seen that eleven of the sherds form a coherent group of 'moderately tempered' material (Kidder and Shepard 1936) which is also moderately porous. The two exceptions are the Fengate Ware vessel P20, which is slightly denser and sparse in filler, and in particular the Grooved Ware pot P62, which is distinctively 'corky' due to the dissolution of calcite material. Otherwise the sherds show similar silt/clay-rich fabrics, but with the exception of P1 whose matrix displays a remarkably strong aggregate birefringence. The data on clast composition can be presented in various combinations. Figure 69a, for example, shows the proportions of grog, argillite/siltstone (ie local), and lithic sandstone/mafic igneous (ie 'foreign') clasts: Fig 69b shows the proportions of argillites/siltstones, lithic sandstones and mafic igneous clasts where P11, rich in lithic sandstone, now stands apart. Alternatively, all the data can be considered through Principal Component Analysis, for which a plot of the first two components is presented in Figure 70.

As pointed out in the earlier discussion, however, no obvious groupings are evident, since all the components are present together in varying proportions in certain sherds. It is therefore concluded that this is a relatively coherent group of sherds in terms of fabric and composition which could have been manufactured from material to be found within 10–50km of Walton. Some variations are evident, in particular in the 'corky fabric' of P62, but this still shows compositional affinities with the remaining sherds.

Analysis of a glass bead from Hindwell Ash and its archaeological interpretation
J Henderson

Introduction

The glass bead (see Fig 49 no 3) measures 7mm in diameter overall with a near-central perforation measuring 2.5mm in diameter. The bead is circular with a slightly flattened section up to 4mm thick. There are traces of wear on both sides indicating that the bead has been strung as one of a group. The glass is a uniform royal blue in colour and the surfaces appear to be slightly pitted with small ?air bubbles.

Scientific analysis of glass and beads can provide a range of technological and archaeological information. It can provide the basis for inferring the kinds of raw materials used, including the primary raw materials and added colourants. Sometimes it is also possible to infer when the glass was made – independently of the dating provided by archaeological contexts – because the chemical composition of ancient glass changed in distinct ways over time; this can be due to changes both in the primary raw materials used, such as sand and alkalies, and also in the colourants and opacifiers with their associated trace impurities. Quite why these changes in glass technology occurred is extremely interesting and several possible reasons for the changes can be suggested but will not detain us here.

Technique of analysis

The translucent blue Hindwell Ash bead was chemically analysed using electron probe microanalysis. This involved the removal of a 1mm sample from the

Table 32: Electron probe microanalysis of the Hindwell Ash glass bead (results are expressed as weight percent of the oxide)

Na_2O	16.4
MgO	0.6
Al_2O_3	2.0
SiO_2	66.8
P_2O_5	0.1
SO_3	0.2
Cl	1.3
K_2O	0.5
CaO	9.2
TiO_2	ND
Cr_2O_3	ND
MnO	ND
Fe_2O_3	1.0
CoO	0.06
NiO	ND
CuO	0.2
ZnO	ND
As_2O_3	ND
SnO_2	ND
Sb_2O_3	0.7
BaO	0.1
PbO	3.4

1 ND = not detected, 2 typical levels of detection in p.p.m. (95.5% probability level) are: Na_2O (760), K_2O (250), CaO (170), Fe_2O_3 (640), CuO (1200), PbO (200).

bead which was mounted in a block of epoxy resin, polished and coated with a thin carbon film to avoid deflection and distortion of the electron beam. The system was calibrated using Corning and National Science Foundation glass standards and chemically analysed using a Cambridge M9 electron microprobe with two wavelength dispersive spectrometers and a defocused electron beam of 80 microns. The results were corrected using a ZAF program. The relative analytical accuracy of the system under the conditions employed was: 4% for soda, 1% for silica, 3% for potassium oxide, 5% for calcium oxide and 2% for lead oxide. For minor elements these levels of accuracy were also acceptable: 2% for magnesia, 1% for aluminia, 3% for phosphorus pentoxide, 10% for ferric oxide and 20% for cupric oxide. A fuller description on the analytical conditions employed is published elsewhere (Henderson 1988).

Analytical results (see Table 32)

The glass bead is of a soda (Na_2O)-lime (CaO)-silica (SiO_2) composition, with 16.4% soda, 9.2% calcium oxide ('lime') and 66.8% silica. It also contains low levels of magnesia (MgO) and potassium oxide (K_2O) both of which are indicators of the kind of alkali used. The bead also contains 3.4% lead oxide (PbO) and a significant impurity (0.7%) of antimony trioxide. The glass is coloured by 0.06% cobalt oxide which was probably originally associated mineralogically with part of the 1.0% ferric oxide (Fe_2O_3) and 0.2% cupric oxide detected in the glass. The antimony oxide detected may also partly have been introduced as a cobalt mineral impurity (Henderson 1985); no manganese oxide was detected. Levels of aluminia (Al_2O_3) at 2.0%, phosphorus pentoxide (P_2O_5) at 0.1%, sulphur trioxide (SO_3) at 0.2% and chlorine (Cl) at 1.3% normally found in soda-lime glass were detected.

Technological inferences

Soda-lime-silica glass was some of the earliest made by man, dating back to the mid 3rd millennium BC. However, during various periods the source of the soda changed, leading to a corresponding change in the associated impurity patterns in the glass, so that it becomes possible to infer a period of production from this alone (Henderson 1995). The Hindwell Ash bead contains low magnesia and potassium oxide levels which suggests that a mineral (as opposed to plant ash) source of alkali was used in its manufacture. The most likely candidate for this is a mineral evaporate called natron, a sodium sesquicarbonate. This is thought to have derived from the Wadi el-Natrun in Egypt (Turner 1956; Henderson 1985), though it is surprising that there is little evidence for any other archaeological links with Egypt during the Bronze and Iron Ages in Europe, when the kind of glass thought to have been made using natron predominated. Ultimately it may be necessary to look to the Classical world to provide a primary point of contact for the exploitation of natron sources in Egypt which was then incorporated in the fused glass used in Europe. Given the consistent levels and types of impurities detected in ancient glasses which are associated with natron, the only, though less likely, interpretation is that another alkali source with the same impurities was used.

The source of silica in the Hindwell Ash bead is likely to have been sand. This can be suggested on the basis of the level of aluminium oxide (Al_2O_3) of 2.0% which was probably introduced into the sand as an impurity (Henderson 1985, 271). The other oxide which was probably introduced with the sand is lime (CaO) as shell fragments. Although the level in the bead is slightly higher than normally detected in soda-lime glass, it is unlikely that dolomite, for example, would have been used as an alternative calcium oxide source in this instance. The composition of beach sand is so variable and constantly changing, that it is impossible to suggest where it would have derived from.

The blue colour of the glass is due to 0.06% cobalt oxide in the presence of 1.0% ferric oxide and 0.2%

cupric oxide: both oxides can potentially colour glass independently given the appropriate chemical environments. Cobalt oxide is the most powerful transition metal colourant and the level detected is typical for a soda-lime glass, producing a marked cobalt blue colour. The technologically interesting thing about the use of cobalt oxide in ancient glasses is that it is possible to suggest the type of cobalt-bearing mineral used in the glass by using the impurities associated with cobalt (Henderson 1985, 278–81). In this case the impurities are iron, copper and antimony (some of the iron may have been introduced in the sand). It is possible therefore that the cobalt was of the triantite ore type (Henderson 1985, 280). Another common cobalt mineral type is rich in manganese and/ or arsenic and neither of these was detected.

A further interesting point can be adduced from the electron probe results about colour, or in this case, potentially a lack of it. Significantly, no manganese oxide was detected in the bead. This suggests that the glass used to make the bead was manufactured before a change in glass technology which occurred in the 2nd century BC when manganese oxide was first introduced in order to decolourise a base glass. The appearance of the glass could then be modified with the addition of colourants and opacifiers. From c 6th century BC antimony oxide was used for decolourising glass, a compound which was largely replaced as a decolouriser by manganese oxide in the 2nd century BC. Although we have suggested that the antimony trioxide was associated with the cobalt used as a colourant, a second and more likely explanation for its presence at rather high levels, is that it was used as a decolouriser in the glass to which a cobalt-rich colourant was added.

Archaeological results

Given that globular glass beads are difficult to date according to their shape and technique of manufacture, chemical analysis of a sample of the glass was carried out in order to attempt to place it in a technological tradition. The most diagnostic chemical characteristics of the glass bead, in terms of a possible date, is the lack of manganese oxide detected and the presence of a relatively high level of antimony trioxide. These chemical characteristics suggest that the glass dates to some time before the 2nd century BC (Henderson and Warren 1983; Henderson 1989), and quite possibly after the 6th century BC. Glass found in Europe which dates to between c 1000 BC and the 7th century BC generally has a distinctly different chemical composition (Braun 1983; Henderson 1989), so we can be fairly confident here that an early to middle Iron Age date for the bead is appropriate.

4 Palaeoenvironmental reports

Phosphate and magnetic susceptibility studies of buried soils and sitch sediments from the Upper Ninepence exavations
John Crowther

Introduction

Phosphate and magnetic susceptibility studies were undertaken on the buried palaeosol beneath the Bronze Age barrow in the hope of gaining additional insight into the nature and pattern of human activity on the old land surface. Investigations were also made of the fill of the ditch (context 8) beneath the barrow; the fill of the Upper Ninepence enclosure ditch (U9D94-II) to the south; and, for comparative purposes, the A and B horizons of a nearby modern soil. Both properties are widely used in archaeological prospection. Phosphate enrichment derives from inputs of organic matter (eg plant material, excreta, urine and, especially, bone) and is typically associated with features such as midden deposits, animal enclosures, burials, etc (see reviews by Proudfoot, 1976; Hamond, 1983). Magnetic susceptibility of soils and sediments is particularly enhanced by burning (Clark 1990; Scollar et al 1990). In the present study conventional low frequency mass-specific magnetic susceptibility (χ) measurements have been complemented by determinations of fractional conversion (χ_{conv}). The latter is a measure of percentage of the maximum potential magnetic susceptibility (χ_{max}) that has been achieved within individual samples, and is more readily interpreted than raw χ data since it takes into account underlying variations attributable to geological and pedogenic factors (Tite 1972; Crowther and Barker 1995). In addition, the organic matter concentration of each sample was estimated by loss-on-ignition (LOI) to check the consistency of the soil horizons/depths sampled, and pH and particle size were determined for selected samples.

Methodology for the analysis of soil phosphate samples

Phosphate-P (total phosphate) was determined by alkaline oxidation with NaOBr using the method described by Dick and Tabatabai (1977); LOI by ignition at 375°C for sixteen hours (Ball 1964); and magnetic susceptibility using a Bartington MS1 meter. χ_{max} was achieved by heating samples at 650°C in reducing, followed by oxidising conditions. The method used broadly follows that of Tite and Mullins (1971), except that household flour was mixed with the soils and lids placed on the crucibles to create the reducing environment (after Graham and Scollar 1976; Crowther and Barker 1995). The percentage χ_{conv} is then calculated as: $(\chi / \chi_{max}) \times 100.0$ (Tite 1972; Scollar et al 1990). Both pH and particle size were determined using standard analytical methods (Avery and Bascomb 1974).

Results and discussion

General character of modern soils

The soils at Walton are developed on drift derived largely from local Silurian sandstones, siltstones and shales. Modern soils in the vicinity of the site are mostly brown earths of the East Keswick 1 association, although locally there is some gleying where the subsoils are less permeable (Rudeforth et al 1984). Analytical data for a profile adjacent to the barrow (Tables 33 and 34) reveal the modern ploughed topsoil to be an acidic (pH 5.5), organic-rich (LOI at 0–15 cm, 6.91%), clay loam. The predominance of silts (64.7%) in the <2mm fraction reflects the high proportion of siltstones in the parent material (see below), and the vulnerability of sand-sized siltstone grains to mechanical disintegration. As would be anticipated, phosphate-P, χ, and χ_{conv} are higher in the topsoil than the subsoil.

Vertical section through buried palaeosol and base of barrow

Concentrations of organic matter within the buried Ah and AEb horizons of the soil are relatively low, with LOI values of 3.06 and 3.05% in samples taken from the topmost 40mm (ie the AEb1 and top of AEb2 horizon covered by thin section MM2; see below). Significant amounts of organic matter will undoubtedly have been lost through decomposition following burial, and therefore the LOI data poorly reflect the absolute concentrations of organic matter that were originally present. However, the relative values are likely to be broadly representative. In this respect the high LOI (6.07%) recorded in the overlying pan is significant in that it suggests the presence of an organic-rich surface layer (cf thin section evidence below). The LOI results also suggest that the AEb horizons of the buried soil extended to a depth of only c 120mm. The modern soil by comparison has a much thicker and more evenly mixed A horizon, which, to a large extent, probably reflects the effects of ploughing.

The pH of the buried soil may well have been affected by post-burial weathering and leaching

127

Table 33 Data on chemical and magnetic properties of samples from modern A and B horizons, the barrow and buried palaeosol

Depth (mm)	LOI (%)	pH (1:2.5, water)	Phosphate-P (mg g⁻¹)	χ (10^{-8} SI kg⁻¹)	χ max (10^{-8} SI kg⁻¹)	χ conv (%)
Modern soil						
A (0–150)	6.91	5.5	1.48	89.2	1450	6.17
A (150–300)	5.87	5.5	1.31	93.0	1400	6.64
B (150–400)	2.99	6.3	0.816	42.4	1280	3.32
*Section through barrow and palaeosoil**						
Barrow	3.32	5.7	2.65	31.8	736	4.32
Fe panning†	6.07	nd	7.32	55.0	6850	0.80
Buried soil‡						
0–20	3.06	5.7	2.62	54.2	1110	4.88
20–40	3.05	5.6	2.37	57.5	1140	5.06
40–60	3.06	5.7	2.39	79.9	1160	6.90
60–80	3.09	5.6	2.51	71.0	983	7.22
80–100	3.16	5.6	2.36	55.4	888	6.24
100–120	2.83	5.5	2.12	47.5	875	5.43
120–170	2.18	5.4	1.92	24.9	826	3.02

* This section is located alongside thin section MM2 (see below): † This includes thin (4 mm) Mn-impregnated Ah horizon: ‡ Depth (mm) below base of iron panning (effectively from the top of the Eb1 horizon identified in thin section)

Table 34 Particle size data for A horizon of the modern soil and buried palaeosol

Depth (cm)	Coarse sand (0.6–2.0 mm)	Medium sand (0.2–0.6 mm)	Fine sand (0.06–0.2mm)	Silt (2–60mm)	Clay (mm)	Texture class*
Modern soil						
A (0–15)	8.1	2.6	2.7	64.7	21.9	CL
Buried soil						
6–8	17.3	5.1	3.6	58.1	15.9	SyZL

* Texture classes: SyZL = sandy silt loam; CL = clay loam.

processes, and therefore needs to be interpreted with caution. The data do however suggest a slightly–moderately acidic, quite heavily leached soil – as is suggested by the thin sections (see below). Variations in phosphate-P down the profile are complicated by the panning. In acid soils such as these, phosphate tends to become fixed by the formation of insoluble compounds with Fe. As a consequence, more phosphate-P will tend to be retained within horizons that are impregnated with Fe, and any phosphates leached from overlying layers (in this case from the barrow) will tend to accumulate here. Even so, the concentration of 7.32 mg g⁻¹ recorded within the pan is very high and certainly tends to suggest some degree of phosphate enrichment at the surface of the buried soil. Interestingly, too, the phosphate-P concentrations of the underlying A horizons of the buried soil (range, 2.12–2.62 mg g⁻¹) and also of the barrow (2.65 mg g⁻¹) are high compared with the modern Ap horizon (1.48 mg g⁻¹ at 0–150mm). These findings

may be indicative of quite high levels of human activity prior to barrow construction.

Unfortunately, the magnetic properties of the top of the buried soil have also been affected by the panning. The very high χ_{max} value (6850 × 10^{-8} SI kg⁻¹) recorded in the pan is clearly a direct reflection Fe accumulation, and the effects of Fe migration will almost certainly have affected the properties of the uppermost layers of the buried soil. The highest χ (79.9 × 10^{-8} SI kg⁻¹) and χ_{conv} (7.22%) values were recorded at between 40 and 80mm, and these are similar to the figures recorded in the A horizon of the modern soil.

Spatial survey of the buried palaeosol

Sampling of the topsoil and subsoil of the buried palaeosol was undertaken on regular grids. Unfortunately, quite extensive areas of the palaeosol,

Table 35 Summary of the analytical data from the survey of the buried palaeosol

	Mean	Minimum	Maximum	Standard deviation
Topsoil (n = 148)				
LOI (%)	3.42	2.68	4.19	0.328
Phosphate-P (mg g^{-1})	2.43	1.04	4.62	0.541
c (10^{-8} SI kg^{-1})	65.1	32.1	154	19.7
χmax (10^{-8} SI kg^{-1})	1200	826	1650	155.3
χconv (%)	5.45	2.21	11.8	1.437
Subsoil (n = 148)				
LOI (%)	2.34	1.55	2.99	0.314
Phosphate-P (mg g^{-1})	1.47	0.524	2.83	0.445
χ (10^{-8} SI kg^{-1})	32.2	10.9	71.3	13.03
χmax (10^{-8} SI kg^{-1})	1080	526	1560	231.6
χconv (%)	2.99	1.06	6.21	1.102

* Excludes 11 samples with LOI^{3}3.00 (see text)

particularly in the southern half of the site, have been disturbed by rabbit burrowing. At each location therefore, a sample was taken of what appeared to be the least disturbed soil within a 1 × 1m grid square. The topsoil survey (at 1m intervals) was confined to the north-west and south-east quadrants, with samples being taken from the top of the palaeosol, or just beneath the iron pan where this was present. In the case of the subsoil, samples were taken from the top of the B horizon (avoiding identifiable features such as pit fill, hearths, etc) at intervals of 5m across the whole area, and of 2m over structures 1 and 3.

Despite the sampling strategy adopted, it is apparent from the LOI data that some of the subsoil samples contain higher than normal concentrations of organic matter (those with LOI >3.0% are certainly suspect). Since disturbance is the most likely cause, these samples (n = 11) have been excluded from subsequent analysis. As would be anticipated, LOI, phosphate-P and χ_{conv} (Table 35) are all significantly higher in the topsoil than the subsoil (Mann-Whitney, $p < 0.001$): the mean values for phosphate-P and c, for example, being 2.43 mg g^{-1} and 65.1 × 10^{-8} SI kg^{-1} respectively in the topsoil, compared with 1.47 mg g^{-1} and 32.2 × 10^{-8} SI kg^{-1} in the subsoil. There is also a significant difference in χ_{max} (Mann-Whitney, $p < 0.001$), but in this case the difference in means between the topsoil (1200 × 10^{-8} SI kg^{-1}) and subsoil (1080 × 10^{-8} SI kg^{-1}) is relatively small, and somewhat difficult to explain.

Although the topsoil and subsoil sampling was undertaken on different grids, 23 of the sampling points did in fact coincide and these enabled the relationship between the two data sets to be investigated. At the time of barrow construction it might be anticipated that there would be a broad relationship between the chemical and magnetic properties of the topsoil and underlying subsoil. Unfortu-

nately, in this survey no significant correlation was found between the topsoil and subsoil data for phosphate-P, χ or χ_{conv}, which suggests that the properties of the soils have been affected by post-burial changes. Clearly, the buried topsoil is more likely to have been disturbed than the subsoil, simply by virtue of its closer proximity to the surface and the greater ease with which it might be burrowed, and the results of the topsoil survey seem to confirm this.

Survey of palaeosol topsoil (north-west and south-east quadrants)

The results of the various surveys are presented in Table 36, Figs 69–70, and below. Of the two quadrants, the south-east was found to have been much more affected by rabbit burrowing, and this was reflected for example in the very fragmentary nature of the iron panning present (cf. substantial and fairly continuous pan in the north-west). LOI is significantly higher in the south-east quadrant than the north-west (Mann-Whitney, $p < 0.001$). Whilst the observed difference might be attributable to faecal input from rabbits, the fact that there is no significant difference in phosphate-P between the two quadrants, and no correlation overall between phosphate-P and LOI, suggests that this is not the case. The reason for the contrast in LOI is unclear, and in any case the difference is relatively small (mean values 3.52 and 3.32% respectively). More striking contrasts are evident in the magnetic susceptibility results: χ, χ_{max} and χ_{conv} all stand out as having generally higher values in the south-east than the north-west quadrant, and in each case the difference in mean values (Table 36) is statistically significant (Mann-Whitney, $p < 0.001$). In view of the topographic setting of the site,

Table 36 Summary of the analytical data for topsoil samples from the south-east and north-west quadrants

	Mean	Minimum	Maximum	Standard deviation
South-east quadrant (n = 69)				
LOI (%)	3.52	2.68	4.19	0.361
Phosphate-P (mg g^{-1})	2.49	1.74	4.62	0.550
χ (10^{-8} SI kg^{-1})	75.6	42.1	154	19.42
χ_{max} (10^{-8} SI kg^{-1})	1240	951	1650	149.0
χ_{conv} (%)	6.09	3.57	11.8	1.422
North-west quadrant (n = 79)				
LOI (%)	3.32	2.72	3.88	0.267
Phosphate-P (mg g^{-1})	2.38	1.04	4.07	0.531
χ (10^{-8} SI kg^{-1})	56.0	32.1	116	14.86
χ_{max} (10^{-8} SI kg^{-1})	1150	826	1490	149.7
χ_{conv} (%)	4.89	2.21	9.13	1.203

the nature of the soil parent material, and the size of area under consideration, the difference in χ_{max} seems unlikely to be attributable to natural variations in geology or in pedogenic processes within the original soil. The development of an iron pan across the top of the buried soil, and its subsequent break-up by rabbit burrowing in the south-east quadrant provides the most likely explanation. Mobilisation and movement of iron from the buried topsoil to the developing pan will have led to a reduction of both χ_{max} and χ within the bulk of the topsoil, and a corresponding increase in χ_{max}, and possibly χ, within the pan itself. Samples taken from the topsoil immediately beneath such a pan (as in the north-west quadrant) will therefore tend to have lower χ_{max} and χ values than in the south-east quadrant where burrowing has broken the pan, thereby reincorporating much of the original iron within the topsoil. Unfortunately, even χ_{conv} is unlikely to provide a reliable indication of the original level of magnetic susceptibility enhancement within the topsoil in this case, since this will depend on the rate of mobilisation of the magnetic minerals relative to the rest of the iron in the soil. In these circumstances, the topsoil survey data must be regarded with extreme caution.

Survey of palaeosol subsoil

By comparison with the topsoils, the subsoils are less likely to have been affected by post-burial pedogenic processes and animal burrowing. Moreover, where appreciable disturbance has occurred then this seems to be reflected in anomalously high LOI values, and the eleven samples that appear to have been affected in this way have been eliminated from the present analysis. In this respect it should be noted that there are no significant differences in LOI, phosphate-P and χ_{conv} between the more disturbed southern half of the site and the northern half (Figs 71 and 72). The absence of a significant correlation between phosphate-P and LOI suggests that the phosphate survey data largely reflect variations in inorganic phosphate (ie there is no evidence of the effects of recent faecal inputs). The key magnetic property, χ_{conv}, is correlated with LOI ($r_s = 0.300$, $p < 0.05$), though the amount of variation explained by the latter is only 6% (based on determination of r^2). Again, therefore, post-burial disturbance would appear to be of minor importance. Thus, the results of the phosphate-P and χ_{conv} surveys seem likely to reflect the properties of the subsoil at the time of burial. Both phosphate-P (range, 0.524–2.83 mg g^{-1}) and χ_{conv} (1.0 –6.21%) exhibit quite marked variability, and interestingly there is a significant, albeit weak, correlation ($r_s = 0.267$, $p < 0.05$) between the two. These findings suggest that traces of phosphate enrichment and magnetic susceptibility enhancement in the original soil may well be present. Certainly those areas with phosphate-P concentrations of [3]2.00 mg g^{-1} and χ_{conv} values of [3]4.0% merit specific consideration in relation to the archaeological evidence. Attention in particular should be drawn to two areas. First, there is a clear grouping of samples with high phosphate-P concentrations in the south-eastern sector of the supposed enclosure. (Is it possible that there was some form of animal pen or midden deposit here?) Secondly, there is a cluster of high χ_{conv} values (including one of 6.21%) in the eastern half of the structure.

Ditch deposits

Samples were taken from the natural at the base of

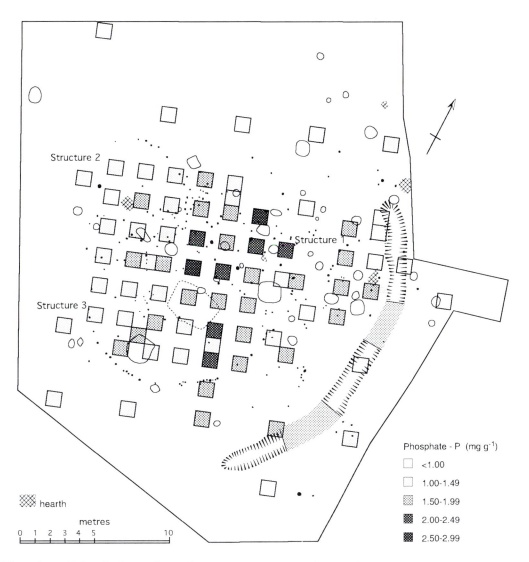

Figure 71 *Phosphate-P levels from the palaeosol subsoil*

each ditch (Upper Ninepence and U9d94-II) and at 5cm intervals up through the sequence of deposits. Both ditches are cut deeply into the underlying subsoil ('natural'), which is characterised by its low LOI, phosphate-P, χ and χ_{conv} (Table 37). The ditch fills are almost identical in terms of organic matter concentration and χ_{max}, which suggests that they are derived from very similar sources. The fact that the LOI figures are so low, with means of 2.81 and 2.71%, respectively, indicates that a substantial proportion of the fills was derived from subsoil, and that the ditches probably remained relatively dry as accumulation took place. Interestingly, despite these close similarities, the fills of the ditch (context 8) at Upper Ninepence have significantly higher (Mann-Whitney, $p < 0.001$) concentrations of phosphate-P (mean, 1.74 mg g^{-1}), and higher χ (47.7 × 10^{-8} SI kg^{-1}) and χ_{conv} (4.72%) values than those of ditch U9d94-II. This finding suggests a much greater anthropogenic influence upon the sediments that accumulated in the former ditch than in the latter.

Report on soil thin sections from Upper Ninepence
John Crowther

Introduction

Four soil thin sections were examined. Two (MM2 and MM5) were taken from the interface between the basal part of the barrow and the top of the buried soil (Fig 73), in the hope that they might provide insight into the nature of the soil and vegetation cover immediately prior to barrow construction, as well as into the character and origins of the material used to make the barrow. The remaining thin sections are from specific contexts of potential archaeological interest: a hearth (hearth 28) deposit (MM7) and a pit fill sequence (pit 188) containing charcoal-rich deposits (MM8). Analytical data relating to MM2 are contained in the report on phosphate and magnetic susceptibility (see above).

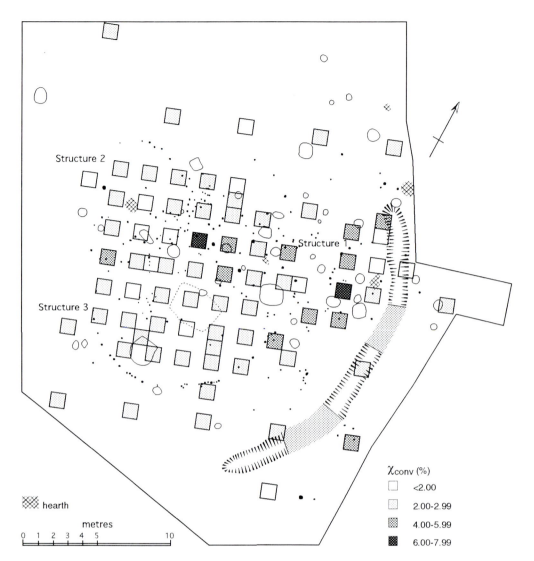

Figure 72 χ conv levels from the palaeosol subsoil

Table 37 Summary of the analytical data from the two sequences of ditch deposits

	Mean	Minimum	Maximum	Standard deviation
Ditch (context 8) at Upper Ninepence				
LOI (%)	2.81	2.02	3.29	0.369
Phosphate-P (mg g^{-1})	1.74	1.15	2.09	0.270
χ (10^{-8} SI kg^{-1})	47.7	29.6	56.8	7.52
χ_{max} (10^{-8} SI kg^{-1})	1020	824	1260	105.3
χ_{conv} (%)	4.72	3.57	5.80	0.778
Neolithic enclosure ditch (U9d94-II)				
LOI (%)	2.71	1.58	3.87	0.650
Phosphate-P (mg g^{-1})	0.529	0.383	0.626	0.062
χ (10^{-8} SI kg^{-1})	13.8	7.84	26.9	5.04
χ_{max} (10^{-8} SI kg^{-1})	1012	663	1560	205
χ_{conv} (%)	1.36	0.71	2.05	0.384

Figure 73 Sampling for soil micromorphology analysis through the remnant mound and subsoils

Methods

The samples were taken in Kubiena boxes, approximately 75 × 50 × 40mm in size (Fig 71). Sample MM2 was taken by the author, whereas the remainder were taken by the excavator. Samples were acetone-dried, prior to impregnation with resin and thin section manufacture (Guilloré 1985; Murphy 1986) – the work being undertaken at the University of Stirling. The thin sections have been described according to Bullock *et al* (1985).

Results and interpretation

Descriptions of the key features of the thin sections are presented below (abbreviations: PPL = plane polarised light; XPL = cross polarised light; OIL = oblique incident light). A coarse/fine limit of 10mm is used for both the mineral and organic components.

MM2: interface between base of barrow and top of buried soil

Buried soil

The precise location of the interface between the barrow and palaeosol is somewhat uncertain because of the extent of Fe (and Mn) panning, impregnation and pseudomorphic replacement of organic matter

which has occurred in this zone. Fe mobilisation and redeposition of this magnitude is common in buried organic/A horizons, especially where water movement and retention has been affected by a marked discontinuity in the character of adjacent materials – in this case between the largely minerogenic material of the barrow and the buried topsoil. The layer (4mm thick) immediately beneath the panning clearly appears to be part of a very thin Ah horizon, the upper part of which is probably impregnated by the panning. It varies from brown to pale grey/yellowish-brown in colour (PPL). It is quite porous (13% void space), which suggests that it has retained much of its original structure and has not been significantly affected by compaction, and has moderately-strongly developed fine crumbs. Fine amorphous organic matter is very abundant and Mn impregnation, which appears to have occurred in association with the organic matter, is abundant. These features all indicate an organic-rich horizon that was very actively worked by soil fauna, and this seems likely to be the actual surface horizon of the buried soil. Although the presence of only rare pseudomorphic plant tissues within the overlying panning (cf within base of barrow) might reflect the presence of only a sparse vegetation cover, it should be noted that post-burial decomposition processes, combined with the intensity of ferruginisation, may give a misleading impression of the extent of the original plant cover.

The Ah horizon overlies AEb horizons. These are

distinguished from the Ah horizon by their speckled pale grey/yellowish-brown colour (PPL), which is typical of leached, clay-depleted horizons; and their much lower concentration of organic matter (only rare coarse and occasional fine organic matter is present) and rare–occasional impregnative Mn nodules. Despite being less organic, these horizons contain abundant ultrafine granules (presumably largely of excremental origin), which clearly indicate high levels of biological activity, including earthworms. Indeed, the presence of a very thin, but distinct, stony layer (AEb1) immediately beneath the Ah horizon is probably attributable to earthworm sorting. Fine and coarse charcoal fragments are rare–occasional down through the buried soil, with the higher concentrations tending to occur at greater depth. This again is indicative of active mixing by earthworms. Thus, whilst the soil appears to have been quite heavily leached, it was not sufficiently acidic as to completely inhibit earthworm activity. The fact that there is such clear horizon differentiation in the top 40mm, with much of the organic matter confined to a thin surface Ah horizon, suggests that this soil had not been subject to significant physical disturbance by human activity (eg ploughing). The presence of small amounts of charcoal, well distributed through the topsoil, suggests a significant period of human activity prior to burial. However, the high porosity of the Ah horizon indicates that this particular location had not been subject to excessive trampling and compaction, as might be associated with the floor of a building or yard area.

Barrow

In the thin section studied, the bottom of the barrow comprises a very thin (20mm) layer of turves. The surfaces of the individual turves are picked out by impregnative Fe panning, within which there are very abundant pseudomorphic plant tissues. Compared with the buried soil, the turves do not have such a clearly identifiable Ah horizon, which suggests that the ground surface from which they were taken was of a different character from the buried soil – possibly from an area where much of the 'natural' Ah horizon had previously been eroded. The overlying matrix largely comprises Eb horizon material, which is speckled pale grey/yellowish-brown in colour (PPL). About one-third of this contains relatively little clay, whereas the rest (presumably derived from deeper in the soil profile from which it was taken) has a rather more pale yellow coloured (PPL) clay. Only rare (amorphous) organic matter is present in these microfabrics. Rare coarse and occasional fine charcoal (some of which is only partially charred) and rare reddened mineral grains in stones confirm the occurrence of burning prior to barrow construction. The lower part of the barrow above the basal turves also includes about 5% of material, occurring in the form of speckled dark

brown and brown (PPL) weakly developed fine granules, that appears to be derived from a former Ah horizon. This contains very abundant coarse and fine organic matter, much of which is in a pellet-like form, together with rare phytoliths and rare–occasional charcoal. The relatively low charcoal concentrations suggest the material to be derived from a location where there had previously been only a low intensity of human activity. The other notable feature of the barrow is the presence of layered, microlaminated yellow clay fills and crescentic coatings within vughs within the matrix, particularly towards the base. These, along with the vughs in which they occur, are clearly products of disturbance and local collapse following barrow construction. Clay movement probably occurred fairly soon after barrow construction. It certainly pre-dates much of the panning, since appreciable amounts of clay were washed down into the Ah horizon of the buried soil.

MM5: interface between base of barrow and top of buried soil (western section)

The sequence revealed in this section of the barrow is broadly similar to that recorded in MM2 (above). It does, however, differ in four significant respects. First, the boundary between the barrow and the old ground surface is less sharp because of post-burial mixing by earthworms. Secondly, whilst the buried soil has been actively worked by soil organisms, no clear stone line is present. Thirdly, although there has been considerable Fe impregnation and pseudomorphic replacement of organic matter, there is only a very limited amount of panning. Finally, the turves themselves appear to be derived from a location where there was a more substantial Ah horizon present. There is thus evidence from the two thin sections (MM2 and MM5) of contrasts in the character of the ground surface in the immediate vicinity of the barrow at the time of construction.

MM7: charcoal-rich layer (context 29) over burnt subsoil (69) associated with hearth (28)

The part of context 29 included within the thin section has been significantly affected by burrowing, and may actually have collapsed into a small animal burrow. About 80% is speckled dark yellowish-brown/brown (PPL) soil from Ah and Eb horizons, whereas the remaining 20% comprises fragments of this microfabric mixed with lighter coloured fragments of subsoil. Although the darker soil now has a predominantly subangular blocky structure, there are traces of crumb-like features associated with earthworm activity. The soil itself exhibits little sign of burning, but contains abundant charcoal, presumably derived from an adjacent hearth. There is no evidence of burnt cereal. The charcoal is moderately broken up and has been thoroughly incorporated into the soil by biological activity. Only about 5% of this part of the context is not significantly charcoal-enriched, and this generally originated from a former Eb horizon. The absence of traces of ash within the context suggests that the hearth debris was subject to weathering and leaching prior to burial by the barrow. Indeed, as is commonly the case, the release of salts from the weathered ash may have served to mobilise clays within the matrix, thereby accounting for the dusty clay coatings recorded within 5% of the vughs. Unlike in the previous two buried soils, there is no evidence in this case of clay movement down from the overlying barrow – presumably the dense floor layer has prevented this.

The underlying subsoil is very stony, with 70% smooth subangular siltstones, up to 30mm in size. The stones are only slightly rubified, which suggests that they were quite deep in the subsoil. Unfortunately, the subsoil appears to have been badly disturbed during sampling, and therefore the structure and porosity cannot be meaningfully assessed. What is interesting, however, is the presence of many silty cappings on the stones. These are mostly charcoal free (ie appear to pre-date anthropogenic activity), and are almost certainly of periglacial origin.

MM8: fills of pit (188)

In view of the abundant fine amorphous organic matter present in the main (upper) fill of the pit, this appears to comprise extremely charcoal-rich Ah horizon material – as might arise where charcoal from a hearth had spread out over the adjacent ground surface and had then been scraped together, incorporating topsoil. There is a particularly charcoal-rich layer at the base of the main fill. The charcoal is mostly of woody material, and there is no evidence of phytoliths or fragments of cereals within the deposit. Any ash that may have been present has been completely weathered, and the fill as a whole has been subject to considerable biological reworking – as reflected in the high proportion of ultrafine and fine granules present within the matrix. The main fill overlies a thin (10mm) lower fill, which is distinguished by its very high sand content and much lower concentrations of organic matter and charcoal. Indeed, the sands and small stones within this layer give rise to an enaulic structure. This layer clearly appears to have been laid down as a separate fill at the base of the pit, but its origin is uncertain. The fill of the pit has been disturbed by burrowing, presumably by small mammals, and the effects of this activity appear to extend down into the top of the underlying natural.

The pit seems to have been cut down into the lower Eb horizon of the original soil. This contains only rare quantities of organic matter and coarse charcoal fragments, but, as with the pit fill, its structure is dominated by biologically-derived ultrafine to fine granules. One puzzling feature of the pit is the presence of a clear band of small stones, 15mm thick, at the top of the Eb horizon. The fact that the finer material which partially fills the interstices between the stones is almost identical in character to the underlying Eb horizon suggests that it might be the result of disturbance caused during the digging of the pit.

Summary of the soil analyses

Pre-barrow soils

The soils are developed on glacial drift derived from local sandstones, siltstones and shales (predominantly siltstones in the thin sections studied). The presence of dusty coatings on stones in the subsoils is indicative of former periglacial conditions.

The soils appear to have been slightly to moderately acidic leached brown earths, with a very thin humic topsoil (Ah horizon), iron- and clay-depleted AEb horizons, and a more clay-rich B horizon.

Human activity on the pre-barrow surface

The buried soils studied do not appear to have been subject to physical mixing (eg by ploughing).

There is, however, substantial evidence of human activity prior to barrow construction. Certain obvious features were found during the excavation, including hearths (eg MM7), pits (eg MM8), postholes, ditches and possible compacted floor surfaces. No traces of cereal remains were identified within the thin sections studied.

The properties and features of the buried soil provide additional insight. For example, charcoal is present and well distributed through the buried topsoil horizons, and there is evidence of phosphate enrichment.

In addition, there appear to have been quite marked local variations in the nature of the topsoil. In places (eg as reflected in the turves within the barrow in MM2) the Ah horizon may have been completely eroded or only very thin, whereas elsewhere there may have been a rather more substantial Ah horizon (eg turves in MM5). Such local variability seems likely to be attributable to human activity.

Materials used in barrow construction

The soil used in constructing the barrow appears to have been derived from an area (presumably nearby) that had some degree of vegetation/turf cover. Thin turves are evident in both thin sections from the base of the barrow. The bulk of the barrow appears to be made up largely of Eb horizon material, mixed with some more organic-rich granules and clay-rich material, presumed to be derived from the former topsoil and B horizons respectively – though it should be noted that turves were identified within the barrow during excavation (see above).

Considerable movement of clay has taken place within the barrow, producing distinctive fills and coatings in many vughs. This probably occurred quite soon after construction, and certainly pre-dates the panning associated with the turves and old ground surface.

Descriptions of the soil thin sections

Key features of thin section MM2: interface between barrow and buried soil

Barrow

This comprises five principal microfabrics:

Microfabric A – very dominant (50% overall, and 70% of upper part of section). Interpreted as being derived from former Eb horizon.

Microfabric
Colour: speckled pale grey/yellowish-brown (PPL); low birefringence with crystallic silt grains (XPL); grey/pale brown (OIL).
Peds: weakly developed very fine–fine subangular blocky peds.
Voids: total void space 13%, comprising planar voids and vughs; planar voids (70% of void space, volume probably exaggerated by disturbance during sampling) – curved, randomly-oriented, not referred, mesoplanes; vughs (30%) – spherical, mesovughs.

Basic mineral components
c/f limit at 10mm; ratio 60:40
Coarse fraction: silt dominant, but includes frequent sand, comprising fragments of siltstone, and very few 2–20mm smooth, subangular stones (siltstones). Overall stone content 5%. Occasional stones contain rare reddened mineral grains (OIL).
Fine fraction: fine silts and clay, yellowish-brown (PPL); low birefringence (XPL); pale brown (OIL).

Organic components
Organic coarse material (>10mm): rare coarse amorphous organic matter; rare charcoal, some partially charred.
Organic fine material (<10mm): rare fine amorphous organic matter; occasional charcoal, some partially charred.

Pedofeatures
Layered, microlaminated yellow clay, with a sharp extinction zone completely fills 25% of the vughs, and forms crescentic coatings within 50% of the vughs.

Microfabric B – frequent (25%). Interpreted as being derived from former Eb horizon.
As Microfabric A, but less yellow clay is evident.

Microfabric C – very few (5%). Interpreted as being derived from former Ah horizon.

Microfabric
Colour: dark brown and brown (PPL); very low birefringence in fine fraction with crystallic silt grains (XPL); brown brown (OIL).
Peds: weakly developed fine granules.
Voids: void space within granules 3%.

Basic mineral components
c/f limit at 10mm; ratio 50:50
Coarse fraction: silt very dominant.
Fine fraction: fine silts and clay, yellowish-brown (PPL); low birefringence (XPL); pale brown (OIL).

Organic components
Organic coarse material (>10mm): occasional coarse amorphous organic matter; rare charcoal; rare phytoliths.
Organic fine material (<10mm): very abundant fine amorphous organic matter, including very abundant pellety organic material; rare–occasional charcoal.

Pedofeatures
No pedofeatures within the peds.

Microfabric D – 10% overall, but dominant in lowermost 20mm of barrow deposit. Interpreted as having same origin as A, with post-deposition iron staining.
As Microfabric A, except that the colour is speckled pale grey/yellowish-brown/orange (PPL), the orange being due to iron staining, chiefly within the clay fraction.

Microfabric E – 10% overall, but dominant in lowermost 20mm of barrow deposit, where it forms bands, up to 5mm thick. Interpreted as being impregnative Fe/Mn panning associated with turves within barrow.

Microfabric
Colour: orange/brown, with many black inclusions of manganese particularly in lowermost band (PPL); no birefringence (XPL); orange/bright brown, with many black inclusions particularly in lower most band (OIL).
Peds: traces of former crumbs are evident, but now completely impregnated with Fe and Mn.
Voids: total void space 3%: mostly planar voids comprising planar voids and vughs; planar voids (75% of void space – volume probably exaggerated by disturbance during sampling); vughs (25%) – spherical, mesovughs.

Basic mineral components
c/f limit at 10mm; ratio 60:40
Coarse fraction: silt dominant, but includes frequent sand, comprising fragments of siltstone and quartzite, and very few 2–20mm smooth, subangular stones (siltstone and quartzite).

Fine fraction: fine silts, clay and amorphous iron compounds; very low birefringence (XPL).

Organic components
Organic coarse material (>10mm): many, and locally very abundant, pseudomorphic plant tissues in which cell walls are marked by ferruginisation; many coarse amorphous organic matter, much of a pellety form; rare charcoal.
Organic fine material (<10mm): abundant fine amorphous organic matter; rare charcoal.

Pedofeatures
Layered, microlaminated orange (iron-stained) clay completely fills 50% of the vughs, and forms crescentic coatings within 25% of the vughs.

Buried soil

This comprises four principal microfabrics:

Microfabric F – forms layer 3mm thick across supposed old ground surface. Interpreted as being impregnative Fe/Mn panning associated with litter/turf layer of old ground surface (but could be bottom turf of barrow).

As Microfabric E, except that there are only rare pseudomorphic plant tissues in the coarse organic fraction.

Microfabric G – forms layer 4mm thick beneath the pan associated with Microfabric F. Interpreted as being the Ah horizon of the buried soil.

Microfabric
Colour: brown and pale grey/yellowish-brown, with very abundant black inclusions of Mn (PPL); low birefringence with crystallic silt grains (XPL); grey/pale brown, with dark grey inclusions of Mn (OIL).
Peds: moderately–strongly developed fine crumbs.
Voids: total void space 13%: 90% compound packing voids and 10% spherical mesovughs.

Basic mineral components
c/f limit at 10mm; ratio 60:40
Coarse fraction: silt dominant, but includes frequent sand, comprising fragments of siltstone, and few 2–20mm smooth, subangular stones (siltstone).
Fine fraction: fine silts, clay and amorphous Fe and Mn compounds; very low birefringence (XPL).

Organic components
Organic coarse material (>10mm): occasional coarse amorphous organic matter, much of it in a pellety form; rare charcoal.
Organic fine material (<10mm): very abundant fine amorphous organic matter; rare charcoal.

Pedofeatures
Layered, microlaminated yellow clay with a sharp extinction zone forming crescentic coatings within 50% of vughs, and occasional coatings on compound packing voids; abundant impregnative Mn, which appears to be associated with organic matter.

Microfabric H – forms layer 20mm thick beneath the supposed Ah horizon associated with Microfabric G. Interpreted as being a stony upper AEb horizon (AEb1) of the buried soil.

Microfabric
Colour: speckled pale grey/yellowish-brown (PPL); low birefringence with crystallic silt grains (XPL); grey/pale brown (OIL).
Peds: weakly–moderately developed fine–medium crumbs, with abundant ultrafine granules.
Voids: total void space 10%: 90% compound packing voids and 10% spherical mesovughs, most of the latter being in the topmost 10mm.

Basic mineral components
c/f limit at 10mm; ratio 80:20
Coarse fraction: common–dominant 2–20mm smooth, subangular stones (siltstone, with occasional quartzite); silt dominant in the fine earth fraction, but includes frequent sand, comprising fragments of siltstone.
Fine fraction: fine silts and clay; very low birefringence (XPL).

Organic components
Organic coarse material (>10mm): rare coarse amorphous organic matter, much of it in a pellety form; rare charcoal.
Organic fine material (<10mm): occasional fine amorphous organic matter; rare charcoal.

Pedofeatures
Layered, microlaminated yellow clay with a sharp extinction zone forms crescentic coatings within 50% of vughs in the uppermost 10mm of the horizon; rare–occasional impregnative Mn nodules, mostly pseudomorphically replacing organic matter.

Microfabric I – extends 20+mm beneath the stony AEb1 horizon associated with Microfabric H. Interpreted as being a lower AEb horizon (AEb2) of the buried soil.

Microfabric
Colour: speckled pale grey/yellowish-brown (PPL); low birefringence with crystallic silt grains (XPL); grey/pale brown (OIL).
Peds: complex: 70% moderately developed very fine–fine subangular peds; 30% ultrafine–fine granules.
Voids: total void space 10%: 60% compound packing voids, 35% planar voids and 5% vughs.

Basic mineral components

c/f limit at 10mm; ratio 65:35
Coarse fraction: silt dominant in the fine earth fraction, but includes frequent sand, comprising fragments of siltstone; few–frequent 2–20mm smooth, subangular stones (siltstone, with occasional quartzite).
Fine fraction: fine silts and clay; very low birefringence (XPL).

Organic components

Organic coarse material (>10mm): rare coarse amorphous organic matter; rare–occasional charcoal.
Organic fine material (<10mm): occasional fine amorphous organic matter; rare–occasional charcoal.

Pedofeatures

Layered, microlaminated yellow clay with a sharp extinction zone forms crescentic coatings within 10% of vughs; occasional impregnative Mn nodules, mostly associated with organic matter.

Key features of thin section MM5: interface between barrow and buried soil

Barrow

This comprises three principal microfabrics:

Microfabric A – very dominant (85% overall). Interpreted as being derived from former Eb horizon.

Microfabric

Colour: speckled pale grey/yellowish-brown (PPL); low birefringence with crystallic silt grains (XPL); grey/pale brown (OIL).
Peds: complex: 80% very fine–fine weakly developed subangular blocky peds; 20% ultrafine-fine granules.
Voids: total void space 12%, comprising planar voids, compound packing voids and vughs; planar voids (50% of void space, volume probably exaggerated by disturbance during sampling) – curved, randomly-oriented, not referred, mesoplanes; compound packing voids (30%); spherical, mesovughs (20%).

Basic mineral components

c/f limit at 10mm; ratio 60:40
Coarse fraction: silt dominant, but with few sand grains comprising fragments of siltstone, and very few 2–20mm smooth, subangular stones (siltstones). Overall stone content 5%.
Fine fraction: fine silts and clay, yellowish-brown (PPL); low birefringence (XPL); pale brown (OIL).

Organic components

Organic coarse material (>10mm): rare coarse organic matter (fragments of plant remains); rare charcoal.

Organic fine material (<10mm): rare fine amorphous organic matter; rare charcoal.

Pedofeatures

Layered, microlaminated yellow clay, with a sharp extinction zone completely fills 5% of the vughs, forms crescentic coatings within 40% of vughs, and forms rare coatings along planar voids.

Microfabric B – few (10%). Interpreted as being derived from former Ah horizon.

Microfabric

Colour: speckled dark brown and brown (PPL); very low birefringence in fine fraction (XPL); brown brown (OIL).
Peds: weakly developed fine granules.
Voids: void space within granules 3%.

Basic mineral components

c/f limit at 10mm; ratio 50:50
Coarse fraction: silt very dominant.
Fine fraction: fine silts and clay, yellowish-brown (PPL); low birefringence (XPL); pale brown (OIL).

Organic components

Organic coarse material (>10mm): occasional coarse organic matter (plant tissue); rare–occasional charcoal.
Organic fine material (<10mm): very abundant fine amorphous organic matter; rare charcoal.

Pedofeatures

Few of the granules contain impregnative Mn nodules.

Microfabric C – 5% overall, but very dominant in 5mm band at base of barrow. Interpreted as comprising turves (with Ah horizon) forming basal layer of barrow. Boundary with surface of buried soil is blurred by mixing by earthworms.

Microfabric

Colour: dark brown and brown (PPL); very low birefringence in fine fraction (XPL); yellowish-brown and dark brown (OIL).
Peds: moderately–strongly developed fine crumbs.
Voids: total void space 10%: 80% compound packing voids and 20% spherical mesovughs.

Basic mineral components

c/f limit at 10mm; ratio 70:30
Coarse fraction: silt very dominant, with few sand grains, mostly siltstone fragments; abundant (12%) subangular 2–6mm stones, mostly siltstones.
Fine fraction: fine silts and clay, yellowish-brown (PPL); low birefringence (XPL); pale brown (OIL).

Organic components

Organic coarse material (>10mm): locally very abundant remains of plant tissue pseudomorphically replaced by Fe; mostly occurs in a single band (representing top of turves within barrow), 1mm in

thickness and including individual intact pieces up to 5mm in length; along 50% of the band the plant tissue has been broken up and fragments are incorporated within adjacent soil. Rare charcoal.
Organic fine material (<10mm): very abundant fine amorphous organic matter, 30% is of a pellety form; rare charcoal.

Pedofeatures
Ferruginised band (see organic coarse material above); occasional impregnative Mn nodules, up to 2mm in diameter; layered, microlaminated yellow clay, with a sharp extinction zone completely fills 20% of the vughs, forms crescentic coatings within 50% of vughs, and forms rare coatings on crumb surfaces.

Buried soil

This comprises three microfabrics:

Microfabric D – forms layer 5mm thick at top of buried soil. Interpreted as comprising turf layer (litter and Ah horizon) of old ground surface. Boundary between barrow and old ground surface of buried soil is blurred by mixing by earthworms.

As Microfabric C except that the band of pseudomorphically-replaced organic coarse material (*representing the turf line*) is less continuous and more disturbed.

Microfabric E – forms 10mm thick layer beneath Microfabric D. Interpreted as being AEb horizon.

Microfabric
Colour: speckled pale grey/yellowish-brown (PPL); low birefringence with crystallic silt grains (XPL); grey/pale brown (OIL).
Peds: moderately developed fine–medium crumbs with abundant ultrafine granules.
Voids: total void space 8% of which: 80% compound packing voids, 15% planar voids and 5% vughs.

Basic mineral components
c/f limit at 10mm; ratio 60:40
Coarse fraction: silt dominant in the fine earth fraction, but includes few sand grains, comprising fragments of siltstone; stone-free.
Fine fraction: fine silts and clay; very low birefringence (XPL).

Organic components
Organic coarse material (>10mm): rare coarse organic matter; rare charcoal, though occasional locally in areas where there has been more active biological working of the soil.
Organic fine material (<10mm): very abundant fine amorphous organic matter; rare charcoal.

Pedofeatures
Layered, microlaminated yellow clay with a sharp

extinction zone forms crescentic coatings within 5% of vughs and rare coatings on crumbs; occasional impregnative Mn nodules, mostly associated with organic matter.

Microfabric F – beneath Microfabric E. Interpreted as being Eb horizon.

Microfabric
Colour: speckled pale grey/yellowish-brown (PPL); low birefringence with crystallic silt grains (XPL); grey/pale brown (OIL).
Peds: complex: 80% moderately developed very fine subangular blocky peds; 20% ultrafine–fine granules.
Voids: total void space 8% of which: 65% compound packing voids, 20% planar voids and 15% vughs.

Basic mineral components
c/f limit at 10mm; ratio 70:30
Coarse fraction: silt dominant in the fine earth fraction, but includes few sand grains, comprising fragments of siltstone; very abundant stones, up to 15mm and mostly subangular siltstones, in uppermost 15mm of this horizon.
Fine fraction: fine silts and clay; very low birefringence (XPL).

Organic components
Organic coarse material (>10mm): rare coarse organic matter; rare charcoal.
Organic fine material (<10mm): occasional fine amorphous organic matter, though locally very abundant where crumbs from Ah horizon are incorporated; rare charcoal.

Pedofeatures
Layered, microlaminated yellow clay with a sharp extinction zone fills 20% of vughs, and forms crescentic coatings within 50% of vughs and many coatings on crumbs; occasional impregnative Mn nodules, mostly associated with organic matter.

Key features of thin section MM7: hearth (context 28) – charcoal-rich layer (29) over burnt subsoil (69)

Charcoal-rich layer (context 29) (top 40mm of thin section)

This context, which appears to have been disturbed by burrowing, comprises two microfabrics:

Microfabric A – 80% of context. Interpreted as comprising mixed charcoal and soil, initially worked by earthworms, that appears to have fallen into a small burrow, and has subsequently developed a subangular blocky structure.

Microfabric
Colour: 95% speckled dark yellowish-brown/dark brown (PPL); low birefringence with crystallic silt

grains (XPL) 5% speckled light grey/light yellowish-brown (PPL); low birefringence with crystallic silt grains (XPL).
Peds: strongly developed very fine–fine subangular blocky peds.
Voids: void space appears to have been exaggerated by sampling; curved, planar unreferred cracks between blocky peds; spherical mesovughs within the peds.

Basic mineral components
c/f limit at 10mm; ratio 65:35
Coarse fraction: silt dominant in the fine earth fraction, but includes few sand grains, comprising fragments of siltstone; 5% stones – smooth subangular siltstones, up to 20mm.
Fine fraction: fine silts and clay; very low birefringence (XPL).

Organic components
Organic coarse material (>10mm): darker part of soil matrix (95% of microfabric) – rare, partially ferruginised plant tissue (up to 200mm); abundant charcoal, including 5% partially charred organic remains (moderately broken up, fragments up to 3mm, and well mixed within the soil). Lighter coloured part (5%) – rare organic matter and occasional charcoal.
Organic fine material (<10mm): darker part of soil matrix – many fine amorphous organic matter; abundant charcoal. Lighter coloured part – occasional fine amorphous organic matter; rare charcoal.

Pedofeatures
Layered, microlaminated brownish-yellow (PPL) dusty clay with a sharp extinction zone forms crescentic coatings within 5% of vughs.

Microfabric B – confined to a 10mm wide pocket within the context (20% of overall context). Interpreted as comprising fragments of Microfabric A (see above) and the underlying subsoil (see below), probably resulting from burrowing activity.

Burnt subsoil (context 69) (lower 40mm of thin section)

NB This part of the soil, which is very stony, appears to have been badly disturbed during sampling, and much of the original structure has been lost.

Microfabric
Colour: speckled light grey/light yellowish-brown/brown (PPL); low birefringence with crystallic silt grains (XPL).
Peds/voids: uncertain because of damage during sampling.

Basic mineral components
c/f limit at 10mm; ratio 90:10

Coarse fraction: silt dominant in the fine earth fraction, but includes many sand grains, comprising fragments of siltstone; 70% stones – smooth subangular siltstones, up to 30mm, slightly rubified.
Fine fraction: fine silts and clay; very low birefringence (XPL).

Organic components
Organic coarse material (>10mm): rare charcoal (up to 600mm).
Organic fine material (<10mm): rare amorphous organic matter; rare charcoal.

Pedofeatures
Many silty cappings (up to 500mm thick) on stones; mostly charcoal free.

Key features of thin section MM8: fills of pit (context 188)

NB It is difficult to relate the thin section to the various contexts identified in the section drawing supplied.

Upper fill (top 45mm of thin section)

Comprises two microfabrics:

Microfabric A: – 85% of fill. Interpreted as deposit of charcoal-rich Ah horizon material.

Microfabric
Colour: speckled light yellowish-brown/dark brown/black (PPL); low birefringence with crystallic silt grains (XPL).
Peds: complex: 50% vughy microstructure and 50% ultra-fine granules.
Voids: total void space 4%; spherical mesovughs and compound packing voids.

Basic mineral components
c/f limit at 10mm; ratio 80:20
Coarse fraction: silt dominant in the fine earth fraction, but includes abundant sand grains, comprising fragments of siltstone and sandstone; 25% stones – smooth subangular siltstones and angular sandstones, up to 20mm.
Fine fraction: fine silts and clay; very low birefringence (XPL).

Organic components
Organic coarse material (>10mm): rare coarse organic material; very abundant coarse charcoal (up to 15mm).
Organic fine material (<10mm): abundant amorphous organic matter; very abundant fine charcoal.

Microfabric B – 15% of fill. Interpreted as fill of animal burrow.

Microfabric
Colour: speckled light brown/brown/black (PPL); low birefringence with crystallic silt grains (XPL).
Peds: complex: 50% vughy microstructure; 50% ultra-fine granules.
Voids: total void space 6%; spherical mesovughs and compound packing voids.

Basic mineral components
c/f limit at 10mm; ratio 75:25
Coarse fraction: silt dominant in the fine earth fraction, but includes abundant sand grains, comprising fragments of siltstone and sandstone; 15% stones – smooth subangular siltstones and angular sandstones, up to 5mm.
Fine fraction: fine silts and clay; very low birefringence (XPL).

Organic components
Organic coarse material (>10mm): rare coarse organic material; many coarse charcoal fragments (up to 4mm).
Organic fine material (<10mm): occasional amorphous organic matter; many fine charcoal fragments.

Lower fill (layer between 45 and 55mm down thin section)

Microfabric
Colour: speckled light grey/brown (PPL); low birefringence with crystallic silt grains (XPL).
Peds: enaulic structure, with skeleton of stones and sands.
Voids: total void space 6%; complex packing voids.

Basic mineral components
c/f limit at 10mm; ratio 95:5
Coarse fraction: sand, mostly quartz, dominant in the fine earth fraction; 15% stones – smooth subangular siltstones and angular sandstones, up to 6mm.
Fine fraction: fine silts and clay; very low birefringence (XPL).

Organic components
Organic coarse material (>10mm): rare coarse organic material; many coarse charcoal fragments (up to 5mm), with very high concentrations in bottom 10mm of this fill.
Organic fine material (<10mm): occasional amorphous organic matter; many fine charcoal fragments.

?Natural soil beneath pit

This appears to have been disturbed by burrowing, with two possible burrows containing Microfabric B extending down through the natural (to the bottom of the thin section). The supposed natural largely comprises Microfabric C, but is overlain by a very stony layer (Microfabric D).

Microfabric C – Interpreted as lower Eb horizon (possibly upper B horizon) of soil in which the pit was dug.

Microfabric
Colour: speckled yellowish-brown (PPL); low birefringence with crystallic silt grains (XPL).
Peds: ultrafine–fine granules.
Voids: total void space 8%; compound packing voids.

Basic mineral components
c/f limit at 10mm; ratio 60:40
Coarse fraction: silt dominant in the fine earth fraction, but with many sand grains; 10% stones – smooth subangular siltstones and angular sandstones, up to 4mm.
Fine fraction: fine silts and clay; very low birefringence (XPL).

Organic components
Organic coarse material (>10mm): rare coarse organic material; rare coarse charcoal fragments (up to 1.2mm).
Organic fine material (<10mm): occasional amorphous organic matter; rare fine charcoal.

Microfabric D: (c 15mm thick stony layer overlying Microfabric C). Provisionally interpreted as being a result of disturbance during pit construction.

This comprises 80% stones (up to 8mm), mostly smooth subangular siltstones, giving rise to an enaulic structure in which 50% of the space between the stones is occupied by Microfabric C and the remainder is void space.

Hindwell Ash charcoals
G Morgan

All contexts at Hindwell Ash were sampled for palaeoenvironmental data and submitted to Leicester University for identification. The following species identified are listed in Table 38.

The charred plant remains from Walton
Astrid E Caseldine and Catherine J Barrow

Introduction

An extensive sampling programme was undertaken to recover charred plant remains. The main site sampled was Upper Ninepence but samples were also taken from Hindwell I and II, Rough Close and Knapp Farm. Samples were taken from a range of features and in all 183 samples were examined.

Table 38 The charcoals from Hindwell Ash. Species present: Oak – *Quercus* spec., Hazel – *Corylus avellana* (or possibly alder), Ash – *Fraxinus excelsior*, Elm – *Ulmus* spec., Hawthorn – *Crataegus* spec., Poplar – *Populus* spec. (or possibly willow), Blackthorn – *Prunus spinosa*.

Context	Species	Diameter (mm)	Rings	Estimated present age	Growth rate/ comments
F5	Hazel	15	8	8	
		20	15	15	
		35	20	25	
	Ash	50 +	15	20 +	
		25	15	15	
	Oak	50 +	8	15 +	
		10	5	5	
		10	14	14	slow
F6	Hazel	35 +	3	5 +	
	Elm	15	10	10	one piece only
	Oak	10	3	5	
		30 +	8	10 +	fast
		50 +	5	10 +	fast
F10	Oak	40 +			fragments
F11	Elm	30 +	4	6 +	
	Poplar type	30 +			fragments
	Hawthorn type	30 +			fragments
	Hazel	30 +			fragments
F12	Oak	30 +			fragments
F20	Blackthorn	10	3	3	
	Hazel	10	3	3	

Methods

The samples were processed by Clwyd-Powys Archaeological Trust using a flotation machine. The minimum mesh size of the sieves used was 250 microns. The samples were sorted and identified at University of Wales, Lampeter, using a Wild M5 stereomicroscope. Identification was by comparison with modern reference material and standard identification texts. The results are summarised in tables 39–48.

Discussion

The majority of the samples were associated with Neolithic activity prior to establishment of the barrow at Upper Ninepence. Plant remains apart from wood charcoal and hazelnut fragments, notably cereals and weed seeds, were scarce, but the results should be set against the paucity of evidence for this period in Wales (Caseldine 1990). Many of the samples were from undated features but a number could be assigned to one of the phases or three

structures recognised, thereby allowing some limited observations to be made.

The sample which produced the greatest number of hazelnut fragments from the site was from pit 10, assigned to the Peterborough phase and first main phase of activity at the site. The only weed seed present in the sample was fat hen (*Chenopodium album*), a plant associated with disturbed ground and cultivation. Two other samples (pits 12 and 200), again comparatively rich in hazelnut fragments, provided firmer evidence for cereal cultivation during this phase. Both samples contained a few glume bases, rachis fragments and spikelet forks of wheat (*Triticum*). Most of the remains were poorly preserved and therefore could not be identified to species level but those that were identifiable further appeared to be probably mainly emmer (*T. dicoccum*), although there was also possibly rachis of bread wheat (*T. cf aestivum*). Two grains of emmer occurred in pit 12. This evidence for the dominance of emmer wheat is in keeping with that from other Neolithic sites in Wales (Caseldine 1990). Weed seeds were scarce but included docks (*Rumex*), possible violet (cf *Viola*), selfheal (*Prunella vulgaris*), possible ribwort plan-

Table 39 Charred plant remains from the Peterborough Phase

Feature		Pits 6	10	12	16	37	200	500	Stake-holes 325
Context		7	11	13	17	38	201	502	326
Taxa **Cereals**									
Triticum dicoccum (emmer wheat)	grain	–	–	2	–	–	–	–	–
	gl. bases	–	–	3cf3	–	–	cf2	–	–
	spklt. fks.	–	–	–	–	–	cf2	–	–
	rachis	–	–	–	–	–	cf1	–	–
T. dicoccum / T. spelta (emmer/spelt wheat)	gl. bases	–	–	1	–	–	–	–	–
	spklt. fks	–	–	1	–	–	–	–	–
	rachis	–	–	–	–	–	2	–	–
T. cf. *aestivum* s.l. (bread wheat)	rachis node	–	–	1	–	–	–	–	–
Triticum sp. (wheat)	grain	–	–	1	–	–	–	–	–
	gl. bases	–	–	2	–	–	–	–	–
	spklt. fks.	–	–	1	–	–	–	–	–
	rachis	–	–	3	–	–	–	–	–
Cerealia indet.	grain	–	–	1	–	–	–	–	–
Other plants									
cf. *Quercus* p. (oak) cupule		–	1	–	–	–	–	–	–
Corylus avellana L. (hazel) nut frags.		10	983	114	186	6	292	23	2
Chenopodium album L. (fat hen)		–	1	–	–	–	–	–	–
Caryophyllaceae (pinks)		–	–	1	–	–	–	–	–
Rumex sp. (docks)		–	–	1	–	–	3	–	–
cf. *Viola* sp. (violets)		–	–	1	–	–	–	–	–
cf. *Trifolium* sp. (clovers)		–	–	1	–	–	–	–	–
Prunella vulgaris L. (selfheal)		–	–	–	–	–	1	–	–
cf. *Plantago lanceolata* L. (ribwort plantain)		–	–	–	1	–	–	–	–
Poaceae (grasses) rhizomes		1	4	2	–	–	–	–	–
Indet. organic		–	6	11	2	–	5	–	–

Table 40 Charred plant remains from structure 1 (Grooved Ware Phase)

Feature	Stakeholes 24	26	57	96	124	279	Postholes 281	92
Context	25	27	58	97	125	280	282	93
Taxa **Cereals**								
Triticum dicoccum / T. spelta (emmer/spelt) gl. bases	1	–	–	–	–	–	–	–
Other plants								
cf *Urtica dioica* L. (common nettle)	–	–	1	–	–	–	–	–
Corylus avellana L. (hazel) nut frags.	–	2	2	77	2	8	4	1
Rubus sp. (bramble) frags	1	–	–	–	–	–	–	–
Stachys type (woundworts)	–	–	1	–	–	–	–	–
Poaceae (grasses)	–	1	–	–	–	–	–	–
Poceae rhizomes	–	–	1	–	1	–	1	1
Organic indet.	–	–	+	–	–	+	–	–

Table 41 Charred plant remains from features containing Grooved Ware pottery

	Pits																Stakeholes			Ditch	Hearth	
Feature	22	33	35	43	55	85	132	136	146	152	154	198	198	198	293	299	277	297	448	478	8	28
Context	23	34	36	44	56	86	133	137	147	153	155	199	289	291	294	300	278	298	449	497	9	29
Taxa																						
Cereals																						
Triticum dicoccum / spklt. fls. *T. spelta* (emmer/spelt)	–	–	1	–	–	–	–	–	–	–	–	–	–	–	–	–	–	–	–	–	–	–
Other plants																						
Quercus sp. (oak) kernel	–	–	–	–	–	–	–	–	–	2	–	–	–	–	–	–	–	–	–	–	–	–
Quercus sp. cupule frags.	–	–	–	–	–	2	2	–	–	–	–	–	–	–	–	–	–	–	–	–	–	–
Alnus glutinosa (L.) Gaertner (alder) catkin	–	–	–	–	–	–	–	–	–	–	1	–	–	–	–	–	–	–	–	–	–	–
Corylus avellana L. (hazel) nut frags.	53	115	–	2	6	7	513	44	1	207	35	33	23	21	1	79	15	66	14	1	3	8
Rumex acetosella (sheep's sorrel)	–	–	–	–	–	–	–	–	–	–	–	–	–	–	–	–	–	1	–	–	–	–
Rumex sp. (docks)	–	2	–	–	–	–	1	–	1	–	1	–	–	–	–	–	–	–	–	–	–	–
Rubus frags (brambles)	–	–	–	–	–	–	–	–	–	–	–	–	–	–	–	–	1	–	–	–	–	–
Rosa sp. (roses)	–	–	–	–	–	–	–	–	–	–	–	2	–	–	–	–	–	–	–	–	–	–
Lotus type (bird's foot trefoil)	–	–	–	–	–	–	–	–	–	–	1	–	–	–	–	–	–	–	–	–	–	–
Plantago lanceolata L. (ribwort plantain)	–	–	–	–	4	–	–	–	–	–	cfl	–	–	–	–	–	–	–	–	–	–	–
Gallium verum / *saxatile* type (lady's/heath bedstraw)	1	–	–	–	–	–	–	–	–	–	–	–	–	–	–	–	–	–	–	–	–	1
Gallium mollugo type (hedge bedstraw)	–	–	–	1	–	–	–	–	–	–	–	–	–	–	–	–	–	–	–	–	–	–
Gallium aparine L. (cleavers)	–	–	–	–	–	–	–	–	–	–	–	–	–	–	–	–	–	1	–	–	–	–
Poaceae (grasses)	–	–	–	–	6	–	–	cfl	–	–	–	–	–	–	–	–	–	–	–	–	–	–
Poaceae rhizomes	3	–	–	–	25	–	–	–	4	–	–	–	–	–	–	1	–	–	–	–	7	–
Leaf bud	–	–	–	–	–	1	–	–	–	–	–	–	–	–	–	–	–	–	–	–	–	–
Thorn	–	–	–	–	–	–	–	–	–	–	–	–	1	–	–	–	–	–	–	–	–	–
Organic indet.	+	+	+	–	–	+	+	+	+	+	+	+	+	+	+	+	+	+	+	–	–	+

Table 42 Charred plant remains from structure 2 (Grooved Ware Phase)

	Postholes								Stake-holes
	(?2)	(?2)	(?2)						
Feature	420	424	438	440	442	452	484	488	505
Context	421	425	439	441	443	453	485	489	506
Taxa									
cf Cerealia indet. (cereal)	–	–	–	–	1	–	–	–	–
Corylus avellana L. (hazel) nut frags.	–	2	2	6	–	14	2	5	3
cf. Rosaceae (rose)	1	–	–	–	–	–	–	–	–
Poaceae (grass) rhizomes	–	–	–	1	1	–	–	–	–

Table 43 Charred plant remains from structure 3 (late Neolithic/early Bronze Age)

	Stakeholes									Pits		
	(?3)	??	(?3)								(?3)	(?3)
Feature	249	253	255	321	323	329	333	346	348	398	41	61
Context	250	254	256	322	324	330	334	347	349	399	42	62
Taxa												
Cereals												
Triticum monococcum/spklt fks/*T. dicoccum* (einkorn/emmer)	–	–	1	–	–	–	–	–	–	–	–	–
T. cf *aestivum* s.l. rachis node (bread wheat)	1	–	–	–	–	–	–	–	–	–	–	–
Triticum sp. gl bases (wheat)	1	–	–	–	–	–	–	–	–	–	–	–
Other plants												
Corylus avellana L. (hazel) nut frags	18	4	1	5	4	9	1	8	–	3	7	6
Rumex sp. (docks)	–	–	–	–	–	–	–	–	–	–	1	1
Rubus (bramble) frags.	–	–	–	–	–	–	–	–	1	–	–	–
cf *Crataegus* sp. (hawthorn) fruit	–	1	–	–	–	–	–	–	–	–	–	–
Vicia sp. (vetches)	–	–	–	–	–	2	–	–	–	–	–	–
Poaceae (grasses)	–	–	–	–	–	–	–	–	–	–	1	–
Poaceae rhizome	–	–	–	–	–	–	–	1	–	–	–	–

tain (*Plantago lanceolata*) and a Caryophyllaceae. Most of these could indicate grassland or disturbed ground but docks and violets can be associated with cultivation. The presence of chaff and weed seeds suggests the samples may represent waste from crop processing but the evidence is too slight to suggest anything more. The other samples from features assigned to the Peterborough phase also contained hazelnuts, but little else. The deliberate collection of hazelnuts as a food resource during the Neolithic is widely recognised, but as hazel is frequent in the charcoal assemblage (see below), it is possible that some of the hazelnuts are present simply because they were collected along with branches of hazel used for fuel. The few charred grass remains in these and later samples could be from grass which became burnt where the fire took place, or from grass used as tinder. Overall the evidence suggests a grassland environment with hazel scrub nearby and perhaps some limited cultivation.

Although the evidence for cereal cultivation is slight during the Peterborough phase, the evidence for cereals from the Grooved Ware phase is even less. Only one wheat glume base was recovered from one stakehole (57) from structure 1, which is attributed

Table 44 Charred plant remains from undated postholes, old ground surface and mound

| Feature | Postholes | | | | | | | | | Mound |
| | 376 | 416 | 418 | 490 | 1020/1020 | 1025/1025 | 1025/1025 | 2025/2025 | | 2 |
Context	377	417	419	491	72	72	72	72	72	2
Taxa										
Corylus avellana L. (hazel) nut frags	10	5	1	9	5	6	3	7	10	62
Atriplex sp. (oraches)	–	–	–	–	–	–	–	–	–	1
Trifolium type (clovers)	–	–	–	–	–	–	–	–	1	2
Spergula arvensis L. (corn spurrey)	–	–	–	–	–	–	–	–	–	1
Lamiaceae (deadnettles)	–	–	–	–	–	–	–	–	–	1
Plantago lanceolata L. (ribwort plantain)	–	–	–	–	–	–	–	–	–	3
Poaceae (grasses)	–	–	–	–	–	–	–	–	–	6
Poaceae large rhizomes	–	–	–	–	–	–	–	–	–	4
Poaceae (grasses) rhizomes	–	1	–	–	2	5	7	1	11	142
Tree bud	–	–	–	–	–	–	–	–	1	–
Flowerheads	–	–	–	–	–	–	–	–	–	6

to the earlier or middle part of the Grooved Ware phase. Similarly, only one pit (33) containing Grooved Ware pottery produced a spikelet fork of wheat and only one possible cereal grain was recovered from structure 2, which is also tentatively assigned to the Grooved Ware phase. Whether this almost complete absence of cereal remains represents a real difference in the economy and diet of the two phases and a greater emphasis on animals rather than cereals is difficult to say when the evidence is so limited, but it is perhaps worth noting. There is some evidence for a change in diet between the two phases as lipid analysis (see above) suggests pig rather than ruminant was the main cooked meat during the Grooved Ware phase. Perhaps consistent with the apparent increased importance in pig is the presence of two fragments of acorn kernel in one of the Grooved Ware pits and cupule fragments in another. Oak is also more frequent in the charcoal record (see below). The presence of alder (*Alnus glutinosa*) is indicated by a catkin. Hazelnut fragments are again widely represented but even these are sparse in a number of samples, particularly from structures 1 and 2. Shrubby species are indicated by remains of bramble (*Rubus*) and rose (*Rosa*). Weed species are again scarce but sheep's sorrel (*Rumex acetosella*), docks (*Rumex*), ribwort plantain (*Plantago lanceolata*), bird's foot trefoil (*Lotus* type), bedstraws (*Galium* spp) – all taxa that can be found in grassland – are present. Essentially, the environment seems to be similar to that during the Peterborough phase but perhaps with more woodland and shrubby species present locally, or different resources being exploited.

Cereal evidence from structure 3, attributed to the late Neolithic or early Bronze Age, also indicates the presence of wheat, including possible bread wheat (*T.* cf *aestivum*). Other remains, including hazelnut fragments, are relatively few.

Samples from the old ground surface produced little apart from a few hazelnut fragments and grass rhizomes. Most of the remaining samples were from undated pits, stakeholes and postholes or animal disturbance. Only three samples produced any cereal evidence but hazelnut fragments were present in most. Occasional weed seeds occurred, including corn spurrey (*Spergula arvensis*) a weed of cultivation. Blackthorn (*Prunus spinosa*) was recorded from two samples.

The sample from context 2 of the mound, considered to be constructed during the early Bronze Age, contained no cereal remains but grass rhizomes were frequent and the weed seeds again included a seed of corn spurrey.

The final three samples from Upper Ninepence were from late features. Two samples were from undated pits in the top of the mound and contained few remains apart from hazelnut fragments and grass rhizomes. The final sample was from hearth 195 dated to 1640 ± 70 BP (SWAN-115). This was the richest sample from the site in terms of charred cereal remains and weed seeds. Much of the grain was indeterminate but wheat, including bread wheat (*Triticum aestivum*) and spelt wheat (*T. spelta*), and hulled barley (*Hordeum*) were present. The bread wheat was confirmed by the presence of chaff. Twisted as well as straight grains of barley indicated six-row as opposed to two-row barley, but the latter

Table 45 Charred plant remains from undated pits and animal disturbance

	Pits																			Animal disturbance	
Feature	14	39	63	77	81	150	164	166	241	259	275	287	295	344	350	370	414	492	503	51	53
Context	15	40	64	78	82	151	165	167	242	260	276	288	296	345	351	371	415	493	504	52	54
Taxa																					
Cereals																					
Triticum dicoccum/gl. bases *T spelta* (emmer/spelt)	–	–	–	–	–	–	1	–	1	–	–	–	–	–	–	–	–	–	–	–	–
Other plants																					
cf. *Quercus* sp (oak) cupule frags.	–	–	–	–	–	–	–	–	–	–	–	–	–	–	–	–	–	–	1	1	–
Corylus avellana L. (hazel) nut frags.	–	4	–	13	1	7	14	6	1	42	5	34	–	2	3	3	2	1	4	2	9
Rumex sp. (docks)	–	–	–	–	–	–	–	–	1	–	–	–	–	–	–	–	–	–	–	–	–
Potentilla / Fragaria (cinquefoils/strawberries)	–	–	–	–	–	–	–	2	2	–	–	–	–	–	–	–	–	–	–	–	–
cf. *Prunus spinosa* L. (blackthorn)	–	–	–	–	–	–	–	–	–	–	–	1	–	–	–	–	–	–	–	–	–
Trifolium sp. (clovers)	–	–	–	–	–	–	–	–	–	–	–	–	–	1	–	–	–	–	–	–	–
Stachys type (woundworts)	–	–	–	–	–	–	–	–	5	–	–	–	–	–	–	–	–	–	–	–	–
Plantago lanceolata L. (ribwort plantain)	–	–	–	–	–	–	–	2	–	–	–	–	–	–	–	–	–	–	–	–	–
cf. Cyperaceae (sedges)	–	–	–	–	–	–	–	–	1	–	–	–	–	–	–	–	–	–	–	–	–
Large Poaceae/Cereal (grass/cereal)	–	–	–	1	–	–	–	–	–	–	–	–	–	–	–	–	–	–	–	–	–
Poaceae (grasses)	–	–	–	–	–	–	–	–	–	–	–	–	–	3	–	–	–	–	–	–	–
Poaceae large rhizomes	1	–	–	–	–	–	–	–	–	–	–	–	–	–	–	–	–	–	–	–	–
Poaceae rhizomes	–	1	–	–	–	1	2	–	21	–	–	–	1	4	–	–	2	–	1	–	–
Fruitstone frag. indet.	1	–	–	–	–	–	–	–	–	–	–	–	–	–	–	–	–	–	–	–	–
Flower	–	–	–	–	–	–	–	1	–	–	–	–	–	–	–	–	–	–	–	–	–
Thorn	–	–	–	–	–	–	–	–	–	–	–	–	–	–	–	1	–	–	–	–	–
Organic indet.	–	–	–	–	–	–	–	–	–	–	–	–	–	–	–	–	–	–	+	–	–

147

Table 46 Charred plant remains from undated sources

	Stakeholes																				
Feature	88	111	122	126	142	168	170	174	176	211	219	239	257	263	301	307	309	315	317	331	494
Context	89	112	123	127	143	169	171	175	177	212	220	240	258	264	302	308	310	316	318	332	495
Taxa																					
Cereals																					
Triticum sp. gl. bases (wheat)	–	–	–	–	–	–	–	–	–	–	–	1	–	–	–	–	–	–	–	–	–
Hordeum sp. hulled indet. grain (barley)	–	–	–	–	–	–	–	–	–	–	–	–	–	–	–	1	–	–	–	–	1
Other plants																					
Corylus avellana L. (hazel) nut frags.	5	–	2	6	2	9	2	1	5	1	1	12	–	5	7	3	6	1	6	–	–
Spergula arvensis L. (corn spurrey)	–	–	–	–	–	–	–	–	–	–	–	–	–	–	–	–	–	–	–	–	1
Persicaria maculosa Gray (redshank)	–	–	–	1	–	–	–	–	–	–	–	–	–	–	–	–	–	–	–	–	–
Rumex sp. (docks)	–	–	–	–	–	–	–	–	–	–	–	–	–	–	–	–	–	–	–	–	–
Prunus spinosa L. (blackthorn) frags.	–	–	–	–	1	–	–	–	–	–	–	–	–	–	–	–	–	–	–	–	–
Vivia cf. *tetrasperma* (L.) Schreber (smooth tare)	1	–	–	–	–	–	–	–	–	–	–	–	–	–	–	–	–	–	–	–	–
Trifolium sp. (clovers)	–	–	–	1	–	–	–	–	–	–	–	–	–	–	–	–	–	–	–	–	–
Plantago lanceolata L. (ribwort plantain)	–	1	–	–	–	–	–	–	–	–	–	–	–	–	–	–	1	–	–	1	–
Poaceae (grasses)	1	–	–	–	–	2	–	–	–	–	–	–	–	–	–	–	–	–	–	–	–
Poaceae large rhizome	–	–	–	–	–	–	–	–	–	–	–	–	1	–	–	–	–	–	–	–	–
Poaceae rhizomes	–	1	–	4	2	–	–	–	–	–	–	–	–	–	–	13	–	–	–	–	1
Flowerhead	–	–	–	–	–	–	–	–	–	–	–	–	–	–	–	–	1	–	–	–	–
Leaf scar	–	–	–	–	–	–	–	–	–	–	–	–	–	–	1	–	–	–	–	–	–
Organic indet.	–	–	–	–	–	–	+	–	–	–	–	–	–	–	–	–	–	–	+	–	–

148

Table 47 Charred plant remains from later features

		Hearth	Pits	
Feature		194	182	186
Context		195	183	187
Taxa				
Cereals				
Triticum spelta	grain	3	–	–
T. spelta / T. aestivum	grain	3	–	–
Triticum aestivum	grain	5cf5	–	–
	rachis nodes	1cf1	–	–
Triticum sp.	grain	19	–	–
	rachis	1	–	–
Hordeum sp. hulled grain	straight	40	–	–
	twisted	21	–	–
	indet.	45	–	–
	rachis	1	–	–
Avena strigosa / A. sativa (bristle oat/oat)	floret base	1	–	–
Cereal indet.	grain	97	–	–
Other plants			–	–
Corylus avellana L. (hazel) nut frags		103	10	75
Chenopodium album L. (fat hen)		21	–	–
Atriplex sp. (oraches)		8	–	–
Chenopodiaceae (goosefoots)		20	–	–
Caryophyllaceae (pinks)		1	–	–
Persicaria maculosa Gray (redshank)		4	–	–
Persicaria lapathifolia (l.) Gray (pale persicaria)		1	–	–
Persicaria sp. (knotweeds)		1	–	–
Fallopia convolvulus (L.) A Love (black bindweed)		2	–	–
Rumex sp. (docks)		144	–	–
Prunus spinosa L. (blackthorn) frags.		8	–	–
Trifolium sp. (clovers)		–	1	–
Ulex sp. (gorse) spines		3	–	–
Lapsana communis L. (nipplewort)		10	–	–
Tripleurospermum inodorum (L.) Schultz-Bip (scentless mayweed)		3	–	–
Avena fatua L. (wild oat) floret base		1	–	–
Avena sp. (oats)		3	–	–
Avena/Large Poaceae		2	–	–
Large Poaceae (grasses)		5	–	–
Small Poaceae		–	3	–
Poaceae large rhizomes		–	–	2
Poaceae stems/rhizomes		–	23	5
Thorns		9	–	–
Pteridium aquilinum (L.) Kuhn (bracken) leaf frags.		3	–	–

Table 48 Charred plant remains from postholes at Hindwell II

Feature	Site B		Site A							
	PH2	PH1	PH1	PH1	PH1	PH2	PH2	PH3	PH3	PH4
Spit	SP4	SP1	SP1	SP3	SP4	SP2	SP3	SP3	SP4	SP2
Taxa										
cf. *Quercus* sp. (oak) kernel	–	–	–	–	1	–	–	–	–	–
Rubus sp. (brambles) frags.	–	–	–	–	–	–	–	1	–	–
Prunus spinosa L. (blackthorn)	–	–	–	–	–	–	–	–	–	2
Plantago lanceolata L. (ribwort plantain)	–	–	1	–	–	–	–	–	–	–
Galium saxatile type (heath bedstraw)	–	–	1	–	–	–	–	–	–	–
Sambucus nigra L. (elder)	–	–	1	–	–	–	–	–	–	–
Large Poaceae (grasses)	1	6	–	–	–	–	–	–	–	–
Small Poaceae	–	7	–	–	1	–	–	1	1	–
Poaceae rhizome/stem frags.	8	245	117	18	34	2	5	49	7	–
Tree leaf buds	–	–	3	–	–	–	–	–	–	–
Organic indet.	–	–	+	–	–	–	–	–	–	–

may be present. There is evidence for the presence of both wild and cultivated oat (*Avena*) from the presence of floret bases. One floret base was possibly of cultivated oat (*A. strigosa/sativa*) whilst another had the typical suckermouth base of wild-oat (*A. fatua*), but winter wild-oat (*A. sterilis*) does have both types of floret base. Docks were the most abundant weed seeds, but Chenopodiaceae were relatively frequent and occasional seeds of redshank (*Persicaria maculosa*), pale persicaria (*P. lapathifolia*) and black bindweed (*Fallopia convolvulus*) also occurred. Hazelnut fragments, as in earlier periods, were again quite frequent and gorse (*Ulex*) spines were present. Since the sample is from a hearth it is possible the grain was from a processed crop either deliberately or accidentally charred. The weed seeds may represent waste from crop processing deliberately used as fuel. The low incidence of chaff in the sample may be because the rachis of free-threshing cereals tends to survive charring less well and the poor state of preservation of the grain would support this. Spelt (*T. spelta*) is generally more common in Wales during the Romano-British period, but large quantities of bread/club wheat were recorded in Romano-British samples from Collfryn (Jones and Milles 1989) and from two corn-dryers at Biglis (Parkhouse 1988). Hulled barley occurs on a number of sites of Romano-British date (Caseldine 1990).

The remaining samples were from the other sites. The samples from Hindwell I and II produced very little apart from grass rhizomes and stems. Hazelnuts were absent but bramble, blackthorn and a possible fragment of acorn kernel were present. No remains other than wood charcoal were recovered from Rough Close and Knapp Farm samples.

Conclusions

Charred plant remains were generally scarce. Evidence for cereal growing during the Neolithic is very limited but there is marginally more for the Peterborough rather than the Grooved Ware phase. However, there is some evidence for both emmer and possibly bread wheat being grown. Hazelnuts were widely represented, if in low amounts, and may have been collected deliberately as a food resource. Alternatively, their presence may have been due to the collection of hazel for fuel. A predominantly grassland environment in the immediate area of the site is indicated, but with some hazel scrubland nearby and perhaps more woodland closer to the site during the Grooved Ware phase, although the evidence could just reflect a difference in areas exploited rather than a change in environment.

The sample from the Romano-British hearth was dominated by free-threshing cereals, bread wheat and barley. The evidence from the site is consistent with that from other parts of Wales.

Walton complex charcoal identifications
Su Johnson

Introduction

Charcoal samples for identification were received from five sites in the Walton complex. The number of samples and the quantity and quality of the charcoal in them varied considerably.

Sub-samples of between ten and seventy fragments were taken for identification, depending on

Table 49 Charcoal from Upper Ninepence. (Fill numbers shown in brackets after feature numbers)

Context		Quercus spp.	Corylus avellana	Pomoideae	Prunus spinosa	Prunus spp.	Salix/ Populus	Euonymus europaeus	Ulex europaeus	Unident. distorted	Bark	Total
Peterborough Ware												
Pits												
10	(11)		47	2	1							50
12	(13)		11	15	2		1			1		30
16	(17)		6	18	5					1		30
200	(201)	1	17	10	2							30
500	(502)		27	1	1	1						30
Grooved Ware												
Pits												
22	(23)		19							1*		20
35	(36)	7	2	1							1	10
85	(86)	6	11	2								20
132	(133)	2	22	2	1		3					30
136	(137)	16	1	2	1							20
146	(147)		42	6	1			1				50
152	(153)	5	5									10
154	(155)	19	18	11	2							50
198	(199)	5	14	11								30
198	(289)	11	9	9								30
198	(291)	3	40	5	2					1		50
293	(292)	20	6	1	1		1			1		30
Stakehole 277	(278)			19						1		20
Structure 1												
Hearth 28	(28)	3		7								10
Stakeholes 26	(27)	3	17									20
57	(57)	16	4									20
Later features												
Pits												
184	(185)	20										20
186	(187)		6	4								10
Hearth 195		8	2	38	10	1			8	2	1	70
Undated pre-barrow												
Pits												
150	(151)	1	9									10
275	(276)	2	15	3								20
370	(371)		2	18								20

Table 50 Charcoal from Hindwell I

Context	Corylus avellana	Pomoideae	Prunus spinosa	Alnus glutinosa	Salix/ Populus	Ulex europeus	Betula spp.	Bark	Total
4222/I/401	5	2	1			2			10
4222/I/501	15	1	2	1			1		20
4222/I/502	10	2	1	3	1	2		1	20

the size of the sample. These sub-samples contained a representative sample of all the fragment sizes present, down to a minimum transverse section of 2mm. The fragments were snapped to expose clean surfaces in three planes which were then examined under a high power microscope.

Upper Ninepence barrow

A total of twenty-seven samples from this site were examined, making this the largest charcoal assemblage from the Walton complex.

Five samples from the Peterborough Ware phase were analysed. Fifty fragments were identified from pit 10 and thirty each from the rest (Table 49).

The samples were similar in composition, all were mainly hazel (Corylus avellana) and Pomoideae (probably hawthorn), and all samples contained a few fragments of blackthorn (Prunus spinosa). Pit 12 produced a single fragment of willow/poplar (Salix/ Populus spp.) and pit 200 a single oak (Quercus spp) fragment.

Hazel was much more common than Pomoideae and blackthorn in pits 10 and 500, but less common in pit 16 whereas the number of fragments from the two groups was more balanced in pits 12 and 200.

The largest group of samples from the site was from the Grooved Ware phase: twelve from pits, three from structure 1 and one from a stakehole. Between 10 and 50 fragments per sample were identified.

Again the range of species in the samples is similar; hazel, Pomoideae and blackthorn, but with the addition (in most samples) of oak. There were also a few occurrences of willow/poplar, and pit 146 contained a single fragment of spindle (Euonymus europaeus).

Most of the pits from this phase contained a range of species, but apart from one that was unidentified, the fragments from pit 22 were exclusively hazel. The fragments from stakehole 277 were again all hazel (with the exception of an unidentified fragment), and here it is tempting to see them as the remains of a hazel stake.

The samples from features associated with structure 1 do not show any significant differences to those from the rest of this phase.

Three samples from undated pre-barrow features were examined. As with the samples above, these contained hazel and Pomoideae and two also produced a few oak fragments.

Samples from later features were also analysed, two from undated pits and one from the Romano-

British hearth 195. Pit 184 contained only oak, and pit 186 yielded hazel and Pomoideae. The sample from hearth 195 was the largest examined and over half the fragments were Pomoideae with roughly equal numbers of oak, blackthorn and gorse (Ulex spp.) as well as a few hazel and unidentifiable fragments.

It is very difficult to make comments about the composition of local woodland on the basis of charcoal. This is because even a large quantity of charcoal may be the remains of only a few branches. There is also the probability that particular species were selected for different purposes, for example the use of small brushwood from shrubby species for fuel rather than larger wood from timber trees, and this would obviously bias the sample. However, given the quantity of hazel, Pomoideae and to a lesser extent, blackthorn, it is likely that there was open woodland and/or scrub in the vicinity. The lack of oak in the samples from the Peterborough Ware phase may indicate that there was not much oak easily available in the area at that time. Possibly it had not yet regenerated after clearance whereas the other species present may have regrown faster. However, without supporting evidence, this should be regarded as highly speculative since other factors, such as the use of different species for fuel and for structural purposes, could account for this lack of oak. It should also be borne in mind that these points are being made on the strength of the contents of only five pits, which is a relatively small sample.

The presence of gorse, presumably used for fuel, in the Romano-British sample suggests open grassland or open woodland type vegetation nearby.

Hindwell I

A total of 50 fragments from three samples from the ditch of the enclosure were examined (Table 50). The species composition of the samples was similar, being mostly hazel, with a few fragments of Pomoideae, blackthorn, alder (Alnus glutinosa) and gorse, and one fragment each of willow/poplar and birch (Betula spp.)

Hindwell II

Ten samples, all from postholes, were examined (Table 51). All the fragments identified were oak, and the unidentified fragments from all the samples had the angular appearance typical of this species. It is

Table 51 Charcoal from Hindwell II

Context	*Quercus* spp.	Total
PR1 SP2	30	30
PH2 SP3	20	20
PR3 SP2	10	10
PH1 SP4	50	50
PH3 SP3	30	30
PH3 SP4	30	30
PH1 SP3	30	30
PH4 SP1	30	30
PH1 SP1	20	20
Post 2 Spit 4	50	50

Table 52 Charcoal from Rough Close

Context	*Quercus* spp.	*Corylus avellana*	Pomoideae	*Prunus spinosa*	*Ulex europeus*	Total
701		3	1	1		5
301	24	1			5	30

Table 53 Charcoal from Knapp Farm

Context	*Corylus avellana*	Pomoideae	*Alnus glutinosa*	*Fraxinus excelsior*	Total
3664/101	3	5	1	1	10

extremely likely that each sample represented the remains of a single, large piece of wood and that what we have here are the remains of the oak posts from the postholes.

Rough Close

Two samples from this site were analysed, one, from a possible pit (701) was a very small sample, containing only a few fragments of hazel, Pomoideae and blackthorn (Table 52). The second was from the dated Mesolithic pit and contained mostly oak, with one hazel fragment and five gorse fragments.

Knapp Farm

A single small sample was analysed. It contained a few fragments of hazel and Pomoideae and one fragment each of alder and ash (*Fraxinus excelsior*) (Table 53).

Palynological investigations in the Walton Basin
Astrid E Caseldine

The pollen evidence from Upper Ninepence, Hindwell

Samples were prepared and examined for pollen from the ditch and palaeosol at Upper Ninepence. Pollen was virtually non-existent in the ditch samples and only a trace survived in the palaeosol samples, precluding a full analysis. Pollen taxa noted included *Alnus*, *Corylus*, Poaceae, Caryophyllaceae, Lactuceae and *Plantago lanceolata*. This evidence, although extremely limited, does suggest the presence of grassland at the site with perhaps some hazel scrub and alder woodland in the vicinity. It is also basically in agreement with the plant macrofossil evidence (see above). However, even these limited results must be treated with caution because of the high level of animal disturbance at the site.

5 Discussion and conclusions

Introduction

The Walton Basin project has produced some spectacular results through a programme of systematic survey, geophysics and excavation. Generally the trial excavations were of mixed success but the larger excavation at Upper Ninepence has produced major Neolithic evidence of national importance, in particular with regard to the Peterborough and Grooved Ware dichotomy, using largely new and to some degree experimental techniques of analysis. In the following discussion, the excavations are considered separately before a final summing up.

The Walton Green cursus

This site bears comparison with the nearby parallel ditches near the Four Stones (the Four Stones cursus) some 2km to the north-west (Gibson 1996a; forthcoming). Like Walton Green, the plan of the possible Four Stones cursus has been recovered from aerial photographs taken over a number of years. The terminals have not yet been located but the parallel ditches can be traced for a distance of 474m and are some 54m apart. The north-east end can be traced as far as the Little Monster Field on Hindwell Farm in which the westernmost arc of the Hindwell palisaded site was found (Gibson 1996a).

The cursus monuments and possible cursus monuments of Wales have been the subject of a recent study (Gibson forthcoming). Eleven possible sites have been recognised, one of which (Holywell) is possibly a bank barrow, and of the rest only three have been excavated to any degree: Walton Green, Sarn-y-bryn-caled (Gibson 1994) and Llandegai (Houlder 1968). These three sites have morphologically similar ditch profiles. They are approximately 3m wide at the gravel surface and around 1m deep. They are also flat bottomed and have clear silting patterns. Sarn-y-bryn-caled appears to have had external banks which are suggested by a rise in the protected gravel surface and by silting patterns from the outside of the monument (Gibson 1994, fig 23), while the others demonstrate silting from the interior.

Superficially, the Walton sites differ from Sarn-y-bryn-caled and Llandegai since the latter two have widths of only 10m and 14m respectively and belong to Loveday's (1985) Elongated Ditch class. These sites contrast with the 60m width of the type Bi Walton Green cursus and the 54m width of the possible Hindwell site. Little meaningful may be said of the lengths of Welsh cursus monuments since only Sarn-y-bryn-caled and Walton Green are known in their entirety. The widths of sites, however, may be broken into three main size-ranges, 10–15m (4 sites – 40%), 20–30m (4 sites – 40%) and 50m or over (2 sites – 20%). Only the narrowest and widest categories include sites which are fairly certainly cursus monuments. The middle range sites are all possible or unlikely identifications.

In keeping with cursus monuments generally, the Welsh sites seem to have association with other ritual sites (Gibson forthcoming). There is a possible henge site to the north-west of the Llandissilio cursus. At Spread Eagle there is a cluster of eight ring-ditches on the gravel terrace some 150m to the east and the parallel ditches seem to be aligned on a ninth large ring-ditch 450m to the north-west and across the river. The possible Llyn-y-Cefn site incorporates a ring-ditch in its south ditch, and at Tyn-y-Cefn there is also a ring-ditch close to the west of the northern end of the monument. At Llandegai, there are two ring-ditches extending the north-western orientation of the cursus, and to the north-east and south-west of the north-west terminal are two henge monuments and a ring-ditch.

The ritual complex at Sarn-y-bryn-caled has been extensively studied (Gibson 1994) and a developmental sequence based on relative and absolute chronologies, as well as site analogy, has been proposed. The cursus appears to be the primary monument, attracting close to its north-east terminal a horseshoe-shaped ring-ditch, a substantial standing post and Peterborough phase pits. These sites are followed by a hengiform ring-ditch, a timber circle, two ring-ditches (both of which show evidence for central pits), and a Beaker-associated henge. The complex was developed over the course of almost two millennia. This complex is, of course, at the south-western end of the second possible cursus at Sarn-y-bryn-caled, though the authenticity of this second site is doubted.

The Hindwell cursus, if such it is, is also set within a ritual landscape. It passes close to the Four Stones stone circle which lies some 20m to the north. To the north-east of the ditches are two substantial round barrows, one of which covers a triple ring-ditch visible on some aerial photographs. Some 20m from the north-eastern end as currently traceable, lies the Hindwell palisaded enclosure (Gibson 1996a) dated to c 2700 Cal BC.

At Walton Green, there is a large barrow covering traces of a ring-ditch 60m to the south-west of the south-west terminal. Flint artefacts have been recovered from the barrow. Less than 1km to the west-north-west of the south-west terminal is the Walton palisaded enclosure. This is of Meldon Bridge type and while it is currently undated, by analogy it is likely to belong to the early third millennium Cal BC and may well pre-date the cursus.

Only the Sarn-y-bryn-caled cursus has been firmly dated; charcoal from the base of the ditch giving a radiocarbon date of 4960 ± 70 BP (OxA–3997) and proving it to be the primary monument in the ritual complex. Loveday's (1985) scheme would prefer to see the narrow sites as earlier and the wide Bi type as later in the monuments' period of currency, and the Sarn-y-bryn-caled date is consistent with this hypothesis. The Bi sites appear to be associated with later Neolithic material such as Grooved Ware from Lechlade (Gibson and Loveday 1989), and Peterborough Ware from Springfield (Hedges and Buckley 1981) and Drayton (Ainslie and Wallis 1987). In this case the limited dating evidence (a Neolithic scraper providing a *terminus ante quem*) from Walton Green is in accordance with the national pattern. The narrower sites tend to be earlier and the C14 dates from Inchtuthil (Barclay and Maxwell 1991) and North Stoke (Case 1982) are consistent with Sarn-y-bryn-caled (Gibson 1994, fig 28).

The Hindwell palisaded enclosure

The palisaded enclosure at Hindwell is truly a remarkable discovery. With an internal area of some 35Ha it is by far the largest Neolithic enclosure in Britain. In Europe Hindwell is only smaller than the early Neolithic, Michelsberg-associated, enclosure at Urmitz, on the Rhine near Koblenz (Boelicke 1977). Clearly much more work needs to be undertaken at Hindwell. The location of entrances, analysis of any internal arrangements and the determination of the function(s) of the enclosure are fundamental research priorities which will involve a substantial project of geophysical survey and trial excavation. The relationships between the Hindwell enclosure and both the Meldon Bridge-type palisaded site at Walton and the neighbouring triple ditches to the east of Hindwell Farm also need investigation.

The reconstruction of the Hindwell enclosure is problematic. The site consists of postholes only and clearly no evidence survives, earthwork or otherwise, for the above ground nature of the site. There was no trace of an inner or outer bank to suggest that the palisade was a revetment. It appears to have been a free-standing fence of uprights. However, we know the depths of the postholes as well as the diameters of the oak posts which they contained. The depths of the postholes, averaging *c* 2m below the gravel surface, suggests that the 0.8m diameter posts probably stood at least 6m above the ground (assuming that at least one third of the post height would have to have been buried to ensure stability). The spacing of the posts in the two excavated sections indicates that there were three posts every 5m therefore, in a monument with a circumference of 2.35km, 1410 posts would have been needed to complete the perimeter. Each post would have weighed in the region of 4.5 tonnes (allowing 1.07 tonnes per cubic metre for green oak), involving the manhandling of some 6300 tonnes of freshly felled oak timbers. Entrances remain to be certainly located though some of the gaps tentatively identified on the aerial photographs may be contenders. Whether these gaps were marked by larger posts, as at Mount Pleasant (Wainwright 1979), remains to be tested.

The original appearance of the Hindwell enclosure also remains uncertain. Gaps between the posts averaged 0.7m. There were no traces of smaller intermediate posts, as encountered at Meldon Bridge (Burgess 1976), and it is impossible to judge whether the posts were free-standing with gaps inbetween, or whether horizontal timbers, pegged to the uprights, formed a solid impenetrable fence. Clearly this knowledge might shed important light on the possible functions of the enclosure; open free-standing posts being more suited to a ritual rather than a defended site.

There are three main types of palisaded enclosure in Neolithic Britain. The first type comprises enclosures with a perimeter of individual postholes such as at Walton, and also at Meldon Bridge, Peeblesshire (Burgess 1976), Forteviot, Perthshire (Harding and Lee 1987, 409–11), Dunragit, Dumfriess (Mercer 1993), Newgrange, Co Meath (Sweetman 1985), and Ballynahatty, Co Down (Hartwell 1991; 1994). The second type includes those like Hindwell with perimeters composed of closely-spaced postpits such as Greyhound Yard, Dorchester, Dorset (Woodward *et al* 1993), and the third type comprises sites with perimeters with uprights set in bedding trenches such as at West Kennet I and II (Whittle 1991; 1992), Orsett, Essex (Hedges and Buckley 1978), Mount Pleasant, Dorset (Wainwright 1979), Knowth, Co Meath (Eogan 1984, 219), Donegore, Co Antrim (inf J Mallory), and possibly Lyles Hill in the same county (Simpson and Gibson 1989), though the exact nature of this latter palisade cannot yet be determined.

In terms of size, the areas of these enclosures can at best be estimated since the only sites with fully known circumferences are Ballynahatty, Forteviot and Mount Pleasant (Table 54). Of the rest, *c* 75% of the Walton perimeter is known and the area can therefore be guessed: similarly at West Kennet I and II, and Dunragit, where the perimeter can be rounded off to provide a rough estimate. Dunragit has been broken into two sites, the outer pit circuit with a scalloped effect and no entrance corridor, and an inner site marked by a more regular double palisade. At Walton and Meldon Bridge the riverine location of each site suggests that the river course was utilised in the perimeter, and at Orsett the palisade appears to follow a line inside the second ditch circuit. The perimeter of Greyhound Yard is less certain but the arc of pits is regular and, combined with similar pits found in Church Street in 1982/3, the area of the enclosure can be estimated, albeit tentatively (Woodward *et al* 1993, 30).

These estimations show that the average area for Neolithic palisaded sites (excluding Hindwell) is 4.5Ha but that there is a large variation in the areas

Table 54 The estimated dimensions of Neolithic palisaded sites. The bracketed values at Meldon Bridge are for the larger posts found in the northern sector of the perimeter. The bracketed values at Mount Pleasant are for the entrance timbers

Site	Estimated area Ha	Estimated post height (m)	Estimated post length (m)	Estimated post diameter (m)	Estimated post weight (tonnes)
Ballynahatty	0.69	3.6	5.4	0.3	0.4
Dunragit outer	6.59 +				
Dunragit inner	1.56				
Forteviot	4.55				
Meldon Bridge	7.21 ?	2.8 (3.4)	4.2 (5.1)	0.4 (0.6)	0.6 (1.5)
Newgrange	0.64	2	3	0.3 ?	0.2 ?
Walton	7.69				
Greyhound Yd	11 ?	6	9	1	7.6
Hindwell	35	4	6	0.8	3.2
Mount Pleasant	4.32	6 (5)	9 (8)	0.4 (1.6)	1.2 (17.2)
West Kennet I	4.35 +	4	6	0.3	0.5
West Kennet II	5.55 ?	4	6	0.5	1.3
Lyles Hill inner	?	<2	<3	0.25	<0.2
Lyles Hill outer	?	<1	<1.5	0.20	<0.08
Knowth E	?	1	1.5	0.25	0.2
Knowth W	?	1	1.5	0.25	0.2
Orsett	1.7 ?	<2	<3	0.25	<0.2
Donegore	2 ?				
Haddenham	8	2.2	3	0.3	0.2

of individual sites. At 35Ha, Hindwell is far greater in size than any other Neolithic palisaded site yet known. Even compared with causewayed enclosures, the size is well in excess of known examples which rarely exceed 8Ha (Palmer 1976). The posts, however, would appear not to be as imposing as those from Greyhound Yard or Mount Pleasant, but compare favourably with the other sites. The Lyles Hill, Newgrange, Knowth and Orsett palisades are much flimsier than the other sites, even allowing for erring on the side of generosity in estimating the post dimensions, and this may suggest either a difference in date or function or both. The Newgrange site is problematic in its interpretation since many postholes were later reused for other purposes of ritual deposition. These smaller sites may justifiably be termed fenced sites to distinguish them from the larger more imposing palisades.

The dating of these sites has recently been discussed (Gibson 1996: 1998a). The British evidence is limited to some thirty dates from ten sites and there appears to be a pattern visible within the date ranges (Table 55). Firstly the smaller fenced sites, Lyles Hill, Donegore and Orsett, are early and date to the earlier Neolithic. Of the more massive sites, the individual posthole sites such as Meldon Bridge and Ballynahatty appear to be earlier, the close-set posthole sites such as Hindwell and Greyhound Yard appear to occupy the middle range just before 2500 Cal BC, with the sites composed of contiguous posts such as Mount Pleasant and West Kennet clustering some time after this date. The sample is admittedly

small and further excavation with judicious dating may further refine or disprove this pattern.

The C14 dates are, however, also supported to an extent by the artefactual evidence. The small fenced sites are all associated with earlier Neolithic pottery, Meldon Bridge with later Neolithic Impressed Ware, West Kennet and Greyhound Yard with Grooved Ware, and Mount Pleasant with Beaker. A sequence of development may therefore be envisaged for these sites from individual posthole construction via close-set posts to contiguous palisades.

Whether this hypothesis will be supported or demolished by subsequent researches remains to be tested, but clearly the most important observation is that, within the later Neolithic, large palisaded enclosures were being constructed and involved considerable outlay in both human and natural resources. They attest to the sophistication of Neolithic engineering, the organisation and motivation of populations and the effectiveness of the stone axe.

The functions of these sites remain to be discovered. The posthole positioning at Meldon Bridge indicates that even the spaced posthole sites very probably presented a solid wall. The evidence is less clear for sites of the close-set type. Nevertheless, the size of the original monument would have presented a physical, if purely visual, barrier. Whether the Hindwell enclosure represents a defended site, a settlement, a ritual enclosure, or whether indeed it possessed a combination of functions, must await further investigation of the interior.

Table 55 Radiocarbon dates from Neolithic palisaded enclosures

Site	Date BP	Lab No	Cal Bc 68%	Cal BC 95%	Context
Meldon Bridge	4280 ± 80	HAR-796	3040–2870 or 2810–2770 or 2720–2700	3300–2600	burnt wood, base of BF3
	4100 ± 130	HAR-797	2880–2800 or 2780–2560 or 2540–2500	3050–2250	charcoal from packing of DF3
Ballynahatty	4293 ± 30	UB-3402	3020–3000 or 2930–2890	3030–2980 or 2930–2880 or 2800–2780	charcoal from posthole packing
	4355 ± 26	UB-3403	3030–2970 or 2940–2920	3040–2910	charcoal from posthole packing
Greyhound Yd	4020 ± 80	HAR-6686	2860–2810 or 2700–2680 or 2660–2460	2900–2300	charcoal from the postpipe
	4090 ± 70	HAR-6687	2870–2810 or 2770–2720 or 2700–2570 or 2530–2510	2890–2490	charcoal from the postpipe
	4080 ± 70	HAR-6688	2870–2810 or 2770–2720 or 2700–2570 or 2540–2500	2880–2800 or 2780–2470	charcoal from the postpipe
	4140 ± 90	HAR-6689	2880–2610	2920–2490	charcoal from the postpipe
	4020 ± 80	HAR-6663	2860–2810 or 2700–2680 or 2660–2460	2900–2300	antler from fill of post-ramp
	4070 ± 70	HAR-6664	2870–2810 or 2750–2720 or 2700–2560 or 2540–2500	2880–2800 or 2780–2460	antler from fill of postpipe
	4060 ± 90	HAR-5508	2870–2810 or 2770–2720 or 2700–2490	2900–2350	charcoal from postpipe at Church St site
Hindwell	3960 ± 70	SWAN-116	2590–2350	2900–2800 or 2700–2200	charcoal from outer rings of post
	4070 ± 70	SWAN-117	2870–2810 or 2750–2720 or 2700–2560 or 2540–2500	2880–2800 or 2780–2460	charcoal from outer rings of post
					charcoal from outer rings of post
					charcoal from outer rings of post
W Kennet 1 outer ditch	3810 ± 50	BM-2579	2450–2430 or 2350–2190 or 2160–2140	2460–2130	antler from ditch
	3620 ± 50	BM-2602	2120–2080 or 2040–1920	2140–1880	antler from ditch
	3860 ± 70	CAR-1289	2460–2280 or 2230–2210	2570–2540 or 2500–2140	bone from ditch
	3900 ± 70	CAR-1290	2500–2290	2580–2190 or 2160–2140	bone from ditch
	3960 ± 70	CAR-1293	2590–2350	2900–2800 or 2700–2200	bone from ditch

Table 55 Radiocarbon dates from Neolithic palisaded enclosures (*cont.*)

Site	Date BP	Lab No	Cal Bc 68%	Cal BC 95%	Context
W Kennet 1 inner ditch	3890 ± 70	CAR-1291	2500–2280	2580–2530 or 2510–2190 or 2170–2140	bone from ditch
W Kennet 2	3620 ± 70	CAR-1294	2130–2070 or 2050–1900	2200–1770	bone from ditch
	4050 ± 70	CAR-1295	2870–2810 or 2740–2730 or 2700–2490	2880–2800 or 2780–2460	bone from ditch
Mt Pleasant	3635 ± 60	BM-662	2140–2070 or 2050–1930	2200–1870	antler in palisade trench
	3645 ± 40	BM-665	2130–2070 or 2050–1970	2140–1910	charcoal from palisade trench
	3955 ± 45	BM-794	2580–2530 or 2510–2450 or 2420–2400	2590–2330	
Lyles Hill Inner	4433 ± 40	UB-3074	3300–3240 or 3110–3030 or 2980–2930	3330–3230 or 3190–2920	
Lyles Hill Outer	3974 ± 50	UB-3062	2580–2460	2900–2800 or 2700–2300	
Orsett	4726 ± 74	BM-1378	3630–3570 or 3540–3370	3690–3350	charcoal from postpipe
	4741 ± 113	BM-1213	3640–3370	3800–3100	charcoal from post central to the entrance
Donegore inner	6066 ± 60	UB-3070	5200–5170 or 5140–5120 or 5070–4900	5210–4840	charcoal from palisade
	4583 ± 50	UB-3073	3500–3470 or 3380–3310 or 3240–3110	3510–3100	charcoal from palisade
Donegore outer	5080 ± 50	UB-3071	3970–3900 or 3880–3810	4000–3780	charcoal from palisade

Upper Ninepence enclosure

The full extent of the Upper Ninepence enclosure, if such it is, has not yet been determined. The enclosure is currently known to describe a sub-polygonal form which is 130m across at its widest point (Fig 18 inset). Silting patterns in the ditch suggest an internal bank, but the enclosure is constructed on a gentle S-facing slope, and does not appear to be in an ostensibly defensive position. Furthermore, the ditch is comparatively narrow and shallow suggesting that any bank derived purely from the spoil from this ditch could not have been very substantial. The site is unlikely therefore to be defensive though it could have been protective if the bank was surmounted by a fence or even a hedge.

Internal arrangements are also unknown. The site is generally under pasture and is rarely ploughed. Cropmarks are rarely seen and when they do appear, they are usually ill-defined. Only the perimeter of the enclosure has been noted on aerial photographs. The enclosure ditch coincides with a ring-ditch on it's eastern arc.

Parallels for the Upper Ninepence enclosure are difficult to find. With the exception of the well-known stone-built enclosures of Dartmoor and the south-west, early Bronze Age (pre-Deverel-Rimbury) enclosures are rare in Britain. The early date for the oft-discussed site at Rams Hill has recently been questioned, as has the precision of the dating of other Bronze Age sites (Needham and Ambers 1994). The subangularity of Upper Ninepence resembles the possible later Bronze Age enclosure at Hog Cliff Hill, Dorset (Ellison and Rahtz 1987), though this site would appear to be later Bronze Age in date. The middle Bronze Age enclosures of South Lodge and Down Farm, recently discussed by Barrett *et al* (1991), share the subangularity of Upper Ninepence, but at 50m and 40m across respectively, they are very small when compared with the present site.

The outer ditches of some double-ditched hengiform monuments, Arminghall, Norfolk, for example, has a slightly irregular and narrow outer ditch (Clark 1936), as does the possible hengiform site at West Cotton, Northamptonshire (Windell 1989). Like Upper Ninepence, this latter site lies on a gentle slope overlooking an area of intense Neolithic and Bronze Age ritual activity – in this case, the Nene Valley – including triple-ditched round barrows like those at Hindwell (PRN 309).

There are also parallels to be found for both the size and the subangularity of Upper Ninepence in the cropmark enclosures of Leicestershire (Hartley 1989, fig 6.5). These sites are generally considered to be Iron Age but few have been securely dated.

Indeed, Upper Ninepence may be added to a small but growing number of final Neolithic or earlier Bronze Age enclosures. In addition to the palisaded sites discussed above, other enclosure types may well belong to this period. The roughly oval enclosure at Plasketlands, for example, remains largely undated, but is assumed to be associated with Neolithic postpits dated to c 3700 Cal BC (Bewley 1993). At Abermule, Powys, a pit associated with middle Neolithic Fengate Ware was located within a rectilinear enclosure, though the dating of the perimeter of this site remains tantalisingly unresolved (Gibson and Musson 1990).

Hindwell Ash barrow

The agricultural regime had clearly had a devastating effect on the surviving archaeology, particularly on the northern semicircle. Where the mound entered the field boundary, and was thus protected from ploughing by its proximity to the fence and by the overlying trig point, the barrow was seen to have a potentially complex and deep stratigraphy. This had, however, been severely plough-truncated in the northern half to the extent that the observed ground surface radius from the centre to the southern perimeter was 15m, while the radius from the centre to the northern perimeter was a mere 9m. The dramatic truncation of the mounds can also be seen in the sections (see Fig 21).

The pre-barrow features located in the natural subsoil below the mound were all small and shallow. Their survival was almost certainly due to the protection offered by the covering mound and any similar data outside the confines of the mound would be unlikely to survive.

The surface indications seemed to suggest that the barrow appeared to survive better in the southern half. Whether this is a correct observation, or whether it is an optical illusion created by siting the mound on a natural knoll, might only be tested by excavation.

From the keyhole work undertaken, however, the barrow appears to have been enlarged with material derived from a ring-ditch forming a circle with an estimated diameter of c 30m. This ditch does not appear to be concentric with either the turf mound or the surviving earthwork, which may imply that

either a sequence of eccentric embellishment has been employed, or that agricultural degradation has so altered the profile of the monument that its apparent centre is far removed from its original position.

Arguments in favour of the former hypothesis may be provided by sites such as Four Crosses in North Powys (Warrilow et al 1986) where the three phases identified at barrow 5 involved the digging of three eccentric ditches. Similar internal eccentricity may be noted in cropmark barrows in the Dyffryn Lane henge complex, also in North Powys (Gibson 1995b), and at Site XII (and to a lesser extent Site XI), Dorchester on Thames, Oxfordshire (Whittle et al 1992, 175). In view of the irregularity of the arc of the Hindwell Ash ditch, obviously the degree of eccentricity at this site cannot be evaluated without further investigation.

Hearths of the later Iron Age or early Roman period were located within the upper levels of the mound. They may have been dug into the mound, or set within its damaged areas, but their stratigraphy is not clearly understood.

Upper Ninepence Neolithic and Bronze Age activity

Introduction

The excavation at Upper Ninepence has demonstrated the wealth of archaeological information which may survive within a context protected from the rigours of modern agriculture by an archaeological feature such as a round barrow. It also demonstrates the vulnerability of such an earth-built monument in an area of intensive arable agriculture. The distribution of the surviving features, particularly the more ephemeral features such as the stakeholes and hearths, is restricted to the area of the mound itself with few lying outside in unprotected contexts (see Fig 31). The buried soil (context 72) similarly did not survive beyond the confines of the barrow mound, though in this case the palaeoenvironmental potential of the context was minimised as a result of animal disturbance.

Phase 1: Mesolithic/Neolithic

The earliest activity recorded at Upper Ninepence is Mesolithic in the form of a possible microlith (L13) from the mound material. In addition there are blades and blade-like flakes as well as a leaf-shaped arrowhead (L24) from unstratified contexts which may further attest a Mesolithic and earlier Neolithic presence. From the surface collection over the mound, an obliquely blunted point and some blades and blade-like flakes may further attest a Mesolithic presence. No recognisable flint artefacts from this period were recovered from stratified contexts below the mound.

Table 56 The Peterborough pits at Upper Ninepence: a summary of contents

Pit	Nos of vessels	Flint waste (burnt)	Retouched pieces	Cores	Artefacts
6	1				
10	1	40 + (2)	2	2	2 arrowheads 2 end-and-side scrapers (1 burnt)
12	3	5	1		
16	3	17 + (1)	1		1 serrated flake 1 piercer
20	1	5 + (2)			1 serrated flake
37	1				
65	2	5 + (3)			
200	2	2			
500	1/2	2			

Phase 2: Middle Neolithic

Shortly before 3000 Cal BC, the hilltop at Upper Ninepence saw a period of activity associated with Peterborough Ware (see Fig 33). This activity is represented by the excavation of at least nine small pits within a restricted area into which ceramics, flint and charred materials were deposited. Pit 500 lay outside this restricted area and contained exclusively Fengate Ware material in a fabric resembling more the grog-filled Grooved Ware than the other material in the Peterborough Ware assemblage. The date for this pit, however, clearly establishes the pottery as Peterborough and confirms the early appearance of Fengate Ware in the archaeological record (Gibson and Kinnes 1997). The artefactual evidence suggests that this material is derived from a domestic context: waste flint debris is present in the lithic assemblage and well-used, and occasionally burnt, scrapers are the predominant tool type (see above). Some of the pottery vessels provide evidence for the cooking of meat derived from ruminant animals (see above). Petrographic analysis of the pottery, while indicating a generally uniform fabric, does suggest that with their schist inclusions, P1, P10 and P20 may all have been derived from approximately 50km outside of the basin, and that the lithic sandstone in P11 may be similarly foreign.

The environmental data (see above) indicates an open environment with cereal cultivation (emmer and bread wheat), grassland and hazel scrub. In view of the faunal evidence suggested by the residue analysis of the pottery and the microwear analysis of the flint, it may be tempting to see the hazel, blackthorn and pomoideae (hawthorn ?) species as representing hedging between the arable and the pasture, but in view of the colonising capabilities of these species, this hypothesis cannot be proven.

The contents of the Peterborough pits vary considerably (Table 56). Generally they contained fragments of 1–3 vessels, but the flint assemblage shows greater diversity. Pit 37, for example, contained no flint waste at all, pits 200 and 500 contained only two waste flakes each, while pits 10

and 16 yielded a far greater amount of waste material as well as artefacts. The apparent differences in content do not appear to be reflected in either the distribution pattern or the shape and dimensions of the pits. It may, however, reflect a difference in ritualistic detail and even an element of deliberate selection (Barrett et al 1991, 79–82).

Whether these pits were excavated specifically to be the repositories of discarded domestic detritus, or whether they had a deeper significance, is at present difficult to determine. A survey of the buried material indicates that the lithic material is waste, well-used or broken, and presumably therefore had become redundant. The ceramic material was all in a sherd state when deposited with no complete vessels represented. The material was, therefore, expendable and at face value represents no great sacrifice on the part of the depositors. Nevertheless, in purely practical terms, the deliberate act of burying this material in pits which were quickly back-filled seems alien to an agrarian community which would have been well-acquainted with manuring regimes. Furthermore, the fact that the pottery vessels are so fragmentary suggests that only a small proportion of the total waste was receiving such well-defined deposition, and if this is the case, then the pits must represent a different and also rare form of rubbish disposal.

The full contents of each pit are not known. In the dry and acid soil, bone and uncharred food remains would not survive. Nor would other organic materials such as leather or fabrics. However, the microwear analysis of the lithic artefacts attests that leather and bone-working were carried out at the settlement, and the presence of ruminant residues akin to sheep fats in the ceramics suggests that woollen fabrics would also have been present. The surviving contents of the pits, ceramics with food traces, stone and charred plant remains probably represent only a fraction of the range of materials that were actually deposited. Nevertheless, both the presumed archaeologically invisible deposits and the surviving materials are united in the fact they derive from the soil: animals feed from the soil, plants grow from it, the raw materials for pottery are dug from it and flint is foraged or quarried from it. The surviving artefacts are also united in that they are spent materials representing a small percentage of the whole.

In the same way that seeds represent a small percentage of the plant but, when returned to the soil, reproduce the resource, so the deposition of fragmentary material in this apparently illogical way may be an attempt to ensure the continuation of the supply of raw materials. Thus symbolically returning a percentage of materials to their source will ensure their constant availability to a society who depended entirely on Earth's bounty. Whether this deposition took the form of a continuous process or whether it was undertaken at specific events or festivals, as at our contemporary harvest festivals, is at present beyond our powers of archaeological detection. To what extent the pit-ritual at Upper Ninepence extended beyond the confines of the later mound is also unknown, but more important is that the activity took place on a physically high point from which the surrounding countryside, the immediate area of local earth-exploitation, could be surveyed. This might ensure that the practitioners in the ritual were physically as well as mentally conscious of the reasons for their ritual.

The best local parallels for the deposition and context of the present assemblage are the finds from Cefn Bryn, Glamorgan (Ward 1987), Llanilar, Ceredigion (Taverner et al forthcoming; Gibson 1995a) and Ysgwennant, Denbighshire (Day 1972). These sites have all produced small quantities of Peterborough Ware from pits sealed by later mounds and have recently been discussed elsewhere (Gibson 1995a). The Llanilar pits in particular are considered by their excavators to have been ritual in function through being filled with burnt (including bagged) settlement-derived material.

At Meole Brace, Shrewsbury, Shropshire, lying adjacent to a ring-ditch, was a distinct cluster of twelve pits associated with Peterborough Ware (Hughes and Woodward 1995). These pits were similar to those from Upper Ninepence in that they were of roughly the same size and also generally single-filled. They also contained fragmentary locally-made vessels, charcoal and occasional burnt pebbles. A similar, if smaller pit group, also with Peterborough Ware and charcoal flecks, was located at Wasperton, Warwickshire (Hughes and Crawford 1995), where the excavators also found difficulty in distinguishing between ritual and domestic. The argument is, however, somewhat academic as it is possible to see domestic material ritually deposited and economics and symbolism are rarely unconnected in primitive societies (Barrett 1994; Grant 1991).

Phase 3: Later Neolithic

The second visible phase of datable archaeological activity centres on c 2700 Cal BC and is manifested by a phase of Grooved Ware-associated pit digging and structural activity. The Grooved Ware appears to be all locally made though the calcite and shell inclusions of P62–3 suggest an element of importation of fillers if not clays. This phase is broadly contemporary with the construction of the Hindwell II palisaded enclosure and this major monument would have been clearly visible, given an open environment, from the hilltop at Upper Ninepence.

The pit digging in this phase was more extensive than in the preceding one, in that the pits were distributed over a wider area (see Fig 33), and the archaeological finds were more prolific. Ten pits are securely dated to the Grooved Ware phase, including the large pit 198 and the subrectangular pit 154 which between them produced fragments of 23 vessels. In addition, seven stakeholes also contained Grooved Ware pottery, though the strict association of the ceramic with these features is less certain. Stakehole 18 was radiocarbon-dated to this phase.

The flint assemblage associated with this phase comprises high quality material but is again used, waste or broken. Indeed, other than the obvious ceramic difference, the finds from the pits in this phase are remarkably similar to those of the former: waste material, pots used for cooking, and carbonised plant material. Once again there is considerable variation in content (Table 57) despite the restricted nature of the surviving material. Pit 22, for example, contained little pottery but an abundance of flint waste and artefacts. By far the largest and deepest feature, pit 198, contained abundant ceramic in its various fills, but remarkably little flint. Pits 132 and 154 were rich in ceramics as well as lithics. It is also from these features that the internally decorated vessels originate. Given the rarity of internally decorated vessels in Grooved Ware assemblages generally (see below), and given the richness of the pit contents, these two comparatively close pits may well represent extra-special depositories of selected redundant material of a nevertheless prestigious nature.

These putatively rich pits (55, 132, 154, 198) occupy the highest point of the site and form a roughly trapezoid arrangement (see Fig 33) resembling the posthole structures at Willington, Derbyshire (Wheeler 1979), though there is no evidence to suggest that the Upper Ninepence pits ever held posts. Pits 293 and 22, however, are also apparently rich yet lie outside this general distribution.

With the change in ceramics comes an apparent change in diet as the lipid analysis suggests that it was pork which had become the predominant cooked meat (see above). This is in keeping with Grooved Ware faunal assemblages elsewhere, for example Durrington Walls, where the preponderance of young pig was regarded as evidence of feasting (Wainwright and Longworth 1971). Other Grooved Ware assemblages, however, suggest a strong element of cattle as well as pig (Pollard 1995; Harding 1988; Barrett et al 1991, 79), but this is not represented by

Table 57 The Grooved Ware pits at Upper Ninepence: a summary of contents

Pit	Nos of vessels (residual Peterborough)	Flint waste (burnt)	Retouched pieces	Cores	Artefacts
22	1	25 + (4)		2	1 chisel arrowhead, 2 end scrapers 4 end-and-side scrapers, 1 misc scraper
35	1	19			
55	7	4			
85	2	9			
132	4	34 + (3)	3	2	1 end scraper
146	1				
150	1	11			
152	1	22 + (3)			
154	8 (1)	32 + (6)	3		1 end-and-side scraper, 1 end scraper 2 misc scrapers, 1 knife
188	1				
198	15 (1)	35 + (2)	4		1 end-and-side scraper
293	4	8 + (2)		1	
300	1				
370	crumbs				

the evidence at Upper Ninepence. The residue analysis of the pottery, while admittedly limited in scope, nevertheless demonstrates a distinct difference between the animal associations of the Peterborough and Grooved Ware phases. Whether this represents a change in husbandry, economy, a change of ritual or indeed an increase in ritual, is at present unclear.

The palaeoenvironmental evidence, sparse though it is, points towards a rather more wooded environment than in the preceding phase, with more oak represented and with less evidence for cereals. Taken with the pig fats in the residue analysis of the ceramics, this may suggest an economy based on browsing animals, though the data are too sparse to be conclusive.

Structures 1 and 2 have been described in detail above. While structure 1 definitely dates to this phase, the chronology of structure 2 is less certain, relying as it does on the finds of residual Grooved Ware from the stakeholes. Nevertheless, the two structures are superficially similar and may be discussed together. In terms of size and construction, the stakehole circles of structures 1 and 2 resemble the Grooved Ware-associated structures at Trelystan Powys (Britnell 1982), though at this site the central hearths were formally edged with stone and heat-crazed stones were recovered from internal pits. (Other than occasional burnt flints, there were no burnt stones from Upper Ninepence.) Also at Trelystan, the perimeter stakes had been driven in at an angle whereas at the present site the stakes were

vertical. Nevertheless, the overall similarity of the four structures concerned is remarkable given their shared cultural backgrounds.

Other stakehole arrangements which bear comparison with structures 1 and 2 are the circular structures at Marden, Wiltshire (10m diameter), Litton Cheney, Dorset (10m diameter) and Hockwold-cum-Wilton, Norfolk (6m diameter). The two former sites lie within larger henge monuments considered to have ritual functions (Wainwright *et al* 1971; Catherall 1976). Neither of these sites have central hearths, and the stakes of the Litton Cheney example are set within a bedding trench. These sites are not ostensibly domestic. At Hockwold-cum-Wilton (Bamford 1982) a slightly dished circular floor area was discovered, with traces of a double stakehole wall around its perimeter, resembling the better preserved structure at Gwithian, Cornwall (Megaw 1976). Both these sites do have internal hearths, but their association with Beaker ceramics places them later than the Upper Ninepence structures.

More numerous parallels for the Upper Ninepence structures may be found in Ireland (see Grogan 1996 for a useful summary). In particular, the stakehole structures with roughly central hearths set within a palimpsest of pits and postholes at Lough Gur are associated with Beaker and Irish Grooved Ware (Gibson 1987; Grogan and Eogan 1987). House 1 at Slieve Breagh (Grogan 1996, fig 4.3) is also of a similar size to structure 1 at Upper Ninepence and appears to have a possible porch to the south. At Newgrange, circular floor areas have been identified around hearth sites located at the base of the great passage grave (Cooney and Grogan 1994). These hearths are associated with Irish Grooved Ware and Beaker ceramics. The identified structures around these hearths did not have stakehole walls but there were internal roofing stakes and they appear to have been arranged in four groups of four each varying between 5m and 6m in diameter.

The Irish circular Neolithic houses range in diameter from 4.5 to 8m in diameter (Grogan 1996 table 4.2) which again corresponds well with the dimensions of structures 1 and 2. Indeed the similarity of the Welsh sites (Upper Ninepence and Trelystan) with the Irish material may be one facet of the strong Hiberno-Cambrian links at this time manifested elsewhere in Wales, for example, by passage graves, Food Vessels, megalithic art and metalwork, and it may be no coincidence to note the presence of Irish style Grooved Ware at Upper Ninepence (see above).

The curving ditch also belongs to this phase but its function remains obscure. The ditch and the problems it presents have been discussed above; suffice it to emphasise here that the spoil from the ditch appears to have been ultimately returned to it (see above). Many of the postholes also date to this period.

Phase 4: ? Final Neolithic/early Bronze Age

The posthole arrangement here designated as structure 3 possibly dates to this period. As with structure 2, the dating is problematic. Grooved Ware has been recovered in a residual state from stakehole 325 on the southern perimeter of the group, but a Grooved Ware phase radiocarbon determination was obtained from charcoal from stakehole 18 which is believed to have formed part of the north-eastern arc. More or less central to the stake circle is the shallow feature 752 believed to represent the site of the primary burial. Stake circles within barrows are common and they are well paralleled in Welsh barrows where the construction, like Upper Ninepence, is of earth or turf. The single circle of close-set posts measuring some 15m in diameter at Six Wells 271', and the irregular circle some 8m in diameter at Six Wells 267', are particularly relevant (Fox 1959). The turf-built barrows at the Brenig cemetery in Denbighshire also have stake circles beneath them (Lynch 1993), though the excavators were uncertain as to whether these features were symbolic or structural. This uncertainty must also persist at Upper Ninepence. Since no traces of the stakeholes were visible within the makeup of the barrow mound, it may well be that the circle is ritual and pre-dates the mound construction. However, the perimeter of the mound was so badly disturbed by rabbit activity that the evidence may have been destroyed. If a vertical revetment similar to those at West Heath, Sussex, (Drewett 1976) is envisaged for Upper Ninepence, then the flimsiness

of the posts suggests that the revetment was probably not very high.

Phase 5: Early Bronze Age

This marks the final construction of the mound at Upper Ninepence. It was composed of turf and topsoil and built directly onto the old ground surface. Fragments of Peterborough Ware and Grooved Ware, as well as flintwork from the mound material, attest the slight truncation of buried features during the scraping up of this soil. Fragments of two early Bronze Age vessels, a probable Collared Urn and a Food Vessel Urn (see below) suggest the presence of former secondary burials in the mound itself, the destruction of which had already been suggested by Dunn some 30 years ago.

The enclosures at Knapp Farm and Hindwell I

The sharp rectangularity of the Knapp Farm enclosure resembles a similarly regular, though slightly more elongated, enclosure approximately 500m to the east at Summergil Bridge (PRN 5137), which lies at the western extent of the Walton marching camp complex. A similar enclosure lies at Walton approximately 900m to the south-east. This enclosure (PRN 5133) lies to the south of the marching camp complex within an area of linear cropmarks interpreted as field boundaries and, like PRN 5137, is slightly more oblong than the Knapp Farm site. Garden enclosure (PRN 4225) lies 750m to the west and, like Knapp Farm, is slightly more square than the Walton and Summergil Bridge sites. All these enclosures are, however, undated and their Iron Age affinity is only assumed. Nevertheless, there does seem to be a growth in enclosed settlements, or enclosed elements of settlements, in the later part of the prehistoric period, and the recut V-shaped ditches of both the Hindwell I (see below) and Knapp Farm sites suggest a common architectural tradition.

Hindwell I is unusual because although there are some 22 possible enclosures presently known within the basin, few are trapezoid and most lack the curvature of the narrower sides of Hindwell I. One site near Lower Harpton (NGR SO278602), which lies just over the English border and immediately outside the study area, does seem to closely mirror Hindwell I (ref CPAT AP 90-MB-1053). This site is orientated roughly north-north-west–south-south-east and is located on the south side of the valley floor in the eastern access to the basin.

Trapezoid enclosures are themselves well-known in Iron Age contexts but such enclosures with concentrically curved ends are rare. Indeed in the comprehensive aerial photographic survey of the well-studied Danebury region, there are no exact parallels despite the identification of over 120 sites (Palmer 1984). Similarly in Warwickshire and the

Upper Thames Valley where comparable air photographic studies have taken place (Hingley 1989; Hingley and Miles 1984).

The Montgomery Small Enclosures survey undertaken by CPAT has similarly identified a large range of enclosure morphology and no sites are directly comparable with the regularity of the Hindwell I site. However, Rhos enclosure (PRN7098) at Trewern near Welshpool, has a mixture of linear and curvilinear ditches forming an approximately trapezoid shape. The innermost of the triple-ditched enclosure at Pen-y-llan, Forden (PRN 3599) is an incomplete cropmark, but does show two diverging straight lateral ditches with an externally convex broad end (the narrower end has not been recorded) and as such is morphologically close to the Hindwell and Lower Harpton sites. Pen-y-llan is a more complex site, being multivallate. These sites are, however, undated.

Concluding remarks

The Walton Basin survey has succeeded in its aims of quantifying and characterising the archaeology of the region. It has also considerably enhanced the sites and monuments record and has identified the chiefly agricultural threats which hang over the earthwork and cropmark archaeology. The analysis of the flint scatters and the monumental record has also allowed multi-period settlements to be identified as well as settlement patterns within the basin in the prehistoric timescale.

While the importance of the archaeology in the basin has been acknowledged for a considerable period, just how rich the archaeological resource is has been highlighted by the present survey. The Hindwell II enclosure is a remarkable site whose presence had not been suspected prior to the survey and its discovery is testimony to the benefits of repeated air photography with terrestrial follow-up. A question remains regarding the relationship between the two enclosures at Hindwell and Walton. A

possible sequence has been suggested above but remains to be proven. The presence of two such sites in close proximity is once more testimony to the importance of the area. The preservation of structural and buried data from beneath the barrow at Upper Ninepence also testifies to the basin's archaeological potential, and the application of new techniques of analysis to the artefacts from this site has yielded information of a type new to Wales. The results of this analysis, as well as the radiocarbon sequence, has a significance well beyond the borders of the Principality and will affect the way that contemporary assemblages are studied elsewhere.

More work remains to be done. The excavation work on the flint scatter at Rough Close was disappointing and some more excavation on scatter areas in different topographical situations might profitably be undertaken. These might need to be on a larger scale than the Rough Close excavation to enable a better understanding of any features that might be encountered. As mentioned above, the relationship between Hindwell II and the Walton palisaded enclosure remains to be defined, and, related to this is the location of any internal features at both sites. Aerial photography has so far been unsuccessful in penetrating the pasture areas of the sites, and so an intensive geophysical survey project covering some 20Ha has been organised for the summer of 1998. The entrance of Hindwell II has similarly not yet been identified and we are a long way from being able to determine with any degree of confidence the function of this internationally important site.

Meanwhile many sites continue to be ploughed irrespective of their protected or unprotected status. The resource is fragile and a large scale programme of education needs to be undertaken amongst the landowners and tenants. There are ready ears and this project has benefited greatly from the cooperation of local farmers, but a more active role needs to be taken by central government. Scheduling is intrusive and, at times, ineffective. More mutually acceptable management agreements need to be negotiated.

Bibliography

Ainslie, R, and Wallis, J, 1987 Excavations on the Cursus at Drayton, Oxon, *Oxoniensia*, **52**, 1–9

Aldhouse-Green, S H R, 1994 Flint and stone artefacts, in A Gibson, 1994

Aldhouse-Green, S H R, forthcoming An Upper Palaeolithic shouldered point and other lithics, in N W Jones, forthcoming

Anon, 1863 Report of the Knighton Meeting, *Archaeologia Cambrensis*, 3rd ser, **IX**, 366

Anon, 1990 Report of the Radnorshire Society Field Section, 1990, *Radnorshire Society Transactions*, **60**, 6–8

Ashbee, P, Smith, I F, and Evans J G 1979 Excavation of three long barrows near Avebury, Wiltshire, *Proceedings of the Prehistoric Society*, **45**, 207–300

Atkinson, R J C, Piggott, C M, and Sandars, N K, 1951 *Excavations at Dorchester, Oxon*. Oxford: Department of Antiquities, Ashmolean Museum

Avery, B W, and Bascomb, C L, (eds), 1974 *Soil Survey Laboratory Methods*. Soil Survey Tech. Monog **6**

Ball, D F, 1964 Loss-on-Ignition as an Estimate of Organic Matter and Organic Carbon in Non-calcareous Soils, *Journal of Soil Science*, **15**, 84–92

Bamford, H, 1982 *Beaker Domestic Sites in the Fen Edge and East Anglia*. East Anglian Archaeology Rep **16**. Dereham: Norfolk Museums Service

Banks, R W, 1874, The Four Stones, Old Radnor, *Archaeologia Cambrensis*, 4th ser, **5**, 215–17

Barclay, G, and Maxwell, G, 1991 Excavations on a Neolithic Long Mortuary Enclosure within the Roman Legionary Fortress at Inchtuthil, Perthshire, *Proceedings of the Society of Antiquaries of Scotland*, **121**, 27–44

Barrett, J, 1994 *Fragments from Antiquity. An Archaeology of Social Life in Britain, 2900–1200 BC*. Oxford: Blackwell

Barrett, J, Bradley, R, and Green, M, 1991. *Landscape, Monuments and Society: The Prehistory of Cranborne Chase*. Cambridge: University Press

Barrett, J, Bradley, R, and Hall, M, (eds), 1991 *Papers on the Prehistory of Cranborne Chase*. Monograph **11**. Oxford: Oxbow Books

Barton, R N E, Berridge, P J, Walker, M J C, and Bevins, R E, 1995 Persistent places in the Mesolithic landscape: an example from the Black Mountain uplands of South Wales, *Proceedings of the Prehistoric Society, **61**, 81–116

Bennett, K D, 1994 *Annotated catalogue of pollen and pteridophyte spore types of the British Isles*. Cambridge: Department of Plant Sciences, University of Cambridge

Bennett, K D, Whittington, G, and Edwards, K J, 1994 Recent plant nomenclatural changes and pollen morphology in the British Isles, *Quaternary Newsletter*, **73**, 1–6

Berridge, P, 1994 The lithics, in H Quinnell and M R Blockley with P Berridge, *Excavations at Rhuddlan, Clwyd, 1969–73, Mesolithic to Medieval*. CBA Res Rep **95**, 95–114. York

Bewley, R H, 1993 Survey and Excavation at a Crop-mark Enclosure, Plasketlands, Cumbria, *Transactions of the Cumberland and Westmorland Antiquarian and Archaeological Society*, **93**, 1–18

Boelicke, U, 1977 Das Neolithische Erdwerk Urmitz, *Acta Praehistorica et Archaeologica*, **7/8**. Berlin: Verlag Bruno Hessling

Bradley, P, 1988 *The Flint Collection from Keep Hill, Herefordshire*. Unpublished post-excavation studies diploma dissertation, University of Leicester

Bradley, P, 1994 *Assemblage Variation and Spatial Patterning of Artefacts in the earlier Neolithic of Southern England with special reference to Causewayed Enclosures*. Unpublished M.Phil. thesis, University of Sheffield

Bradley, P, 1996 Flint, in G Hey, *Yarnton Floodplain B: Post-Excavation Assessment*. Unpublished document prepared for English Heritage

Bradley, P, forthcoming Worked flint, in A Barclay and C Halpin, *Barrow, Hills Radley, Volume 1: The Prehistoric Monument Complex*. Oxford Archaeological Unit: Thames Valley Landscape Series

Bradley, R, Chowne, P, Cleal, R M J, Healy, F, and Kinnes, I, 1993 *Excavations on Redgate Hill, Hunstanton, Norfolk, and at Tattershall Thorpe, Lincolnshire*. East Anglian Archaeology Report **57**. Norwich: Norfolk Museums Service Field Archaeology Division and Heritage Trust of Lincolnshire

Brassil, K, and Gibson, A M, forthcoming A Grooved Ware pit group and a Bronze Age multiple inhumation at Hendre, Rhydymwyn, Clwyd, in A McSween and R Cleal (eds), *Grooved Ware in Context*. Oxford: Oxbow books

Braun, C. 1983. Analysen von Gläsern aus der Hallstattzeit mit einem exkurs über romische Fenstergläser, in O-H Frey (ed) *Glasperlen der verrömischen Eisenzeit I*. Marburger Studien zur Vor- und Frühgeschichte, vol **5**. Phillip von Zabern, Mainz, 129–78

Britnell, W J, 1982 The excavation of two round barrows at Trelystan, Powys, *Proceedings of the Prehistoric Society*, **48**, 133–202

Brown, A, 1991 Structured deposition and technological change among the flaked stone artefacts from Cranborne Chase, in Barrett *et al* (eds), 1991, 101–34

Bullock, P, Federoff, N, Jongerius, A, Stoops, G, and Tursina, T, 1985 *Handbook for Soil Thin Section Description*. Wolverhampton: Waine Research Publications

Burgess, C B, 1972, Goatscrag: a Bronze Age rock shelter cemetery in North Northumberland with notes on other rock shelters and craglines in the area, *Archaeologia Aeliana*, 4th ser, **50**, 28ff

Burgess, C B, 1976 Meldon Bridge: a Neolithic defended promontory complex near Peebles, in C B Burgess and R F Miket (eds*)*, 151–80

Burgess, C B, 1980 The Bronze Age in Wales, in J A Taylor (ed), 1980, 243–86

Burgess, C B and Miket, R, (eds), 1976 *Settlement and Economy in the Third and Second Millennia BC*, Report **33**. Oxford: British Archaeological Reports

Burl, H A W, 1988 *Four-Posters. Bronze Age Stone Circles of Western Europe*. Oxford: British Archaeological Reports **195**

Case, H J, 1982, The Linear Ditches and Southern Enclosure, North Stoke, in H J Case and A W R Whittle (eds), *Settlement Patterns in the Oxford Region: Excavations at the Abingdon Causewayed Enclosure and Other Sites*. CBA Res Rep **44**, 60–75

Caseldine, A, 1990 *Environmental Archaeology in Wales*. Lampeter: St David's University College

Catherall, P D 1976, Excavations at Litton Cheney, Dorset, in C B Burgess and R Miket (eds) 1976, 81–100

Charlesworth, J K 1957 *The Quaternary Era with Special Reference to its Glaciation*. London: Edward Arnold

Charters, S, Evershed, R P, Goad, L J, Leyden, A, and Blinkhorn, P W, 1993a Identification of an adhesive used to repair a Roman jar, *Archaeometry*, **35**, 91–101

Charters, S, Evershed, R P, Goad, L J, Leyden, A, Blinkhorn, P W, and Denham, V, 1993b Quantification and distribution of lipid in archaeological ceramics: implications for sampling potsherds for organic residue analysis and the classification of vessel use, *Archaeometry*, **35**, 211–23

Charters, S, Evershed, R P, Blinkhorn, P W, 1995, Evidence for the mixing of fats and waxes in archaeological ceramics, *Archaeometry*, **37**, No 1, 113–27

Children, G, and Nash, G, 1994 *The Prehistoric Sites of Herefordshire*, Monuments in the Landscape **I**. Woonton Almeley: Logaston Press

Clark, A J, 1990 *Seeing Beneath the Soil*. London: Batsford

Clark, G, 1936 The Timber Monument at Arminghall and its Affinities, *Proceedings of the Prehistoric Society*, **2**, 1–51

Cleal, R, 1991 Cranborne Chase – the earlier prehistoric pottery, in Barrett *et al* (eds), 1991, 134–200

Clifford, E M, 1930 A prehistoric and Roman site at Barnwood, near Gloucester, *Transactions of the Bristol and Gloucestershire Archaeological Society,* **52**, 201–54

Cooney, G, and Grogan, E, 1994 *Irish Prehistory: A Social Perspective*. Dublin: Wordwell

Crowther, J, 1996 *Phosphate and magnetic susceptibility studies of buried soils and ditch sediments from the Upper Ninepence Excavation, Walton Basin, Powys*. Unpub. Report for Clwyd-Powys Archaeological Trust

Crowther, J, and Barker, P, 1995 Magnetic Susceptibility: Distinguishing Anthropogenic Effects from the Natural, *Archaeological Prospection*, **2**, 207–15

Crummy, P, 1992 *Excavations at Culver Street, the Gilberd School and Other Sites in Colchester 1971–85*. Colchester Archaeological Report No **6**. Colchester: Colchester Archaeological Trust Ltd

Cunliffe, B, 1987 *Hengistbury Head Dorset. Volume 1: the Prehistoric and Roman Settlement, 3500BC – AD500*. Monograph **13**. Oxford: Oxford University Committee for Archaeology

Cunliffe, B, 1991 *Iron Age Communities in Britain*, 3rd edn. London: Routledge

Cunnington, M E, 1929 *Woodhenge*. Devizes: Simpson and Co

Cunnington, M E, 1931 The 'Sanctuary' on Overton Hill, near Avebury, *Wiltshire Archaeological and Natural History Magazine*, **45**, 300–35

David, A, 1989 Some aspects of the human presence in west Wales during the Mesolithic, in C Bonsall (ed), *The mesolithic in Europe*, 241–253. Edinburgh: Edinburgh University Press

Davies, E, 1905 *A General History of the County of Radnor Compiled from the Manuscript of the Late Reverend Jonathan Williams*. Brecon: Davies and Co

Day, W, 1972 The Excavation of a Bronze Age Burial Mound at Ysgwennant, Llansilin, Denbighshire, *Archaeologia Cambrensis*, **121**, 17–50

De Niro, M J, and Epstein, S, 1978 Influence of diet on the distribution of carbon isotopes in animals, *Geochim. et Cosmochim. Acta*, **42**, 495–506

Dick, W A, and Tabatabai, M A, 1977 An Alkaline Oxidation Method for the Determination of Total Phosphorus in Soils, *Journal of the Soil Science Society of America*, **41**, 511–14

Dinn, J, and Evans, J, 1990 Aston Hill Farm, Kemerton: excavation of a ring ditch, middle Iron Age enclosures, and a grubenhaus, *Transactions of the Worcestershire Archaeological Society,* **12,** 5–66

Donahue, R E, 1994 The current state of lithic microwear research, in N Ashton and A David (eds), *Stories in Stone,* 156–68. Oxford: Lithic Studies Society

Drewett, P, 1976 The Excavation of Four Round Barrows of the Second Millennium BC at West Heath, Harting, 1973–5, *Sussex Archaeological Collections,* **114,** 126–50

Dunn, C J, 1964 Flints from the Radnor Basin, *Radnorshire Society Transactions,* **34,** 42–50

Dunn, C J, 1965 Further archaeological discoveries in the Radnor Basin, *Radnorshire Society Transactions,* **35,** 10–20

Dunn, C J, 1966 Surface finds from a barrow and its immediate vicinity near Walton, Radnorshire, *Radnorshire Society Transactions,* **36,** 9–14

Dunn, C J, 1974 *Radnorshire Barrows: East of the River Ithon.* Undergraduate dissertation, University of Cardiff (CPAT copy)

Dunn, C J, 1988 The barrows of east-central Powys, *Archaeologia Cambrensis,* **137,** 27–42

Dunning, G C, 1932 Bronze Age settlements and a Saxon hut near Bourton on the Water, Gloucestershire, *Antiq J,* **12,** 279–93

Dunning, G C, 1976 Salmonsbury, Bourton on the Water, Gloucestershire, in D W Harding (ed), *Hillforts: Later Prehistoric Earthworks in Britain and Ireland,* 75–118. London

Dutton, G H, 1903 Notes on glacial and alluvial deposits near Cardiff, *Transactions of the Cardiff Naturalists Society,* **36,** 109–15

Ellison, A, and Rahtz, P, 1987 Excavations at Hog Cliff Hill, Maiden Newton, Dorset, *Proceedings of the Prehistoric Society,* **53,** 223–70

Enser, M, 1991 Animal carcass fats and fish oils, in J B Rossell and J L R Pritchard, (eds), *Analysis of Oilseeds, Oils and Fatty Foods,* 329–394. London: Elsevier

Eogan, G, 1984. *Excavations at Knowth (I).* Dublin: Royal Irish Academy

Evans, J G, and Smith, I F, 1983 Excavations at Cherhill, North Wiltshire, 1967, *Proceedings of the Prehistoric Society,* **49,** 43–118

Evershed, R P, and Charters, S, 1995 Interpreting lipid residues in archaeological ceramics: preliminary results from laboratory simulations of vessel use and burial, *Materials Research Society Symposium Proceedings,* **352**

Evershed, R P, Heron, C, and Goad, L J, 1991 Epicuticular wax components preserved in potsherds as chemical indicators of leafy vegetables in ancient diets, *Antiquity,* **65,** 540–4

Evershed, R P, Heron, C, Charters, S, and Goad, L J, 1990 Analysis of organic residues of archaeological origin by high temperature gas chromatography/mass spectrometry, *Analyst,* **115,** 1339–42

Evershed, R P, Heron, C, Charters, S, and Goad, L J, 1992 The survival of food residues: New methods of analysis, interpretation and application, *Proceedings of the British Academy,* **77,** 189–208

Evershed, R P, Stott, A W, Raven, A, Dudd, S N, Charters, S, and Leyden, A, 1995 Formation of long-chain ketones in ancient pottery vessels by pyrolysis of acyl lipids, *Tetrahedron Letters,* **36,** No 48, 8875–8

Evershed, R P, Mottram, H R, Dudd, S N, Charters, S, Stott, A W, Gibson, A M, Conner, A, Blinkham, P W, and Reeves, V, 1997 New criteria for the identification of animal fats preserved in archaeological pottery, *Naturwissenschaften,* **84,** 402–6

Fischer, A, 1989 Hunting with flint-tipped arrows: results and experiences from practical experiments, in C Bonsall (ed), *The Mesolithic of Europe,* 29–39. Edinburgh: Edinburgh University Press

Fischer, A, Hansen, P V, and Rasmussen, P, 1984 Macro and micro wear traces on lithic projectile points, *Journal of Danish Archaeology,* **3,** 19–46

Ford, S, Bradley, R, Hawkes, J, and Fisher, P, 1984 Flint working in the metal age, *Oxford Journal of Archaeology,* **3** (1), 157–73

Fox, C, 1959. *Life and Death in the Bronze Age.* London: Routledge Kegan Paul

Gibson, A M, 1982 *Beaker Domestic Sites. A Study of the Domestic Pottery of the Third and Early Second Millennia BC in the British Isles,* BAR Brit Ser **107.** Oxford: British Archaeological Reports

Gibson, A M, 1987 Beaker Domestic Sites Across the North Sea: A Review, in J-C Blanchet (ed), *Les Relations Entre le Continent et les Isles Britanniques à l'Age du Bronze: Actes du Colloque de Lille dans le Cadre du 22ème Congres Préhistoriques de France, 2–7 Septembre 1984.* 7–16. Amiens: Revue Archaeologique de Picardie/Société Préhistoriques Française

Gibson, A M, (ed) 1989 *Midlands Prehistory: Some Recent and Current Researches into The Prehistory of Central England,* BAR Brit Ser **204.** Oxford: British Archaeological Reports

Gibson, A M, 1990 *The Neolithic Pottery from Ogmore, Glamorgan.* Report prepared for the National Museum of Wales

Gibson, A M, 1993a Radiocarbon date for a Fengate sherd from Brynderwen, Llandyssil, Powys, *Archaeology in Wales,* **33,** 34–5

Gibson, A M, 1993b *Kisses' Barn Farm, Polesworth, Warwickshire: The Prehistoric Pottery.* Report prepared for Warwickshire Museums Field Archaeology Unit

Gibson, A M, 1994 Excavations at the Sarn-y-bryn-caled cursus complex, Welshpool,

168

Powys, and the timber circles of Great Britain and Ireland, *Proceedings of the Prehistoric Society,* **60**, 143–223

Gibson, A M, 1995a First impressions: a review of Peterborough Ware in Wales, in I Kinnes and G Varndell (eds), *Unbaked Urns of Rudely Shape. Essays on British and Irish Pottery for Ian Longworth,* 23–39, Monograph **55**. Oxford: Oxbow Books

Gibson, A M, 1995b The Carreg Bueno prehistoric landscape, Berriew, *Montgomeryshire Collections,* **83**, 41–58

Gibson, A M, 1995c Walton. *Current Archaeology,* **12**, 444–5

Gibson, A M, 1996a A Neolithic Enclosure at Hindwell, Radnorshire, Powys, *Oxford Journal of Archaeology,* **15** (3), 341–8

Gibson, A M, 1996b The Later Neolithic Structures at Trelystan, Powys, Wales: Ten Years On, in T Darvill and J Thomas (eds), *Neolithic Houses in Northwest Europe and Beyond.* Neolithic Studies Group Seminar Papers 1, 133–41. Monograph **57**. Oxford: Oxbow Books

Gibson, A M, 1997 Survey in the Walton Basin (Radnor Valley), Powys, *Transactions of the Radnorshire Society,* **67**, 20–62

Gibson, A M, 1998a Hindwell and the Palisaded Enclosures of Britain and Ireland, in A M Gibson and D D A Simpson (eds), *Prehistoric Ritual,* 68–79. Stroud: Alan Sutton

Gibson, A M, 1998b *The Walton Basin Project, 1993–1997.* Report No **283**, CPAT

Gibson, A M, 1998c The Walton Basin Project, in H Clevis and J de Jong (eds), *Archaeology and Landuse, Three Case Studies,* 8–33, Municipality of Zwolle, Heritage and Archaeology

Gibson, A M, forthcoming The Cursus Monuments and Possible Cursus Monuments of Wales: Avenues for Future Research or Roads to Nowhere?, in A Barclay and J Harding (eds), *Pathways and Ceremonies: The Cursus Monuments of Neolithic Britain.* Oxford: Oxbow Books

Gibson, A M, and Kinnes, I A, 1997 On the Urns of a Dilemma: Radiocarbon and the Peterborough Problem, *Oxford Journal of Archaeology,* **16** (1), 65–72

Gibson, A M, and Loveday, R, 1989 Excavations at the Cursus Monument at Aston on Trent, Derbyshire, in A M Gibson (ed), *Midlands Prehistory. Some Recent and Current Researches into the Prehistory of Central England.* 27–50. BAR **204**. Oxford: British Archaeological Reports

Gibson, A M, and Musson, C R, 1990 A cropmark enclosure and a sherd of later Neolithic pottery from Brynderwen, Llandyssil, Powys, *Montgomeryshire Collections,* **78**, 11–15

Graham, I D G, and Scollar, I, 1976 Limitations on Magnetic Prospection in Archaeology Imposed by Soil Properties, *Archaeo-Physika,* **6**, 1–124

Grant, A, 1991 Economic or Symbolic ? Animals and Ritual Behaviour, in P Garwood, D Jennings, R Skeates and J Toms (eds), *Sacred and Profane. Proceedings of a Conference on Archaeology, Ritual and Religion, Oxford, 1989,* 109–114. Monograph **32**. Oxford: Oxford University Committee for Archaeology

Green, H S, 1980 *The Flint Arrowheads of the British Isles,* BAR **75**. Oxford: British Archaeological Reports

Green, H S, 1986 The flintwork, in W Warrilow, G Owen and W Britnell, 1986

Green, H S, Guilbert, G, and Cowell, M, 1983 Two Gold Bracelets from Maesmelan Farm, Powys, *Bulletin of the Board of Celtic Studies,* **30** (III–IV), 394–8

Grimes, W F, 1960 *Excavations on Defence Sites, 1939–1945. I: Mainly Neolithic–Bronze Age,* Ministry of Works Archaeological Reports No **3**. London: HMSO

Grimm, E C, 1991, *Tilia and Tilia-graph.* Springfield: Illinois State Museum

Grogan, E, 1996 Neolithic Houses in Ireland, in T Darvill and J Thomas (eds), *Neolithic Houses in Northwest Europe and Beyond,* 41–60. Monograph **57**. Oxford: Oxbow Books

Grogan, E, and Eogan, G, 1987 Lough Gur Excavations by S. P. O'Riordain: Further Neolithic and Beaker Habitations on Knockadoon, *Proceedings of the Royal Irish Academy,* **87C**, 299–506

Guilloré, P, 1985 *Methode de Fabrication Mechanique et en Series des Lames Minces.* Paris: Institut National Agronomique

Hamond, F W, 1983 Phosphate Analysis of Archaeological Sediments, in T Reeves-Smyth and F W Hamond (eds), *Landscape and Archaeology in Ireland,* 47–80, BAR **116**. Oxford: British Archaeological Reports

Hannan, A, 1993 Excavations at Tewksbury 1972–74. *Transactions of the Bristol and Gloucestershire Archaeological Society,* **111**, 21–75

Harding, P, 1988 The Chalk Plaque Pit, Amesbury, *Proceedings of the Prehistoric Society,* **54**, 320–327

Harding, A F, and Lee, G E, 1987 *Henge Monuments and Related Sites of Great Britain. Air Photographic Evidence and Catalogue.* BAR **175**. Oxford: British Archaeological Reports

Hartley, F, 1989 Aerial Archaeology in Leicestershire, in A M Gibson (ed), 1989, 95–105

Hartwell, B, 1991 Ballynahatty – a Prehistoric Ceremonial Centre, *Archaeology Ireland,* **5** (4), 12–15

Hartwell, B, 1994 Late Neolithic ceremonies, *Archaeology Ireland,* **8** (4), 10–13

Healey, E, 1982 The flintwork, in W Britnell, 1982

Healey, E, 1993 The lithic artefacts of Mesolithic date and the Neolithic and Bronze Age flintwork, in F Lynch, 1993, 22–32, and 187–95

Healy, F, Heaton, M, and Lobb, S J, 1992 Mesolithic site at Thatcham, Berkshire. *Proceedings of the Prehistoric Society, 58*, 41–76

Hedges, J, and Buckley, D, 1981 *Springfield Cursus and the Cursus Problem*. Chelmsford: Essex County Council

Henderson, J, 1985 The raw materials of early glass production, *Oxford Journal of Archaeology*, **4** (3), 267–91

Henderson, J, 1988 Electron probe microanalysis of mixed-alkali glasses, *Archaeometry*, **30** (1), 77–91

Henderson, J, 1989 Scientific analysis of ancient glass, and its archaeological interpretation, in J Henderson (ed), *Scientific analysis in Archaeology, and its interpretation*, Oxford University Committee on Archaeology Monograph no **19**, UCLA Institute of Archaeology, Archaeological Research Tools 5, 30–58

Henderson, J,1995 Ancient vitreous materials, *American Journal of Archaeology*, **99** (1), 117–21

Henderson, J, and Warren, S E, 1983 Prehistoric lead glasses, in A Aspinall and S E Warren (eds), Proceedings of the 22nd Symposium on Archaeometry, Bradford, UK, 168–80

Heron, C, and Evershed, R P, (1993) The analysis of organic residues and the study of pottery use, in M Schiffer (ed), *Archaeological Method and Theory* 5, 247–84. Arizona: University of Arzona Press

Hingley, R, 1989 Iron Age Settlement and Society in Central and Southern Warwickshire: Directions for Future Research, in A M Gibson (ed), 1989, 122–57

Hingley, R, and Miles, D, 1984 Aspects of Iron Age Settlement in the Upper Thames valley, in B Cunliffe and D Miles (eds) *Aspects of the Iron Age in Central Southern Britain*, 52–71. Monograph **2**. Oxford: University of Oxford Committee for Archaeology

Holgate, N, and Hallowes, K A K, 1941 The igneous rocks of the Stanner-Hunter district, Radnorshire, *Geological Magazine, 78*, 242–67

Holgate, R, 1988 *Neolithic Settlement in the Thames Basin*. BAR Brit Ser **76**, Oxford: British Archaeological Reports

Houlder, C, 1968 The henge monuments at Llandegai, *Antiquity*, **42**, 216–21

Hughes, G, and Crawford, G, 1995 Excavations at Wasperton, Warwickshire, 1980–85. Introduction and Part 1: the Neolithic and early Bronze Age, *Transactions of the Birmingham and Warwickshire Archaeological Society, 99*, 9–45

Hughes, G, and Woodward, A, 1995 Excavations at Meole Brace 1990 and at Bromfield 1981–91. Part 1, a ring ditch and neolithic pit complex at Meole Brace, Shrewsbury, *Shropshire History and Archaeology*, **70**, 1–170

Hurst, H, 1972 Excavations at Gloucester 1968–71: first interim report, *Antiq J*, **52**, 24–69

Jacobi, R M, 1980 The early Holocene settlement of Wales, in J A Taylor (ed), 1980, 131–206

Jones, G, and Milles, A, 1989 Iron Age, Romano-British and Medieval plant remains, in W Britnell, The Collfryn Hillslope Enclosure, Llansantffraid Deuddwr, Powys: Excavations 1980–1982, *Proceedings of the Prehistoric Society*, **55**, Microfiche 3–5

Jones N W, 1992 *New Radnor – The Porth, Powys (Preliminary Report on Excavations 1991–1992)*. Report No **39**: CPAT

Jones, N W forthcoming Excavations within the Medieval Town at New Radnor, Powys, 1991–2, *Archaeol J*, **155**

Keeley, L H 1980 *Experimental Determination of Stone Tool Uses: a Microwear Analysis*. Chicago: University of Chicago Press

Kidder, A V, and Shepard, A O, 1936 The pottery of Pecos, 2, in *Papers of the Phillips Academy, Southwestern Expedition No **7**, 389–587

Levi Sala, I, 1986a Experimental replication of post-depositional surface modification on flint, in L Owen and G Unrath (eds), *Technical Aspects of Microwear Studies on Stone Tools*, 103–9. *Early Man News* 9/10/11

Levi Sala, I, 1986b Use wear and post-depositional surface modification: a word of caution, *Journal of Archaeological Science, 13*, 229–44

Loveday, R, 1985 *Cursuses and Related Monuments of the British Neolithic*. Unpublished PhD thesis, University of Leicester

Loveday, R, 1989 The Barford ritual complex: further excavations (1972) and a regional perspective, in A M Gibson (ed), 1989, 51–84

Lynch, F, 1970 *Prehistoric Anglesey*. Llangefni: Anglesey Antiquarian Society

Lynch, F, 1980 Bronze Age monuments in Wales, in J A Taylor (ed), 1980, 233–41

Lynch, F, 1991 *Prehistoric Anglesey*, 2nd edn. Llangefni: Anglesey Antiquarian Society

Lynch, F, 1993 *Excavations in the Brenig Valley. A Mesolithic and Bronze Age Landscape in North Wales*. Cambrian Archaeological Monographs No **5**. Cardiff: Cambrian Archaeological Association and Cadw: Welsh Historic Monuments

Manby, T G, 1974 *Grooved Ware Sites in the North of England*. BAR **9**. Oxford: British Archaeological Reports

Manby, T G, 1975 Neolithic Occupation Sites on the Yorkshire Wolds, *Yorkshire Archaeological Journal*, **47**, 23–59

Manley, J, and Healey, E, 1982 Excavations at

Hendre, Rhuddlan: the mesolithic finds, *Archaeologia Cambrensis*, **131**, 18–48

Matter, L, 1992. Determination of the animal of origin of dairy products and raw and cooked meats by GC analysis of the fatty acid methyl esters (FAME) obtained by transesterification, *Journal of High Resolution Chromatography*, **15**, 514–16

Matter, L, Schenker, D, Husmann, H, Schomburg, G, 1989 Characterisation of animal fats via the GC pattern of FAME mixtures obtained by transesterification of the triglycerides, *Chromatographia*, **27**, 31–6

Matthews, C L, 1976 *Occupation Sites on a Chiltern Ridge. Excavations at Puddlehill and Sites near Dunstable, Bedfordshire. Part I: Neolithic, Bronze Age and Early Iron Age*. BAR **29**. Oxford: British Archaeological Reports

Megaw, J V S 1976 Gwithian Cornwall: Some Notes on the Evidence for Neolithic and Bronze Age Settlement, in C B Burgess and R Miket (eds), 1976, 51–66

Mercer, R J 1981 *Grimes Graves, Norfolk. Excavations 1971–72: Volume I*. Department of the Environment Archaeological Report No **11**. London: HMSO

Mercer, R J, 1993 Secretary's Report, *Monuments on Record, Annual Review 1992–3*. Edinburgh: RCAHMS

Moore, P D, Webb, J A, and Collinson, M E, 1991 *Pollen Analysis*. Oxford: Blackwell Scientific Publications

Mottram, H R, 1995 Stable isotope analysis as an aid to determining the origin of fats absorbed in ancient pottery. Third year thesis

Murphy, C P, 1986 *Thin Section Preparation of Soils and Sediments*. Berkhamsted: A B Academic Publishers

Musson, C R, 1994 *Wales from the Air – Patterns Past and Present*. Aberystwyth: RCHAMW

National Library of Wales Manuscript No 13174A – Manuscript record of a tour by Iolo Morgannwg begun in March, 1802

Needham, S, and Ambers, J, 1994 Redating Rams Hill and Reconsidering Bronze Age Enclosure, *Proceedings of the Prehistoric Society*, **60**, 225–244

Nier, A O, and Gulbransen, E A, 1939 Variations in the relative abundances of the carbon isotopes, *Journal of the American Chemical Society*, **61**, 697–8

Odell, G H, and Cowan, F, 1986 Experiments with spears and arrows on animal targets, *Journal of Field Archaeology*, **13**, 195–212

O'Kelly, M J, Cleary, R M, and Lehane, D, 1983 *Newgrange, Co Meath, Ireland. The Late Neolithic/Beaker Period Settlement*, BAR Int Ser **190**. Oxford: British Archaeological Reports

Oswald, A, (ed) 1969 Excavations for the Avon/Severn Research Committee at Barford, Warwickshire, *Transactions of the Birmingham Archaeological Society, 83*, 1–65

Palmer, R, 1976 Interrupted ditched enclosures in Britain: the use of aerial photography for comparative studies, *Proceedings of the Prehistoric Society*, **42**, 161–86

Palmer, R, 1984 *Danebury: An Iron Age Hillfort in Hampshire. An Aerial Photographic Interpretation of its Environs*. London: RCHME

Parkhouse, J, 1988 A preliminary note on environmental samples, in D M Robinson (ed), *Biglis, Caldicot and Llandough*, 64, BAR **188**. Oxford: British Archaeological Reports

Peacock, D P S, 1968 A Petrological Study of Certain Iron Age Pottery from Western England, *Proceedings of the Prehistoric Society*, **34**, 414–27

Philp, B J, 1973 *Excavations in West Kent, 1960–1970*. Second Research Report in the Kent Series. Dover: Kent Archaeological Rescue Unit

Piggott, S, 1962 *The West Kennet Long Barrow: Excavations 1955–56*, Ministry of Works Archaeological Reports No **4**. London: HMSO

Pitts, M W, and Jacobi, R M, 1979 Some Aspects of Change in Flaked Stone Industries of the Mesolithic and Neolithic of Southern Britain, *Journal of Archaeological Science*, **6**, 166–70

Pocock, R W, and Whitehead, T H, 1953 *British Regional Geology: The Welsh Borderland*. London: HMSO

Pollard, J, 1995 Structured Deposition at Woodhenge, *Proceedings of the Prehistoric Society*, **61**, 137–56

Proudfoot, V B, 1976 The Analysis and Interpretation of Soil Phosphorous in Archaeological Contexts, in D A Davidson and M L Shackley (eds), *Geoarchaeology*, 93–113. London: Duckworth

Pye, W R, 1975 Fron Ddyrys, Radnorshire, *Archaeology in Wales*, **15**, 40

Pye, W R 1979 Hindwell, Walton: an Early Roman Fort, *Transactions of the Radnor Society*, **49**, 10–23

Rahtz, P, 1962 Neolithic and Beaker sites at Downton, near Salisbury, Wiltshire. *Wiltshire Archaeological and Natural History Magazine*, **58**, 116–41

Rankine, W F, and W M, 1960 Further excavations at a Mesolithic site at Oakhanger, Selbourne, Hants. *Proceedings of the Prehistoric Society*, **26**, 246–62

Rayner, D H, 1981 *The Stratigraphy of the British Isles*. 2nd edn. Cambridge: Cambridge University Press

Rudeforth, C C, Hartnup, R, Lea, J W, Thompson, T R E, and Wright, P S, 1984 *Soils and their Use in Wales*. Bulletin 11, Harpenden: Soil Survey of England and Wales

Saville, A, 1979 Further excavations at Nympsfield chambered tomb, Gloucestershire, 1974,

Proceedings of the Prehistoric Society, **45**, 53–91

Savory, H N, 1976 *Guide Catalogue of the Iron Age Collections*. Cardiff: National Museum of Wales

Savory, H N, 1980 The neolithic in Wales, in J A Taylor (ed), 1980, 207–32

Scollar, I, Tabbagh, A, Hesse, A, and Herzog, I, 1990 *Archaeological Prospecting and Remote Sensing*. Cambridge: Cambridge University Press

Shennan, S J, Healy, F, and Smith, I F, 1985 The excavation of a ring-ditch at Tye Field, Lawford, Essex, *Archaeological Journal*, **142**, 150–215

Shepherd, W, 1972 *Flint. Its Origins, Properties and Uses*. London: Faber and Faber

Silvester R J, 1994a *Radnorshire Historic Settlements*. Report No **92**: CPAT, Welshpool

Silvester R J, 1994b *New Radnor: A Topographical Survey*. Report No **101**: CPAT, Welshpool

Simpson, D D A, and Gibson, A M, 1989 Lyles Hill, *Current Archaeology*, **10**, 214–5

Smith, C A, and Lynch, F M, 1987 *Trefignath and Din Dryfol. The Excavation of Two Megalithic Tombs in Anglesey*. Cambrian Archaeological Monographs No **3**. Cardiff: Cambrian Archaeological Association

Smith, I F, 1965 *Windmill Hill and Avebury. Excavations by Alexander Keiller 1925–1939*. Oxford: Clarendon Press

Smith, I F, 1968 Report on late Neolithic pits at Cam, Gloucestershire, *Transactions of the Bristol and Gloucestershire Archaeological Society*, **87**, 14–28

Stanford, S C, 1982 Bromfield, Shropshire – Neolithic, Beaker and Bronze Age sites, 1966–79, *Proceedings of the Prehistoric Society*, **48**, 279–320

Sweetman, D P, 1985 A Late Neolithic/Early Bronze Age Pit Circle at Newgrange Co Meath, *Proceedings of the Royal Irish Academy*, **85** (C), 195–221

Taverner, N, Marshall, E C, Murphy, K, and Williams, G H, forthcoming A Neolithic and Early Bronze Age Site at Llanilar, Dyfed

Taylor, J A, (ed), 1980 *Culture and Environment in Prehistoric Wales*, BAR Brit Ser **76**. Oxford: British Archaeological Reports

Thornton, M D, Morgan, E D, Celoria, F, 1970 The composition of bog butter, *Science and Archaeology*, **2/3**, 20–4

Tite, M S, 1972 The Influence of Geology on the Magnetic Susceptibility of soils on Archaeological Sites, *Archaeometry*, **14**, 229–36

Tite, M S, and Mullins, C, 1971 Enhancement of Magnetic Susceptibility of Soils on Archaeological Sites, *Archaeometry*, **13**, 209–19

Tixier, J, Inizan, I, and Roche, H, 1980 *Préhistoire de la Pierre Taillée. I, Terminologie et Technologie*. Paris: Cercle de Recherches et d'Etudes Prehistoriques

Turner, W E S, 1956 Studies in ancient glass and glassmaking processes. Part V. Raw materials and melting processes, *Journal of the Society of Glass Technology*, **40**, 277T–300T

Tyler, A, 1976 *Neolithic Flint Axes from the Cotswold Hills*, BAR Brit Ser **25**. Oxford: British Archaeological Reports

Ungar-Hamilton, R, 1988 *Method in Microwear Analysis: Prehistoric Sickles and other Stone Tools from Arjoune, Syria*. BAR Int Ser **S435**. Oxford: British Archaeological Reports

Wainwright, G J, 1962 The excavation of an earthwork at Castell Bryn Gwyn, Llanidan Parish, Anglesey, *Archaeologia Cambrensis*, **111**, 25–58

Wainwright, G J, 1963 A reiteration of the microlithic industries in Wales, *Proceedings of the Prehistoric Society*, **29**, 99–132

Wainwright, G J, 1972 The excavation of a Neolithic settlement on Broome Heath, Ditchingham, Norfolk, England, *Proceedings of the Prehistoric Society*, **38**, 1–97

Wainwright, G J, 1979 *Mount Pleasant, Dorset: Excavations 1970–71*. Research Report **37**. London: Society of Antiquaries

Wainwright, G J, and Longworth, I H, 1971 *Durrington Walls: Excavations 1966–68*. Research Report **29**. London: Society of Antiquaries

Wainwright, G J, Evans, J G, and Longworth, I H, 1971 The excavation of a late neolithic enclosure at Marden, Wiltshire, *Antiq J*, **51**, 177–239

Ward, A, 1987 Cefn Bryn, Gower, *Archaeology in Wales*, **27**, 39–40

Warrilow, W, Owen, G, and Britnell, W J, 1986 Eight ring-ditches at Four Crosses, Llandysilio, Powys, 1981–85, *Proceedings of the Prehistoric Society* **52**, 53–88

Wheeler, H, 1979 Excavation at Willington, Derbyshire, 1970–1972, *Derbyshire Archaeological Journal*, **99**, 58–220

White, S I, 1980 Capel Eithin, Cefn Du, Llanfihangelysceifiog, *Archaeology in Wales*, **20**, 12–18

White, S I, 1981 Excavations at Capel Eithin, Gaerwen, Anglesey, 1st interim report, *Transactions of the Anglesey Antiquarian Society and Field Club*, 1981, 15–27

Whittle, A W R, 1991 A Late Neolithic Complex at West Kennet, Wiltshire, England, *Antiquity*, **65**, 256–62

Whittle, A W R, 1992 *Excavations at West Kennet, near Avebury, 1992. Preliminary Report*. Privately circulated

Whittle, A W R, Atkinson, R J C, Chambers, R, and Thomas, N, 1992 Excavations in the Neolithic and Bronze Age complex at Dorchester-on-Thames, Oxfordshire,

172

1947–1952 and 1981, *Proceedings of the Prehistoric Society*, **58**, 143–202

Windell, D, 1989 A Late Neolithic 'Ritual Focus' at West Cotton, Northamptonshire, in A M Gibson (ed), 1989, 85–94

Woodward, P J, Davies, S M, and Graham, A, 1993 *Excavations at Greyhound Yard and the Old Methodist Chapel, Dorchester, 1981–4.* Monograph **12**. Dorchester: Dorset Natural History and Archaeological Society

Wymer, J, 1962 Excavations at the Maglemosian sites at Thatcham, Berkshire, England, *Proceedings of the Prehistoric Society*, **28**, 329–61

Index *by Susan Vaughan*

Illustrations are denoted by page numbers in italics or by *illus* where figures are scattered throughout the text.